'This is an important and timely book that urges us as scholars and citizens to rethink our assumptions about neoliberalism today. It is a nuanced and wide-ranging volume that uses the powerful concept of authoritarian neoliberalism to develop a truly global map of the ways in which state, market and everyday life are being tied together in new and often-damaging ways.'

Jacqueline Best, Author of Governing Failure: Provisional Expertise and the Transformation of Global Development Finance *and Professor of Political Studies at the University of Ottawa, Canada*

'This pioneering collection places at its centre neoliberalism's key sites of reproduction and contestation. By taking the reader from state settings into households, work places and neighbourhoods, it theorises neoliberalism's authoritarian guises in the face of crises and popular opposition. A beautifully composed collection, this edited book is a must read for anyone interested in an explicitly political reading of neoliberalism's power and its disguises.'

Insa Koch, Author of Personalizing the State: An Anthropology of Law, Politics, and Welfare in Austerity Britain *and Associate Professor of Law and Anthropology at the London School of Economics, UK*

'Bruff and Tansel provide a timely edited volume that defends and advances the analytical purchase of their concept of authoritarian neoliberalism at a moment when liberal democratic states are dismantling rights regimes and creating novel forms of social and political control to guarantee the conditions for a more savage regime of capital accumulation in the global North and South. The rigorously theorised and empirically grounded chapters provide insights into how authoritarian neoliberalism is restructuring households, urban landscapes, and civil societies in diverse conjunctures ranging from Europe, US, Morocco, Turkey to Mexico, but it also provides glimpses of social forces that could possibly mount radical alternatives to contemporary capitalism. A must read for grounded contemporary critical theorists and theoretically inclined activists alike.'

Alfonso Gonzales, Author of Reform without Justice: Latino Migrant Politics and the Homeland Security State *and Director of the Latin American Studies Program at the University of California, Riverside, USA*

'This volume is a very important contribution to critical political economy scholarship as it offers both nuanced reflections on the articulation of neoliberalism and authoritarianism, and rich case studies on the varieties of authoritarian neoliberalism from across the globe.'

Alexander Gallas, Author of The Thatcherite Offensive: A Neo-Poulantzasian Analysis *and Assistant Professor of Politics at the University of Kassel, Germany*

Authoritarian Neoliberalism

Authoritarian Neoliberalism explores how neoliberal forms of managing capitalism are challenging democratic governance at local, national and international levels.

Identifying a spectrum of policies and practices that seek to reproduce neoliberalism and shield it from popular and democratic contestation, contributors provide original case studies that investigate the legal-administrative, social, coercive and corporate dimensions of authoritarian neoliberalism across the global North and South. They detail the crisis-ridden intertwinement of authoritarian statecraft and neoliberal reforms, and trace the transformation of key societal sites in capitalism (e.g. states, households, workplaces, urban spaces) through uneven yet cumulative processes of neoliberalization.

Informed by innovative conceptual and methodological approaches, *Authoritarian Neoliberalism* uncovers how inequalities of power are produced and reproduced in capitalist societies, and highlights how alternatives to neoliberalism can be formulated and pursued. The book was originally published as a special issue of *Globalizations*.

Ian Bruff is Lecturer in European Politics at the University of Manchester, UK. He has published on capitalist diversity, European capitalisms, neoliberalism and social theory. He is currently researching the foundations of neoliberal thought and is the Managing Editor of the *Transforming Capitalism* book series.

Cemal Burak Tansel is Lecturer in International Politics in the Department of Politics at the University of Sheffield, UK. His research focuses on the historical sociology of state formation and capitalist development in the Middle East and the political economy of development. He is the Editor of *States of Discipline: Authoritarian Neoliberalism and the Contested Reproduction of Capitalist Order* (2017).

Rethinking Globalizations

Edited by Barry K. Gills, University of Helsinki, Finland and Kevin Gray, University of Sussex, UK.

This series is designed to break new ground in the literature on globalization and its academic and popular understanding. Rather than perpetuating or simply reacting to the economic understanding of globalization, this series seeks to capture the term and broaden its meaning to encompass a wide range of issues and disciplines and convey a sense of alternative possibilities for the future.

The Role of Religion in Struggles for Global Justice
Faith in Justice
Edited by Peter J. Smith, Katharina Glaab, Claudia Baumgart-Ochse and Elizabeth Smythe

Vivir Bien as an Alternative to Neoliberal Globalization
Can Indigenous Terminologies Decolonize the State?
Eija Ranta

Feminist Global Political Economies of the Everyday
Edited by Juanita Elias and Adrienne Roberts

The Politics of Destination in the 2030 Sustainable Development Goals
Leaving No-one Behind?
Edited by Clive Gabay and Suzan Ilcan

BRICS and MICs
Implications for Global Agrarian Transformation
Edited by Ben Cousins, Saturnino M. Borras Jr., Sergio Sauer and Jingzhong Ye

Migration, Civil Society and Global Governance
Edited by Carl-Ulrik Schierup, Branka Likic-Brboric, Raúl Delgado Wise and Gülay Toksöz

Authoritarian Neoliberalism
Philosophies, Practices, Contestations
Edited by Ian Bruff and Cemal Burak Tansel

For more information about this series, please visit:
www.routledge.com/Rethinking-Globalizations/book-series/RG

Authoritarian Neoliberalism

Philosophies, Practices, Contestations

Edited by
Ian Bruff and Cemal Burak Tansel

Routledge
Taylor & Francis Group
LONDON AND NEW YORK

First published 2020
by Routledge
2 Park Square, Milton Park, Abingdon, Oxon, OX14 4RN

and by Routledge
52 Vanderbilt Avenue, New York, NY 10017

Routledge is an imprint of the Taylor & Francis Group, an informa business

First issued in paperback 2021

British Library Cataloguing in Publication Data
A catalogue record for this book is available from the British Library

ISBN13: 978-0-367-37544-7 (hbk)
ISBN13: 978-1-03-208802-0 (pbk)

Typeset in Minion Pro
by Newgen Publishing UK

Publisher's Note
The publisher accepts responsibility for any inconsistencies that may have arisen during the conversion of this book from journal articles to book chapters, namely the inclusion of journal terminology.

Contents

Citation Information

The following chapters were originally published in *Globalizations*, volume 16, issue 3 (April 2019). When citing this material, please use the original page numbering for each article, as follows:

Chapter 1

Authoritarian neoliberalism: trajectories of knowledge production and praxis
Ian Bruff and Cemal Burak Tansel
Globalizations, volume 16, issue 3 (April 2019) pp. 233–244

Chapter 2

Framing the neoliberal canon: resisting the market myth via literary enquiry
Ian Bruff and Kathryn Starnes
Globalizations, volume 16, issue 3 (April 2019) pp. 245–259

Chapter 3

Managerial power in the German model: the case of Bertelsmann and the antecedents of neoliberalism
Mareike Beck and Julian Germann
Globalizations, volume 16, issue 3 (April 2019) pp. 260–273

Chapter 4

Authoritarian neoliberalism and capitalist transformation in Africa: all pain, no gain
Graham Harrison
Globalizations, volume 16, issue 3 (April 2019) pp. 274–288

Chapter 5

Neoliberal co-optation and authoritarian renewal: social entrepreneurship networks in Jordan and Morocco
Nadine Kreitmeyr
Globalizations, volume 16, issue 3 (April 2019) pp. 289–303

Chapter 6

Authoritarian neoliberal rescaling in Latin America: urban in/security and austerity in Oaxaca
Alke Jenss
Globalizations, volume 16, issue 3 (April 2019) pp. 304–319

Chapter 7

Reproducing authoritarian neoliberalism in Turkey: urban governance and state restructuring in the shadow of executive centralization
Cemal Burak Tansel
Globalizations, volume 16, issue 3 (April 2019) pp. 320–335

Chapter 8

Reconfiguring the state: executive powers, emergency legislation, and neoliberalization in Italy
Adriano Cozzolino
Globalizations, volume 16, issue 3 (April 2019) pp. 336–352

Chapter 9

The new EU industrial policy: authoritarian neoliberal structural adjustment and the case for alternatives
Angela Wigger
Globalizations, volume 16, issue 3 (April 2019) pp. 353–369

Notes on Contributors

Mareike Beck is a Doctoral Researcher in International Relations at the University of Sussex, UK. Her thesis analyzes the international history of German banking and speculation since the 1960s. Her broader research interests include the political economy of debt and financial development, microfinance and German political economy.

Ian Bruff is Lecturer in European Politics at the University of Manchester, UK. He has published on capitalist diversity, European capitalisms, neoliberalism, and social theory. He is currently researching the foundations of neoliberal thought.

Adriano Cozzolino is a Teaching Assistant at the University of Naples L'Orientale, Italy. He is currently researching the dynamics of state transformation, particularly the rise of executive power, in the neoliberal phase of capitalism in the European Union space.

Julian Germann is Lecturer in International Relations and Director for the Centre for Global Political Economy (CGPE) at the University of Sussex, UK. His current areas of research include the historical sociology of global governance and contestation, the political economy of capitalist crisis management, and US and German foreign economic policy.

Graham Harrison teaches in the School of Government and International Affairs at the University of Durham, UK.

Alke Jenss is a Senior Researcher at the Arnold-Bergstraesser-Institut at the University of Freiburg, Germany, and co-coordinates the institute's research cluster Contested Governance. Her current research focuses on the production of security and insecurity, the Latin American 'war on drugs' and its relation to transnational infrastructure masterplans, and multi-scalar governance from a state theory perspective.

Nadine Kreitmeyr is Assistant Professor in Middle East and Comparative Politics in the Graduate School of Social Sciences at the Middle East Technical University in Ankara, Turkey. Her research focuses on the interplay of authoritarianism and neoliberalism in the Middle East and North Africa.

Kathryn Starnes is Lecturer in International Relations at Manchester Metropolitan University, UK. She is currently researching IR narratives via postcolonial approaches to Gothic literature to explore practices of epistemic violence.

Cemal Burak Tansel is Lecturer in International Politics in the Department of Politics at the University of Sheffield, UK. His research focuses on the historical sociology of state formation and capitalist development in the Middle East and the political economy of development.

Angela Wigger is Associate Professor of Global Political Economy at Radboud University, the Netherlands. Her research focuses on the global economic crisis, crisis responses and political resistance, with a particular focus on the EU's 'competitiveness' fetish and the issue of debt.

Preface

Work on this special issue stems from a joint section on authoritarian neoliberalism that we convened for the September 2016 European International Studies Association conference in Izmir, Turkey. In response to our section call, we received many interesting submissions and were looking forward to discussions in Izmir. However, the conference was cancelled in July 2016 on account of both the failed coup attempt in Turkey and the subsequent punitive state of emergency, which in turn built upon an increasingly authoritarian trajectory taken by the Justice and Development Party.

Undeterred, we agreed that a Section Call should be submitted for the September 2017 EISA conference in Barcelona. This produced 12 well-attended panels and approximately 50 presentations across the conference. Around the time of the conference, the city itself became a key site for the manifestation of the crisis-ridden and highly contested assertion of national state power in Spain, as it took place only a few weeks before the independence referendum and subsequent invocation of emergency provisions by the Spanish state (such as the notorious Article 155). For some involved in the independence struggle, at stake was not just local sovereignty but transformed and democratized forms of self-governance as well.

Almost all of the chapters in this edited volume were either presented at the 2017 conference or would have been presented at the 2016 conference. The final versions of the chapters, which were originally published in a special issue of the journal *Globalizations* (2019, volume 16, issue 3), were produced in late spring/early summer 2018. The volume is a reprint of the special issue, and papers are reproduced in the same form they appear in the *Globalizations* issue.

We would like to thank Barry Gills, editor of the journal *Globalizations* and one of the editors of the *Rethinking Globalizations* series, for enthusiastically supporting this project from our original conversations with him in late 2016 to the publication of this volume; Shelley Barry, for overseeing the smooth process of producing the special issue once it had been accepted; and Lydia de Cruz at Routledge for managing the transition from special issue to published book. Finally, much love and thanks to Laura Chambers and Lauren Selfe for continued support.

Ian Bruff and Cemal Burak Tansel
Manchester and Sheffield
June 2019

1 Authoritarian neoliberalism: trajectories of knowledge production and praxis

Ian Bruff and Cemal Burak Tansel

ABSTRACT

This introduction to the special issue takes as its point of departure three centres of gravity that have shaped the study of neoliberalism but have also established barriers to further progress in these debates. By promoting an intersectional materialist research agenda which challenges extant ideational, modernist and empiricist tendencies in scholarship on neoliberalism, the essay contextualizes the special issue articles by outlining and clarifying key aspects of our understanding of authoritarian neoliberalism. In particular, we reflect on themes related to conceptualization and periodization, which are of importance for both this special issue but also for broader questions of knowledge production and praxis. Through doing so, we argue that there are two distinct yet connected trajectories within the research agenda on authoritarian neoliberalism: one which focuses on the intertwinement of authoritarian statisms and neoliberal reforms; and another which traces various lineages of transformation of key societal sites in capitalism (e.g. states, households, workplaces, urban spaces). Recognition of this *spectrum* of authoritarian neoliberal practices is important as it helps us uncover how inequalities of power are produced and reproduced in capitalist societies, and pushes us to consider more fully how other worlds can be made possible. Nevertheless, it is affirmed that we must remain open to what an emancipatory society might look like, and what struggles would be most appropriate, in and across various socio-spatial contexts.

Understanding neoliberalism: moving away from three centres of gravity

The conceptual value and political utility of neoliberalism continue to be significant fault-lines in academic and public debates. On the one hand, many scholars increasingly question whether 'neoliberalism as a broad, catch-all term [can] adequately serve so many different phenomena and theoretical conceptualizations' (Venugopal, 2015, p. 165). On the other hand, the claim that public policies and state strategies that have been variously described as 'neoliberal' in the past three decades continue to dominate is accepted not only by scholars, but also by those who have often been portrayed as the architects of those policies (see Ostry, Loungani, & Furceri, 2016). Coupled with the fact that 'neoliberalism' has not lost its popular and analytical resonance after the 2007–8 global economic crisis *and* throughout a state of 'permanent austerity' enacted especially but not only in Europe (Bailey, 2015), it is urgent that we consider these crucial questions:

- How do the practices, policies and ideas that are associated with 'neoliberalism' reproduce themselves in the face of crises and popular opposition?
- In what ways are such attempts at reproduction – in the current period, increasingly authoritarian and coercive – productive of new forms of crisis due to their contradictory nature?
- What lineages of transformation of key societal sites in capitalism (e.g. states, households, workplaces, urban spaces) can be traced to inform both our understanding of neoliberalism but also strategies for critiquing and resisting it?
- How do social struggles and various forms of resistance shape the manifestations of authoritarian neoliberalism, and how could they be utilized to generate visions of a more equitable future?

While debates on the conceptualization and utilization of neoliberalism continue to produce vibrant points of analytical contention, the term 'authoritarian neoliberalism' is fast becoming an established part of critical social science scholarship, as shown by its deployment across numerous disciplinary and critical perspectives (for example, Bruff, 2014, 2016; Bruff and Wöhl, 2016; Gonzales, 2016; Smith, 2018; Tansel, 2017b, 2018; Wigger and Buch-Hansen, 2015; Yeşil, 2016; and the contributions in Tansel, 2017a).

In our work, we locate the term at the intersection of a range of social relations and utilize it to highlight how contemporary capitalism is governed in a way which tends to reinforce and rely upon practices that seek to marginalize, discipline and control dissenting social groups and oppositional politics rather than strive for their explicit consent or co-optation. Such practices include the repeated invocations of 'the market' or 'economic necessity' to justify a wide range of restructurings across various societal sites (e.g. states, households, workplaces, urban spaces), the growing tendency to prioritize constitutional and legal mechanisms rather than democratic debate and participation, the centralization of state powers by the executive branch at the expense of popular participation and other nodes of governance, the mobilization of state apparatuses for the repression of oppositional social forces at a range of scales, and the heightened pressures and responsibilities shifted onto households by repeated bouts of crisis and the restructuring of the state's redistributive mechanisms. Nevertheless, for us, authoritarian neoliberalism is also understood as a crisis-ridden, contradictory set of practices which enhance the capacities and potentials for resistance as well as for domination. While the political and socio-economic developments that triggered the conceptualization of authoritarian neoliberalism tend to be understood from within a framework of progressive politics – such as the emphasis on the emergence of new sites of solidarity and autonomous movements seeking to prefigure a better world (see Huke, Clua-Losada, & Bailey, 2015) – we argue that resistances are multi-form and not always emancipatory, as signalled, for example, by the rise of new radical Right populism (see Konings, 2012).

Our aim in this collection of contributions to the rich debate on neoliberalism is to advance three main considerations, which together propose a departure from some of the limitations inherent to the well-established approaches in the literature. This is, by no means, a wholesale dismissal of the extant body of work on neoliberalism, but should be seen as an extension of a collective effort to move away from three centres of gravity that have shaped the study of neoliberalism but have also established barriers to further progress in these debates. With this objective in mind, and with a view to forging a stronger dialogue with cognate approaches to and critiques of neoliberalism in various branches of the social sciences, our contributions are framed thus:

(1) We advocate an explicitly 'political' reading of neoliberalism, promoting an intersectional materialist research agenda in contrast to predominantly ideational approaches which have often

been at the centre of debates about neoliberalism (for example, Mirowski & Plehwe, 2009; Peck, 2010). The role of ideas and discourses is not to be discounted, and these works have been essential for advancing our understanding of neoliberalism beyond simplistic 'free market' narratives which also have a habit of essentializing states as inherently socially protective. However, these accounts, by virtue of their very focus, tend to underplay the connection between such ideas and discourses with capitalist development and statehood – plus with unequal social relations across society – and particularly their imbrication with coercive practices which seek to support and protect capital accumulation in the name of 'free markets' (Cahill, 2014). Moreover, these contributions place implicit faith in the potential of a new set of *better* ideas and discourses to displace and replace neoliberal practices. While laudable in a general sense, the works in this tradition do not say enough about the fact that '[m]aterial circumstances are the net of constraints, the "conditions of existence" for practical thought and calculation about society' (Hall, 1996, p. 44), thus saying too little about *how* and *why* certain ideas come to dominate policy and preferences at particular points in time, as well as how and why they come to be contested (cf. Bieler & Morton, 2008).

(2) The special issue responds to the call made by Connell and Dados (2014, p. 134) to '[move] beyond the self-referentiality of Northern social science [and] towards a more democratic structure of theory on a world scale', which, for us, includes a more thorough examination of global South cases hitherto viewed as marginal to the study and especially the (re)constitution of neoliberalism. Neoliberalism in the global South has come to mean much more than what can be captured through the use of the traditional 'structural adjustment programme' analytical prism. Therefore, the special issue offers a wide range of empirical case studies that cover more ground than the Anglo-American centre of gravity that has long dominated the literature (see also Klein, 2007). In doing so, it challenges modernist and Eurocentric dichotomies about the *forms* taken by neoliberalism, which tend to contrast democratic capitalism in the global North with authoritarian development in the global South – i.e. as if 'capitalism' and 'development' can be neatly separated and mapped on to the world in an either/or fashion (see Tansel, 2017b). It is clear that countries such as the UK and the US, and relatedly Australia, Canada, Ireland and New Zealand, are important examples of neoliberalization, but this does not justify a strong focus on these spaces over others – a choice that effectively limits the potential for furthering our understanding of neoliberalism as well as skewing its conceptualization.

(3) Our contributions move the debate decisively beyond the empiricist tendencies of some accounts of neoliberalism's resilience since 2007–8, which have largely superimposed commentary about the increasingly authoritarian forms taken by a resilient neoliberalism onto theoretical frameworks and approaches established prior to 2008 (for example, Ban, 2016; Schmidt & Thatcher, 2013; Streeck, 2014). In various ways, the articles in the special issue take stock of the important contributions made by these accounts, but also aim to co-produce a research agenda more attuned to the significance of post-2008 shifts in socio-economic, legal and political landscapes. As we explore in detail below, highlighting this character of the crisis as a key conjuncture does not mean that the current trajectory of neoliberalism signifies a radical break from its pre-crisis orientation. Nor do we wish this consideration to be seen as a move that separates the association of neoliberalism from capitalism. Nevertheless, we contend that the crisis – and its accompanying aftershocks at various levels of governance and across a range of societies – did play an important role in heightening the extant anti-democratic tendencies of neoliberalism as well as generating new and mutated mechanisms that reproduce such tendencies. As such, our contributions complement some of the recent additions to the literature on neoliberalism

(Soederberg, 2014; Springer, 2016; Wacquant, 2009) and simultaneously act as a call for the further shedding of *some* of the notions and assumptions which advanced our understandings of neoliberalism in the 1990s and 2000s, but ultimately require amendments in light of concrete political and socio-economic changes (e.g. the dominant focus on 'marketization' as a driver of neoliberalism).

Built on these premises, the special issue brings together contributions that further refine our conceptualization of the term 'authoritarian neoliberalism' and flesh out how the processes that we associate with it manifest in concrete contexts. In many ways, we utilize the space provided by this special issue to expand on the collective step taken towards formulating 'authoritarian neoliberalism' as a research agenda in *States of Discipline: Authoritarian Neoliberalism and the Contested Reproduction of Capitalist Order* (Tansel, 2017a), and to offer a targeted exercise in mapping practices, ideas and struggles that shape contemporary capitalism. Before covering the details of our contributions, we would like to take this opportunity to reflect on a number of issues related to the conceptualization and periodization of the concept, which we think are of importance not only for the current contributions at hand, but also for broader questions of knowledge production and praxis.

Embracing messiness, or why it is healthy to work with imperfect concepts

The 11th European International Studies Association conference, organized in Barcelona in September 2017,[1] hosted a well-attended section on authoritarian neoliberalism. The call for this section attracted enough interest to enable 12 panels to take place across the conference, including a roundtable on *States of Discipline* (Tansel, 2017a). It was gratifying to witness such interest in the book and the concept, yet we were also struck by the tendency for certain types of well-meaning questions to be asked more than others – an experience which has been mirrored when we have delivered presentations elsewhere.

These questions often revolved around the desire for greater definitional clarity (for example, what we understand authoritarianism to be) and more precise conceptualizations of various elements of the research agenda (for instance, the exact relationship between consent and coercion). Some colleagues voiced the concern that authoritarian neoliberalism represents a top-down approach which neglects everyday life and the possibilities for grassroots change. Many of these questions prompted us to reflect on how we adopted, deployed and defined the concept, but also to think carefully about how we articulated and communicated our arguments in our work. As such, they produced helpful dialogues that displayed both the vibrancy of the debates around the concept and the existence of a number of issues that 'authoritarian neoliberalism', at least in its current incarnation, was not – and *should* not be – able to explain.

Nevertheless, given the persistence of certain requests for clarification, we realized that some of these exchanges spoke to the formalized nature of knowledge production that is encouraged and, indeed sanctioned, in many parts of the social sciences – for instance, the privileging of modes of reasoning which embody and promote an incessant drive for *categorizability*. In principle, this categorization drive opens up the possibilities for dialogue between protagonists in various literatures, for having an analytical common ground helps provide a basis for the debates that unfold. But what happens when the very basis for the debates, the categories themselves, start mutating in front of our eyes and we are forced to reflect on the way we understand the world? Here we concur wholeheartedly with Buttigieg (1990, p. 81), when he argues that 'if the relationship among the fragments [of our knowledge] were permanently fixed, then the concepts and theories would crystallize into dogmas'. We can, for example, trace the negative analytical consequences of utilizing neoliberalism in an inflexible way in how dominant Anglocentric conceptions have struggled to explain the complexities of cases emanating from the global South. Similarly, the governance of neoliberalism in the aftermath of the 2007–8 crisis has accentuated the need to rethink the relationship between the capitalist state and the role of the law in regulating and reproducing dominant policy paradigms, with law all too often being understood in a descriptive and analytically/politically neutral manner.

It is important to highlight that we acknowledge the value of crafting arguments which are well-informed, coherent and persuasive, but on the other hand, we agree with Mason (2011, p. 80) on the importance of adopting a less orthodox approach to concept formation, which should not be seen as antithetical to analytical 'rigour':

> if we want to create flashes of insight we need researchers to be active and imaginative agents ... when they ask themselves how they can get hold of some pivotal, incisive, crucial or vital things ... They need to make inventive and even ingenious decisions about which might be particularly compelling lines of enquiry and this cannot be done with deductive reasoning and following predefined methodological procedures alone.

Therefore, we would like to reiterate our contention that authoritarian neoliberalism does capture important global trends that warrant our attention, but it is not a template conceptualization that can be uncritically applied across the world or across time. Hence the discussion in our work of practices, repertoires and spectrums rather than an attempt to formulate strict typologies and models. Moreover, observe the evolution in Bruff's work to acknowledge the relative absence of feminist scholarship in his earlier contributions (compare Bruff, 2014 with Bruff & Wöhl, 2016), and the explicit statement in Tansel's introduction to *States of Discipline* that the volume should not be seen as the culmination of a completed research project, with 'the particular gendered, racialized and localized effects of authoritarian neoliberalism, as well as their relationship with the contemporary forms of indebtedness, financialization, migration and globalized conflict' requiring greater future scrutiny (Tansel, 2017b, p. 18).

This leads us to a more specific point about the intellectual inspirations for our initial forays into this area of work. In both cases (Bruff, 2014; Tansel, 2017a), parity of esteem was accorded to Antonio Gramsci, Stuart Hall, and Nicos Poulantzas. Tellingly, while Gramsci and especially Poulantzas are referenced in questions asked of us at conferences, Hall is frequently conspicuous by his absence. What might this be emblematic of? For us, it is the aforementioned, formalized modes of reasoning: as a scholar associated with Cultural Studies and sometimes Sociology, Hall – we infer – must be seen as someone who can only help us gain insight into the *cultural* aspects of authoritarian neoliberalism, such as the role of the media in promoting debt-laden consumerism. Such a set of assumptions is highly problematic for embodying dichotomies such as culture/politics, state/society and formal/informal, refracting the notion of authoritarian neoliberalism through narrow prisms. More damagingly, it neglects the fact that, *precisely because* he viewed the world he studied as constituted by a plurality of sites and practices, Hall can be understood as a politicized and politicizing scholar in all respects.[2] Politics does not just reside in the state, policy-making, election campaigns, and so on; it is immanent to all social relationships and sites. Not for nothing was he the person to coin the term 'Thatcherism' prior to Thatcher becoming Prime Minister, and to identify its contradictions earlier than almost anybody else.

Crucially for our purposes, on neoliberalism Hall argued that the 'term "neoliberal" is not a satisfactory one ... However, I think there are enough common features to warrant giving it a *provisional* conceptual identity, provided this is understood as a first approximation' (Hall, 2011, p. 10; original emphasis). This is not simply because Hall is imploring us to understand neoliberalism in its multiple instantiations, though that is part of the story. It also means that:

> No project achieves 'hegemony' as a completed project. It is a process, not a state of being. No victories are permanent or final. Hegemony has constantly to be 'worked on', maintained, renewed, revised. Excluded social forces, whose consent has not been won, whose interests have not been taken into account, for the basis of counter-movements, resistance, alternative strategies and visions ... and the struggle over a hegemonic system starts anew. They constitute what Raymond Williams called 'the emergent' – and are the reason why history is never closed but maintains an open horizon towards the future. (Hall, 2011, p. 26)

In other words, and in contrast to approaches which project resistance to neoliberalism as something that is thrust *upon* the capitalist state by forces from *outside* that are analytically and methodologically *separate* from politics and governance (e.g. Foucault, 2008; Gill, 2000; Harvey, 2005), we instead see social struggles as traversing all parts of society, including the state. More to the point, it is possible to envision and place at the heart of our research the potentials for things to be different in the future if we reject over-formalized forms of knowledge of production and instead embrace the inevitable *messiness* inherent to the study of socio-economic, legal, and political landscapes that are shifting in front of us, in our own lifetimes (cf. Montesinos Coleman, 2015). The research agenda of authoritarian neoliberalism, for all of its apparent pessimism and seeming focus on domination, reveals that the way we live today is not inevitable because it is actively constructed by competing social forces, and that our modes of living could be different in the future for the same reason.

As noted earlier in the article, resistance in the current period is multi-form and points to a range of possible future 'post-neoliberal' developments, from regressive to transformative. Additionally, if we are committed to acknowledging and understanding practices, repertoires and spectrums rather than attempting to formulate strict typologies and models, then it is imperative that we remain open to what an emancipatory society might look like, and what struggles would be most appropriate, in and across various socio-spatial contexts. Nevertheless, we close this section by affirming a core motivation for pursuing the research agenda on authoritarian neoliberalism: by becoming more attuned to how inequalities of power are produced and reproduced in capitalist societies, we are able to consider more fully how other worlds can be made possible. The world *could* be more equitable if, in the process of understanding, critiquing and challenging authoritarian neoliberalism, we can find a way to reconstruct states and societies according to values such as equality, justice, dignity, and solidarity.

Two strategies for unpacking the lineages of authoritarian neoliberalism

This living and evolving character of the concept also raises some important questions about understanding the novelty and historicity of the practices that we associate with authoritarian neoliberalism. Some critical treatments of the concept we have come across in conference discussions focus on this issue, highlighting the dangers of disassociating non-democratic practices from a broader history of neoliberalism and capitalism – a concern often accompanied by the call to recognize that neoliberalism and capitalism have always been 'authoritarian'. This is an important point, which reminds us to pay attention to, for example, the tensions created by the political organization of capitalism which continually build barriers against substantial democratization, as well as to the fact that many instances of neoliberal reforms across the world materialized through the deployment of highly coercive state strategies. Yet, we are not entirely convinced how this issue applies to the way in which we have attempted to formulate the concept, as our own sketches have been shaped by two complementary sensitivities that stress both the 'authoritarian' continuities and the qualitative transformations in the lineages of actually existing neoliberalisms.

With regards to the novelty of authoritarian neoliberalism – and in particular, of the practices that have become more visible in the aftermath of the global economic crisis – we have maintained that these developments should not be seen as amounting to a wholesale break from neoliberal practices prior to 2007 (Bruff, 2014, p. 116). On the contrary, we have repeatedly contextualized such practices within the longer trajectory of neoliberalism, and insisted that the focus on *authoritarian* neoliberalism:

> should *not* be read to the effect that the deployment of coercive state apparatuses for the protection of the circuits of capital accumulation is a *new* phenomenon, nor should it lead to the assumption that the pre-crisis trajectories of neoliberalization have been *exclusively consensual.* (Tansel, 2017b, pp. 2–3; original emphases)

At the same time, our collective work with colleagues has demonstrated that neoliberal projects have increasingly relied on a constellation of legal, administrative and coercive state apparatuses to both legitimize and shield themselves from political and social contestation. Such measures and practices could be interpreted as merely updated incarnations of capitalism's (or neoliberalism's) inherent authoritarian tendencies, but we think it is crucial to conduct a more surgical analysis and examine carefully how these practices differ from established logics of capitalist statecraft. Put bluntly, rejecting the authoritarian character of contemporary capitalism on the grounds that capitalism itself possesses non-democratic tendencies is a counter-productive strategy. While it is important to take into account systemic imperatives in explaining why capitalism produces authoritarian governance, we cannot reduce all instances and forms of authoritarian practices to a general capitalist law of motion. Doing so obscures a vast spectrum of governance techniques and potential ways to resist and overcome them, and risks producing, in the process of invoking the need to produce a more accurate picture of periodization, an ahistorical account of temporally seamless authoritarian capitalist statecraft.

Furthermore, authoritarian neoliberalism captures two distinct research trajectories: one focusing on the intertwinement of authoritarian statisms and neoliberal reforms; and another which traces various lineages of transformation of key societal sites in capitalism (e.g. states, households, workplaces, urban spaces), via spatially and temporally uneven yet cumulative neoliberalization processes that are observable across different cases. These are not mutually exclusive orientations, but they ultimately prioritize a different set of research questions and would suggest different political strategies when considering questions of resistance. In the first trajectory, the concept could be deployed to explore how neoliberalization in authoritarian states produces a symbiotic configuration whereby the reforms are enacted and protected through existing mechanisms of authoritarian statecraft. The historical trend of neoliberalization through authoritarianism is an important part of the story of Latin American and Middle Eastern cases (Bedirhanoğlu & Yalman, 2010), and more recent research has demonstrated the significance of this co-constitutive relationship in the cases of China and Cambodia (Lim, 2017; Springer, 2017). In the second trajectory, the focus is more decisively on sets of neoliberal practices employed not only in authoritarian states but also in formally democratic regimes to further protect spaces and circuits of capitalist accumulation, and how such practices are dependent for their effectiveness on their ongoing, varying and frequently conflictual entanglement with key societal sites such as households, workplaces, and urban spaces. Here, the particular administrative and legal efforts to limit the social and political space for contesting those ideas/policies, as well as to facilitate a broader realignment of public power away from democratic politics, takes priority.

Contributions to this special issue are situated within these two trajectories, and by doing so, reveal both the continuities in some of the neoliberalization processes under scrutiny, and the qualitative changes experienced in the others – particularly (but not only) in relation to executive centralization and legislative activism, and conflictual entanglements between these evolutions and other key societal sites.

Outlining the special issue

The special issue contains eight articles in addition to this introductory essay, and they can be considered in pairs. The papers by Ian Bruff & Kathryn Starnes and by Mareike Beck & Julian Germann take issue with the position of 'the market' in neoliberal thought and practice. Bruff & Starnes utilize a literary-theoretical approach to argue that neoliberalism, even in 'pure' theory texts by key intellectuals such as Friedrich Hayek and Milton Friedman, has never been about free markets. Bruff & Starnes emphasize the crucial role of states and households instead; in contrast, Beck & Germann's article points to the importance of corporate hierarchies and management techniques in the emergence of German neoliberalism. This enables them to claim that Germany was not a latecomer to neoliberalism; nor was it necessarily distinct from 'Anglo' countries because of the role of ordoliberal ideas (as suggested by many commentaries on neoliberalism with German characteristics).

Graham Harrison and Nadine Kreitmeyr provide regional overviews of African and MENA (Middle East and North Africa) countries. In doing so, they highlight how seemingly more inclusive governing strategies can give the impression of a move away from neoliberalism to more enlightened politico-economic projects. However, Harrison notes that more 'developmental' strategies, while facilitating greater chances of sustained capital accumulation than their neoliberal equivalents, do not necessarily lead to the more democratic or equal society that critics of neoliberalism often assume. Conversely, Kreitmeyr argues that the growth of social entrepreneurship networks may suggest a pluralization and partial liberalization of these societies, but are presently serving to forge paths of authoritarian renewal via neoliberal co-optation. As such, both papers remind us of the importance of conceptual reflection when considering the term 'authoritarianism' as well as that of 'neoliberalism'.

The papers by Alke Jenss and Cemal Burak Tansel continue the challenge to modernist dichotomies, but zoom in from the regional to the urban scale. This is important, for struggles around security and housing have been central to (in Jenss' article) 'austerity urbanism' and to what Tansel understands as the commodification of public space and housing. More specifically, Jenss extends previous work on authoritarian neoliberalism by considering the coloniality of power in local forms of statehood in southern Mexico, and the consequences this has for studying localized expressions of formal and informal social relations. Tansel's article contests another common binary, between national and local levels of governance in the production of neoliberal reforms. He shows how the selective mobilization of executive powers, particularly through judicial and administrative restructuring, have been utilized in Turkey to increase the scope of commodification of urban land and in housing, as well as to strengthen the presence of state coercion across multiple sites.

The final two papers consider a well-known theme in debates on authoritarian neoliberalism, the Eurozone crises and responses to them at supranational, national and local scales. Nevertheless, Adriano Cozzolino and Angela Wigger paint a different picture of their cases compared to the norm. Cozzolino continues Tansel's discussion of executive centralization, showing that the narrowing down of political space to contest policy, via constitutionalization, emergency laws and administrative restructuring, has been ongoing in Italy since the late 1970s. Therefore, while these processes have intensified in the last decade, Cozzolino's analysis dovetails with our points about periodization in this essay. Wigger's critique of the European Union's so-called new industrial policy shows that real change will not come from EU institutions as currently configured, but instead from entirely different practices which have as their premise democratically-managed social relations of (re)production; moreover, such understandings are currently proliferating in European solidarity economy initiatives.

Inevitably, collections such as this special issue cannot cover all aspects of the topic and related themes. Therefore, we will use the conclusion to discuss the objectives of the special issue and where future research on authoritarian neoliberalism could take us.

Conclusion and pointers for future research

The special issue aims to fulfil the following objectives:

Advancing new conceptual and methodological tools to bolster the study of neoliberalism

In addition to its focus on conceptualizing authoritarian neoliberalism, this collection features empirical case studies built on approaches and methods that are relatively under-utilized in the literature (e.g. literary theory, archival research, legal analysis). The articles further promote interdisciplinary dialogue by echoing some of the cognate debates in Anthropology and Area Studies (see Eriksen, Laidlaw, Mair, Martin, & Venkatesan, 2015; Guarneros-Meza & Geddes, 2010).

Rectifying a number of significant empirical and geographical lacunae in accounts of neoliberalism

The special issue articles on Middle Eastern, African and Latin American cases help to decentre the dominant narrative on neoliberalism. We present these cases not as empirical 'additions' to an otherwise unproblematized theoretical edifice, but the building blocks of our new research agenda that takes local histories, socio-economic conditions and political struggles seriously. We further believe that these case studies will be of utmost importance to the broader International Political Economy and Economic Sociology literatures, given the extent to which the former in particular has been complicit in overlooking the Middle East and Africa as sites of analysis (be it through neglect of the cases or the failure to avoid the capitalism/development binary discussed earlier).

Informing political struggles and envisioning alternative futures

Reform of or alternatives to capitalism have achieved greater prominence in recent years, reaching beyond academic literatures to inform popular debates (see Mason, 2015; Piketty, 2014). They have also led to a revival in autonomist and related writings on self-organization and new forms of resistance (see Federici, 2012; Holloway, 2016). However, many still understand the struggle against neoliberalism to be resistance against marketization. This special issue challenges assumptions which associate too strongly neoliberalism with economics or free markets *per se*, as part of a broader attempt to rethink progressive politics and strategies. As a result, the special issue invites us to consider the significance of a broader range of resistances. This does not downplay more formal forms of politics, but it does mean that we ought not to restrict ourselves to political parties, trade unions, and established civil society organizations. A broader perspective would also address, for instance, labour activisms which challenge legal restrictions and neglectful trade unions (such as in China), place-based struggles that embody radically different understandings of development (such as among indigenous peoples in Latin America), spatially diffused but socially connected movements against racialized coercion and militarized forms of policing (such as Black Lives Matter), community-centred responses and resistances to intensified crises of social reproduction (such as the PAH's actions in Spain to prevent evictions and fight for the right to housing), and finally the wide range of solidarity economy initiatives that exist across the world which attempt to prefigure the world that they wish to see. To be clear, this does not obviate the need to engage with more formalized forms of politics, but we should adjust our worldview in order to understand and discuss the *interconnections* between various resistances and struggles and how they inform and shape each other.

Hence, by making important conceptual and methodological advances and through addressing a number of empirical and geographical lacunae, the possibilities for scholarship on authoritarian neoliberalism to inform political and social struggles and to envision alternative futures are significantly increased. In particular, every article in the special issue undermines established 'facts' about neoliberalism in thought and in practice, pointing in the process towards new avenues for research and for political and social praxis. Moreover, every article cautions readers about the inevitably loaded nature of terms such as 'markets', 'democracy', 'authoritarianism', 'households', 'competition', and 'social', thus hopefully helping to foster a dialogue which does not take such concepts for granted when considering strategies of critique and resistance.

This leads us to future research on authoritarian neoliberalism. This list is not exhaustive, but all would help enrich further the work already being done: genealogies of authoritarian neoliberalism in earlier contributions from a range of neoliberal intellectuals; the intertwining of more commercial and more securitized forms of power, especially in terms of violence and policing; understandings of and struggles over the term 'public', be it in terms of public services, public spaces, public goods, and so on; enhanced connections and dialogues between a greater range of critical-theoretical approaches (for example, historical materialist, feminist, postcolonial, anarchist); the notion of the 'non-market', so central to neoliberalism yet also the potential basis for an alternative society in the future (e.g. the solidarity economy); and anthropologies of resistance in their particular socio-spatial contexts. Much work lies ahead of us.

Notes

1. Around the time of the conference, the city itself became a key site for the manifestation of the crisis-ridden and highly contested assertion of national state power, and embodied the fundamental incoherence of the Spanish state in its localized expressions. Moreover, for some involved in the independence struggle, at stake was not just local sovereignty but transformed and democratized forms of self-governance as well.
2. Many thanks to Kathryn Starnes for this point.

Acknowledgements

We would like to thank the participants of the section 'Authoritarian Neoliberalism: Dominations, Crises, Resistances', organized at the 11th European International Studies Association conference in Barcelona (13–16 September 2017), and in particular to Victoria Basham, Katharina Bodirsky, Sébastien Rioux and Ilona Steiler for their feedback and contributions. Additionally, the Critical Political Economy Research

Network has been valuable for Ian Bruff in particular, across many years. Many of the ideas expressed in this piece have been shaped by our conversations with David Bailey, Andreas Bieler, Mònica Clua-Losada, Brecht De Smet, Juanita Elias, Laura Horn, Johannes Jäger, Lara Montesinos Coleman, Adam David Morton, Reecia Orzeck, V. Spike Peterson, Adrienne Roberts, Roberto Roccu, Alfredo Saad-Filho, Susanne Soederberg, Simon Springer, Liam Stanley, Kathryn Starnes, Angela Wigger, Stefanie Wöhl, and Yuliya Yurchenko. We extend our gratitude to them for their generous support. Finally, we would like to thank the editors of *Globalizations*, especially Barry Gills, for supporting the proposal for this special issue.

Disclosure statement

No potential conflict of interest was reported by the authors.

References

Bailey, D. (2015). Resistance is futile? The impact of disruptive protest in the 'silver age of permanent austerity'. *Socio-economic Review, 13*(1), 5–32.

Ban, C. (2016). *Ruling ideas: How global neoliberalism goes local.* Oxford: Oxford University Press.

Bedirhanoğlu, P., & Yalman, G. L. (2010). State, class and the discourse: Reflections on the neoliberal transformation in Turkey. In A. Saad-Filho & G. L. Yalman (Eds.), *Economic transitions to neoliberalism in middle-income countries* (pp. 107–127). Abingdon: Routledge.

Bieler, A., & Morton, A. D. (2008). The deficits of discourse in IPE: Turning base metal into gold? *International Studies Quarterly, 52*(1), 103–128.

Bruff, I. (2014). The rise of authoritarian neoliberalism. *Rethinking Marxism, 26*(1), 113–129.

Bruff, I. (2016). Neoliberalism and authoritarianism. In S. Springer, K. Birch, & J. MacLeavy (Eds.), *The handbook of neoliberalism* (pp. 107–117). New York: Routledge.

Bruff, I., & Wöhl, S. (2016). Constitutionalizing austerity, disciplining the household: Masculine norms of competitiveness and the crisis of social reproduction in the Eurozone. In A. Hozić & J. True (Eds.), *Scandalous economics: Gender and the politics of financial crises* (pp. 92–108). Oxford: Oxford University Press.

Buttigieg, J. A. (1990). Gramsci's method. *Boundary 2, 17*(2), 60–81.

Cahill, D. (2014). *The end of laissez-faire? On the durability of embedded liberalism.* Cheltenham: Edward Elgar.

Connell, R., & Dados, N. (2014). Where in the world does neoliberalism come from? The market agenda in Southern perspective. *Theory and Society, 43*(2), 117–138.

Eriksen, T. H., Laidlaw, J., Mair, J., Martin, K., & Venkatesan, S. (2015). Debate: The concept of neoliberalism has become an obstacle to the anthropological understanding of the twenty-first century. *Journal of the Royal Anthropological Institute, 21*(4), 911–923.

Federici, S. (2012). *Revolution at point zero: Housework, reproduction, and feminist struggle.* Oalkland: PM Press.

Foucault, M. (2008). *The birth of biopolitics: Lectures at the Collège de France, 1978–1979* (G. Burchell, Trans.). New York: Palgrave Macmillan.

Gill, S. (2000). Towards a postmodern prince? The battle in Seattle as a moment in the new politics of globalisation. *Millennium: Journal of International Studies, 29*(1), 131–140.

Gonzales, A. (2016). Neoliberalism, the Homeland Security state, and the authoritarian turn. *Latino Studies, 14* (1), 80–98.
Guarneros-Meza, V., & Geddes, M. (2010). Local governance and participation under neoliberalism: Comparative perspectives. *International Journal of Urban and Regional Research*, *34*(1), 115–129.
Hall, S. (1996). The problem of ideology: Marxism without guarantees. In D. Morley & K.-H. Chen (Eds.), *Stuart Hall: Critical dialogues in cultural studies* (pp. 25–46). London: Routledge.
Hall, S. (2011). The neoliberal revolution. *Soundings*, *48*, 9–28.
Harvey, D. (2005). *A brief history of neoliberalism*. Oxford: Oxford University Press.
Holloway, J. (2016). *In, against, and beyond capitalism: The San Francisco lectures*. Oakland: PM Press.
Huke, N., Clua-Losada, M., & Bailey, D. J. (2015). Disrupting the European crisis: A critical political economy of contestation, subversion and escape. *New Political Economy*, *20*(5), 725–751.
Klein, N. (2007). *The shock doctrine: The rise of disaster capitalism*. London: Allen Lane.
Konings, M. (2012). Imagined double movements: Progressive thought and the specter of neoliberal populism. *Globalizations*, *9*(4), 609–622.
Lim, K. F. (2017). Variegated neoliberalization as a function and outcome of neo-authoritarianism in China. In C. B. Tansel (Ed.), *States of discipline: Authoritarian neoliberalism and the contested reproduction of capitalist order* (pp. 255–273). London: Rowman & Littlefield International.
Mason, J. (2011). Facet methodology: The case for an inventive research orientation. *Methodological Innovations Online*, *6*(3), 75–92.
Mason, P. (2015) *Postcapitalism: A guide to our future*. London: Allen Lane.
Mirowski, P., & Plehwe, D. (Eds.). (2009). *The road from Mont Pelerin: The making of the neoliberal thought collective*. Cambridge: Harvard University Press.
Montesinos Coleman, L. (2015). Ethnography, commitment, and critique: Departing from activist scholarship. *International Political Sociology*, *9*(3), 263–280.
Ostry, J. D., Loungani, P., & Furceri, D. (2016). Neoliberalism: Oversold? *Finance & Development*, *53*(2), 38–41. Retrieved from http://www.imf.org/external/pubs/ft/fandd/2016/06/pdf/ostry.pdf
Peck, J. (2010). *Constructions of neoliberal reason*. Oxford: Oxford University Press.
Piketty, T. (2014) *Capital in the twenty-first century*. Harvard, MA: Harvard University Press.
Schmidt, V. A., & Thatcher, M. (Eds.). (2013). *Resilient liberalism in Europe's political economy*. Cambridge: Cambridge University Press.
Smith, C. (2018). Race and the logic of radicalisation under neoliberalism. *Journal of Sociology*, *54*(1), 92–107.
Soederberg, S. (2014). *Debtfare states and the poverty industry: Money, discipline and the surplus population*. Abingdon: Routledge.
Springer, S. (2016). *The discourse of neoliberalism: An anatomy of a powerful idea*. London: Rowman & Littlefield International.
Springer, S. (2017). Klepto-neoliberalism: Authoritarianism and patronage in Cambodia. In C. B. Tansel (Ed.), *States of discipline: Authoritarian neoliberalism and the contested reproduction of capitalist order* (pp. 235–254). London: Rowman & Littlefield International.
Streeck, W. (2014). How will capitalism end? *New Left Review*, *2*(87), 35–64.
Tansel, C. B. (Ed.). (2017a). *States of discipline: Authoritarian neoliberalism and the contested reproduction of capitalist order*. London: Rowman & Littlefield International.
Tansel, C. B. (2017b). Authoritarian neoliberalism: Towards a new research agenda. In C. B. Tansel (Ed.), *States of discipline: Authoritarian neoliberalism and the contested reproduction of capitalist order* (pp. 1–28). London: Rowman & Littlefield International.
Tansel, C. B. (2018). Authoritarian neoliberalism and democratic backsliding in Turkey: Beyond the narratives of progress. *South European Society and Politics*, *23*(2), 197–217.
Venugopal, R. (2015). Neoliberalism as concept. *Economy and Society*, *44*(2), 165–187.
Wacquant, L. (2009). *Punishing the poor: The neoliberal government of social insecurity*. Durham: Duke University Press.
Wigger, A., & Buch-Hansen, H. (2015). EU competition regulation: A case of authoritarian neoliberalism? In P. F. Kjaer & E. Hartmann (Eds.), *The evolution of intermediary institutions in Europe: From corporatism to governance* (pp. 81–98). London: Palgrave Macmillan.
Yeşil, B. (2016). *Media in new Turkey: Origins of an authoritarian neoliberal state*. Chicago: University of Illinois Press.

2 Framing the neoliberal canon: resisting the market myth via literary enquiry

Ian Bruff and Kathryn Starnes

ABSTRACT
There is widespread recognition that neoliberal rhetoric about 'free markets' stands in considerable tension with 'really existing' neoliberalizing processes. However, the oft-utilized analytical distinction between 'pure' economic and political theory and 'messy' empirical developments takes for granted that neoliberalism, at its core, valorizes free markets. In contrast, the paper explores whether neoliberal intellectuals ever made such an argument. Using Friedrich Hayek and Milton Friedman as exemplars, our reading of canonical neoliberal texts focuses on author framing gestures, particular understandings of the term 'science', techniques of characterization, and constructions of epistemological legitimacy. This enables us to avoid the trap of assuming that these texts are about free markets and instead enquires into their constitution as literary artefacts. As such, we argue that the remaking of states and households rather than the promotion of free markets is at the core of neoliberalism. Our analysis has significant implications. For example, it means that authoritarian neoliberalism is not a departure from but actually more in line with the 'pure' neoliberal canon than in the past. Therefore, neoliberalism ought to be critiqued not for its rhetorical promotion of free markets but instead for seeking to reorganize societies in coercive, non-democratic and unequal ways. This also enables us to acknowledge that households are central to resistance to neoliberalism as well as to the neoliberal worldview itself.

Introduction

Despite widespread recognition that neoliberalism's rhetorical valorization of the 'free market' stands in considerable tension with 'really existing' neoliberalization processes, underlying respect for such claims persists. This is a consequence of the common focus on the contradictions between 'pure' neoliberal ideology and 'messy' empirical developments, whereby the role for the state and associated institutions is larger than anticipated in neoliberal ideology, leading to much attention being placed on studies of 'actually existing neoliberalism' (Brenner & Theodore, 2002; see also Cahill, 2014; Harvey, 2005). Therefore, while disagreements over whether neoliberalism is (for example) a set of ideas, a political programme, an ideological worldview or simply the discursive justification for the current phase of capitalism are important, the intellectual foundations of neoliberalism tend to be neglected. This is all the more significant when one considers the fact that the 'public intellectual' role played by key neoliberal thinkers such as Friedrich Hayek and Milton Friedman is often the focus of the analysis (for example, Friedman, 1962; Hayek, 1944). The literature overlooks the essential foundations for these political interventions, reflecting the *de facto* acceptance of 'in principle' claims about the 'free market'.

This paper contends that we need to re-examine the canonical texts of neoliberal thought in order to arrive at a more satisfactory understanding of neoliberalism, in theory and in practice. It is not enough, though, simply to re-read these publications. Instead, we demonstrate the benefits of re-examining the canon of neoliberal thought as literary artefacts rather than simply political or economic arguments. This reveals that free markets serve as a literary device that is at once a product of the text's constitution *and* what the text claims to objectively examine.[1] This device allows the authors to maintain a claim to represent 'actually existing' free markets in their writings while constituting free markets in an image that serves the aims of their narrative. The constitution of free markets as novel, even marvellous, depoliticizes the neoliberal project by making the project appear as objective representation of 'free market' reality rather than 'free markets' being instead understood as the product of constitutive authorial practices. There are further analytical implications, too. Most notably, our literary-theoretical approach reveals that neoliberalism has *never* been about free markets: the heavy intellectual burden borne in canonical neoliberal texts is actually the remaking of states and households in the name of the 'free market' image (for a similar approach, regarding Economics as a discipline, see Watson, 2017). Free markets are valorized as the ideal organizing principle for any capitalist society, but that is as far as it goes.

This means that scholarly, political and policy debates need substantial modification as a result. Many have argued that neoliberalism's economic and political dominance since the 1980s has been challenged in the last decade: witness the failure of pro-market policy paradigms regarding financial regulation, the bail-outs of financial institutions by national governments, and the state interventions to prop up economies for years afterwards (for example, deficit spending from 2008 to 2010 and Quantitative Easing programmes thereafter). More recently, there has been the rise to prominence of a range of political leaders and parties (for example, Donald Trump, Left and Right populism in Europe) openly hostile to what are viewed as axioms of neoliberalism, such as free trade globally and free markets domestically. In contrast, we understand the current period of authoritarian neoliberalism as actually *closer* to the neoliberal vision than in the past. The notion that the last decade has witnessed developments that are contrary to neoliberal principles can make sense only if one understands neoliberalism to be about free markets, which we reject (see also Bruff, 2014, 2016a; Tansel, 2017). It is thus necessary to critique neoliberalism not for its rhetorical promotion of free markets but instead for seeking to orchestrate societies in coercive, non-democratic and unequal ways (see also Beck & Germann, 2018; Wigger, 2018).

Crucially, such societal orchestration has states and households, together, at its heart. Below, we utilize the insights of feminist political economy scholarship to argue that the remaking of households in a manner which denies social justice is as important to neoliberalism as is the remaking of states in an anti-democratic manner.[2] The centrality of households to capitalism is of course a long-standing concern of feminist scholarship (Benería & Feldman, 1992; Dalla Costa & James, 1975; Mies, 1986), yet dominant modes of feminist analysis of neoliberalism – while still important – tend to detach 'households', 'states' and 'markets' into discrete categories (Bakker & Gill, 2003; Fraser, 2013; Walby, 2009). This article advocates a more integral approach, as outlined by authors such as Peterson (2010), Federici (2012), Roberts (2013), and Soederberg (2018). To be clear, these scholars focus on neoliberalism in practice, but their work informs this article's literary-theoretical analysis of neoliberal thought.

The paper is structured as follows. The next section offers a brief and critical review of the existing literatures on neoliberalism; subsequently, we outline our literary-theoretical approach, which discusses the roles of authorship, framing gestures, and foundational assumptions. Next, using canonical contributions by Friedrich Hayek and Milton Friedman as exemplars of neoliberal thought more broadly, our reading shows how both authors utilize techniques of characterization and constructions of epistemological legitimacy to make their case for a science of economics. We then argue that this matters because of how it masks their strong reliance on the remaking of states and households in highly specific ways.[3] The paper concludes with some comments on the 'in principle' and 'real world' implications of our analysis.

Taking for granted neoliberalism's utopian vision

The dominant approach within the literatures is that neoliberalism's genesis in the mid-twentieth century – in an era characterized by the growing role in capitalism for 'non-market' domains such as the state, trade unions, and welfare programmes – meant that from the beginning its worldview covered all areas of social life. Inextricably bound up with this worldview, however, was the recognition that such domains could not be eliminated or drastically reduced in scope and power overnight. Therefore, a common denominator across various literatures on neoliberalism is that, from its originary moments onwards, it has been a profoundly contradictory project of social transformation. On the one hand, there is a 'utopian vision of a free society and free economy' (Peck, 2010, p. 7); on the other hand, this vision transmutes 'into various arguments for the existence of a strong state as both producer and guarantor of a stable market society' (Mirowski, 2013, p. 54). Examples of the latter include vigilance against 'distortions' of the market by groups such as trade unions, and the maintenance of 'law and order' in times of economic crisis and/or protests against a smaller economic and social role for the state.

Consequently, discussions of neoliberalism have focused on 'actually existing neoliberalism' (cf. Brenner & Theodore, 2002), and for two main reasons. One, the scope for 'market-oriented' political rule to exist in a variety of forms has turned out to be very significant, meaning that the possibilities for empirical studies of uneven, messy processes of neoliberalization have proved almost endless. Two, by enhancing our understanding of neoliberalism in empirically rich ways, the literatures also provide the basis for a critique of neoliberalism's utopian vision, especially its fundamental unrealizability. Consequently, debates and controversies have revolved around what are the putative essences of neoliberalization, which in turn inform how neoliberalism should be critiqued: a class project (Harvey, 2005), a drive to subordinate society to the market (Mirowski, 2013), an ongoing process of market-oriented regulatory restructuring (Peck, 2010), an anti-democratic political rationality (Brown, 2015), a discourse latent with transformative violence (Springer, 2016).

Clearly, our understanding of neoliberalism is more sophisticated than in the past – for example, in suggesting ways of overcoming unhelpful dichotomies such as state/market, which imply or actually propose essences that are intrinsic to various societal domains (cf. Bruff, 2011). However, the closest one gets to enquiring into, rather than taking for granted, neoliberalism's rhetorically 'pure' claims about free markets is to argue that the *effects* of seeking to realize the utopian vision is to empower the state in new ways, promote de-democratization and economization, and so on. Hence, the possibility that neoliberal thought pays as much attention to 'non-market' domains as neoliberalism in practice has not been adequately explored (cf. Bruff, 2016b).

Furthermore, and importantly, there is often the absence in the literatures of 'non-market' domains that are not 'public' societal sites such as the state, which has implications for the study of neoliberal thought and practice.[4] Some contributions have been helpful for showing that the so-called 'return of the state' after 2008 and the emergence of various forms of ostensibly anti-neoliberal populism do little to reverse the neoliberal tide that has been incoming since the 1970s, not least because the state never went away (Davies, 2014; Jessop, 2013; Konings, 2012). However, 'public' societal sites are heavily prioritized, skewing analysis and critique towards questions of state power and political authority. As noted in the introduction, there is a long tradition of feminist political economy work on the centrality of households to capitalism, and there has been much recent research on neoliberalism as well (see also Harcourt, 2017). The integral approach advocated by this article not only has analytical benefits, i.e. for gaining a richer understanding of the texts discussed below and thus of neoliberalism in thought and in practice. It also, as we consider briefly in the conclusion, enables us to acknowledge that households are central to resistance to neoliberalism as well as to the neoliberal worldview itself (cf. Bruff & Wöhl, 2016).

The question, then, is how to enquire into the possibility that neoliberal thought pays just as much attention to 'non-market' domains, such as states and households, as neoliberalism in practice. In our view, this necessitates the literary-theoretical approach discussed next, which enables us to explore carefully the practices of writing these texts and thus the means by which the texts are produced.

Authoring texts through framing gestures

The approach we outline below facilitates a thorough interrogation of the forms taken by the argument, the narrative techniques deployed, and the modes of articulation present in and across neoliberal texts. In particular, we are interested in understanding the significance of foundational assumptions in texts viewed as canonical contributions to neoliberal thought: if 'some kind of assumptions (as to what we are thinking *about*) must be made before we can even begin to think' (Thompson, 1995, p. 48, emphasis in original), then it is incumbent upon us to focus on the texts where such assumptions are most likely to be visible. It does not follow that they are explicated in clear and systematic ways, but it is essential that they are identified and analyzed – the qualities of texts deemed canonical become the qualities looked for in texts which are produced subsequently (Harries, 2001, p. 45).

We propose to treat canonical neoliberal texts as literary endeavours: how they are written is as important to critical enquiry as their content. As Starnes (2016, p. 156) explains, subtle gestures within the text reiterate foundational assumptions as uncontroversial to the extent that they become ontological features, no longer available as grounds for debate or critique. Recognizing how this happens requires making seemingly familiar ways of writing unfamiliar, and looking as much at *how* authors write as at *what* they write – for example, how authors construct themselves as experts and position their texts within disciplinary literatures (see also Starnes, 2018). As a result, we view the authoring of texts as a creative and productive process. This does not mean that we subscribe to a traditional understanding, i.e. that authors are singular, unique and self-possessed creators of the texts published in their name, somehow working in isolation from the 'socio-historical conditions within which a writer exists' (Morton, 2003, p. 30; cf. Gramsci, 1985). Instead, we find useful Benjamin's (1970 [1934]) exploration of how authors are implicated in the process of producing texts beyond those they themselves author, through what he refers to as 'techniques of production.' Benjamin advocates treating texts as literary artefacts, which requires examining not just content, but also literary technique, or the processes that show how content and form are entwined in all modes of writing (pp. 87–88).

Hence, we emphasize the role and position of the 'expert' within the text under consideration. This shapes the production of knowledge and the conditions for critique of that knowledge – and thus production of future knowledge. It also enables us to examine how these techniques of literary production are enacted within a text: for example, where authors either implicitly or explicitly comment on the writing process within the text. Such framing gestures have a specific role in the constitution of the 'rules' of epistemological legitimacy, which shape the conditions of possibility for future contributions to the field and thus for critique of the 'expert' who helped create or contribute to the field in the first place.

In order to illustrate the advantages of the approach outlined above, we examine 'The Use of Knowledge in Society' (Hayek, 1948a; originally published in 1945) and 'The Methodology of Positive Economics' (Friedman, 1953a). Both papers have, since their publication, been understood as seminal contributions – they have been cited thousands of times each, and also serve as the philosophical foundations for Hayek and Friedman's broader intellectual and political agendas. As such, they are highly appropriate texts for the purposes of this article. In exploring the texts, we looked at how the framing gestures employed by Hayek and Friedman allow them to produce a specific image of the science of economics as an enterprise that takes the study of free markets as its raison d'etre. However, this apparently natural equation between science and markets is in fact a technique of authorship which obscures the simultaneous constitution of specific, submerged images of states and households in the same text. This 'forgetting' may be unintentional, often blending into the assertive practices of academic writing in which authors make space for their text in the literature by referring to their role as an expert, or not acknowledging the fully contestable nature of the decisions they make. Nevertheless, it is clear that, by virtue of their treatment of the question of a putative science of economics as one resolved by the image of the market, Hayek and Friedman propose the market as naturally occurring while themselves participating in its constitution.

But how do they actually go about this task? As we explain in the next section, both authors follow a similar line of argument. Firstly, they proclaim a *scepticism* about the possibilities for a science of economics, a scepticism which derives from the scientific method itself. Secondly, they use this proclamation to state that their own contribution is *modest*, because it recognizes the fallibilities inherent to all knowledge claims. Thirdly, they make a *proposal* which comprises an alternative understanding of markets in capitalism compared to what they claim to be the dominant view. Fourthly and finally, they use their avowed scepticism and modesty to defend their proposal against possible criticism on the grounds that such criticism is unscientific, thereby *foreclosing* critique in the process. Therefore, in a creative and authorially distinctive manner, Hayek and Friedman's framing gestures delegitimize critiques of their position as unscientific and thus inadmissible arguments, leaving the way clear for a naturally occurring market to represent the 'normal' way to understand their contribution to science. While this argument may not seem unfamiliar, the literary-theoretical approach outlined above reveals what is masked by such gestures, helping form the basis of a more appropriate critique of neoliberalism.[5]

Hayek and Friedman: scepticism, modesty, proposal, foreclosure

Both texts under consideration focus on the possibilities of creating a science of economics. Hayek discusses the problems of scientific knowledge (for example, 1948a, pp. 79–81), whereas Friedman's essay is 'concerned primarily with certain methodological problems that arise in constructing the "distinct positive science"' Keynes called for (1953a, p. 3). Nevertheless, while ostensibly about scientific methods, these texts also engage with ontological themes concerning the science of economics' object of study and epistemological questions regarding the kinds of knowledge production which are deemed admissible by both authors.

This reading of Hayek in particular may prove unusual, because it demonstrates his preoccupation with direct observation and thus empiricism – famously, he disagreed with Karl Popper on the supposed unity of the scientific method and thus the possibilities for universal knowledge claims. Hayek begins by stating that 'knowledge of the circumstances of which we must make use never exists in concentrated or integrated form, but solely as the dispersed bits of incomplete and frequently contradictory knowledge which all the separate individuals possess' (1948a, p. 77). This lies at the heart of his science of economics: while accounting for differences between the natural and social sciences, Hayek nevertheless frames these dissimilarities not as the limits of the scientific method but instead as an ontological premise regarding who in society is most likely to have appropriate forms of knowledge of societal circumstances. Hence, his *scepticism* about the possibility of creating a science of economics focuses on questioning the scientific status of supposed experts, primarily because even their knowledge of the world is particular rather than universal (p. 80).

This means that Hayek's critique does not reject a science of economics, but merely dismisses the possibility for generalizable conclusions to underpin decision-making; he is not as different from Popper as is usually assumed. Consequently, he questions the possibility of anyone being expert enough to plan or manage economies on epistemological grounds of *modesty*: we can produce knowledge about our circumstances only via our own direct observation of them. Hayek thus argues that planning can successfully be undertaken only by those able to observe directly the 'relevant changes and the resources immediately available to meet them' (p. 84). Ultimately it is the problem of representation which troubles Hayek, not science itself. He therefore advocates a kind of extreme empiricism in which decisions must only be based on that which is directly observable and undistorted by the knowledge held by others (for example, experts).

It is at this point that Hayek's position becomes more problematic. By entering into the act of writing in order to proclaim his scepticism about the knowledge claims of others and to affect a commitment to epistemological modesty, Hayek implicitly frames himself as an expert. This leaves him apparently exempt from the problems inherent to representation of knowledge and thus allows him to act as the arbiter of what counts (relative importance of particular things with which the 'man on the ground' is concerned) and what does not (the wider conditions and context for this 'economic calculus'). Therefore, when Hayek then *proposes* the price system in competitive markets as a solution to the impossibility of full and empirically verifiable knowledge in the hands of individual humans (pp. 85–86), he endorses the impersonal market as a mechanism for the aggregation of particular knowledges born out of individuals' direct observation of prices.

By making the proposal in this way, Hayek's position as expert becomes clear: only through his understanding of science can it be possible to appreciate markets in the appropriate manner. For example, he describes the price mechanism as a 'marvel' on the basis of its accuracy in spite of being free from deliberate human design (p. 87). He then argues that the price mechanism has been stumbled upon, rather than constituted through human practices. Hayek thus treats it as an ontological fact, failing to acknowledge his own role in its reiteration and claiming he cannot possibly have the 'expert' knowledge to view it completely. This forgets, of course, the constitution of Hayek as just such an expert, qualified to choose those examples, plus his concomitant role in constituting the price mechanism's status as 'accurate'. Consequently, the proposal falls foul of Hayek's self-proclaimed scepticism and modesty, because he engages explicitly in the kind of representation of knowledge that, earlier in the paper, he inveighed against forcefully.

What is Hayek doing, then? We argue that he frames an 'appropriate' science of economics as possible only if that science understands markets as the singular legitimate source of human knowledge and activity – he *forecloses* critique of his own position as, by default, unscientific. By declaring that markets have spontaneously emerged over time free from human interference, Hayek posits them as ontological facts rather than as images constituted by his own literary techniques. Hence, the marvel of the market is depoliticized via Hayek discounting his own political decisions about what is relevant and what is not for a science of economics to be credible. For example, his claim that the price mechanism is indispensable for rational calculation in the face of economic complexity even goes so far as to explicitly deny the politics in its constitution and thus to dismiss critiques on political grounds (p. 89). Hayek then explains that the 'remaining dissent [from other economists] *seems clearly* to be due to purely intellectual, and more particularly methodological differences' (p. 89, added emphasis). The final passages in the article are devoted to debunking just one such critique (which is derisorily dismissed) and reinforces further Hayek's extreme empiricism, which he attributes to 'the unavoidable imperfection of man's knowledge and the consequent need for a process [i.e. the market] by which knowledge is constantly communicated and acquired' (p. 91).

To summarize, while Hayek can be (and indeed is often) read as critiquing the possibilities of constructing an 'objective' science of economics, he is in fact himself depoliticizing and stripping out the possibility of subjective bias within economics (knowingly or not). He does this by arguing that the only legitimate knowledge is not that which acknowledges the possibility of political expression, bias or questions of perspective in its representation, but that which is directly observed. In order to make this argument, Hayek rests on a partial and inherently political constitution of the market mechanism as ontological, neutral and, crucially, exempt from critique on 'unscientific' political grounds. Furthermore, by claiming only a methodological purpose for his text, Hayek obscures the epistemological and ontological claims his text establishes, immunizing them from (delegitimized) critique and framing future discussion of his argument around how markets function rather than the means by which he makes these claims about markets in the first place.

We have already noted that Hayek's disagreements with Popper on the nature and status of scientific knowledge is significantly over-played. The same can be said about the differences between the 'Austrian' and 'Chicago' schools of neoliberal thought – Hayek being associated with the former, Friedman with the latter. While it is clear that distinctions can be drawn (cf. Kirzner, 1997) – for example, the potential for individuals to have full information about their circumstances – an examination of Friedman's text reveals strong overlaps. For instance, Friedman begins with a discussion of the distinctions between what he terms positive (his preferred version) and normative economics. Through this, he acknowledges that even 'positive economics' analysis has normative relevance and implications, which, along with the nature of economics as explicitly concerned with humans, poses a challenge to the development of a science independent of ethical positions or normative judgements (p. 4). Among the obstacles to the generation of empirical evidence that will allow the positive science of economics to advance is language, which is used to construct hypotheses, categorize materials, and shape our understanding (p. 7). Ultimately, Friedman's *scepticism* revolves around the role that interpretation plays in the representational process of using language to shape and communicate any available empirical evidence.

This leads to the claim that '[s]elf-proclaimed "experts" speak with many voices and can hardly all be regarded as disinterested … "expert" opinion could hardly be accepted solely on faith even if the "experts" were nearly unanimous and clearly disinterested' (p. 4). Hence, Friedman forefronts his *modesty* in such matters, for he acknowledges the role of judgement in assessing competing knowledge claims. Moreover, he uses this epistemological restraint as the basis for an appeal to direct observation as a means of making such judgements. Empirical evidence is cited as the criteria by which arguments are accepted or rejected and, starkly, is 'alone' in being able to show whether analytical categories 'have a meaningful empirical counterpart' (p. 7).

Hence, Friedman proceeds along similar lines to Hayek. Also with Hayek, it is at this stage that the argument becomes more difficult to sustain without damage being done to the principles embodied in the text's opening remarks. For example, he *proposes* that 'the only relevant test of the *validity* of a hypothesis is comparison of its predictions with experience' (pp. 8–9; original emphasis). While seemingly innocuous, this sets the stage for an extensive discussion of scientific procedure which delineates, in highly specific ways, acceptable and unacceptable forms of knowledge production. Friedman thus frames himself both as an expert in such matters and as someone who is somehow immune to the ethical and normative issues which he earlier argued were an inevitable part of all scientific research. This becomes more apparent when discussing the stages of constructing and testing hypotheses. Friedman acknowledges that the initial stage is always reliant on previous decisions, the context of old hypotheses, and is thus subject to the knowledge and interests of the investigator. Consequently, these 'two methodologically distinct stages [of construction and testing] are always proceeding jointly' (p. 14). He then claims, however, that the notion that starting assumptions are relevant to the validity of the hypothesis being tested is:

> fundamentally wrong and productive of much mischief. Far from providing an easier means for sifting valid from invalid hypotheses, it only confuses the issue, promotes misunderstanding about the significance of empirical evidence for economic theory, produces a misdirection of much intellectual effort devoted to the development of positive economics, and impedes the attainment of consensus on tentative hypotheses in positive economics. (p. 14)

The implications emerge later in the text. Firstly, Friedman asserts that '[i]t is only a short step' from the discussion of scientific procedure to the – in his view, widely accepted – hypothesis that firms seek rationally to maximize profits and have full knowledge of the information needed to make such an attempt (p. 21). Moreover, while he acknowledges that evidence supporting such a hypothesis is hard to document, its failure to be contradicted is by default the evidence for its scientific worth. On the surface, this is an example of Friedman's commitment to scientific procedure, whereby a hypothesis remains accepted until it is proven to be false. Yet, later on, a more plausible reason appears. Here, via a series of assertions, dismissals and unsubstantiated claims, Friedman tackles attempts in existing scholarship to contradict this hypothesis. According to him, theories of imperfect or monopolistic competition – for which a wide range of empirical evidence is available, both then and now – possess 'none of the attributes that would make [them] a truly useful general theory' (p. 38). They are deficient, logically meaningless, offer no analytical tools, and therefore must be considered incompetent (pp. 38–39).

Why does Friedman treat alternative approaches and analyses with such contempt, especially when they appear to offer the possibility for precisely the kind of scientific dialogue that he calls for? For us, it is because he adopts a similar approach to Hayek. While Friedman's invocation of markets is more concrete and applied – considering questions of company strategy and inter-firm competition (or lack of) – compared to Hayek's more abstract claims about the price mechanism, the effect is remarkably alike. Hence, he also frames an 'appropriate' science of economics as possible only if that science understands markets as the singular legitimate source of human knowledge and activity – Friedman *forecloses* critique of his own position as, by default, unscientific. He does this via implicit ontological claims about the assumed rational actions of firms and thus, more broadly, about the markets the firms are part of; epistemologically, he asserts that any deviation from the process of hypothesis testing as outlined in the text renders that piece of research irrelevant. Hence his concluding argument that normative judgements 'impede objectivity' and thus the formulation of scientifically informed analysis (p. 40), which can be understood as an attempt to delegitimize alternative worldviews (be they on the nature of firms and markets or on the principles governing research). It is clear that, contrary to the pretensions offered early in the text, Friedman understands himself as an expert, and an expert whose judgement is superior to those within economics who believe that normative questions are relevant in a range of ways.

To summarize, while Friedman can be (and indeed is often) read as defending an objective, value-free version of social science research, he in fact saturates his arguments about science with his own value-laden assertions (knowingly or not). He acknowledges the inevitability of normative influences and ethical implications of the analytical judgements that are made, but ignores his own self-interest when arguing that the influence of interests and the difficulty of accuracy in starting assumptions and representations is of no consequence for a science of economics to be 'good'. In order to make this argument, Friedman ultimately rests on a partial and inherently political constitution of the market which he defends as ontological, neutral and exempt from 'incompetent' and unscientific critique. Furthermore, as with Hayek the text obscures these epistemological and ontological claims, immunizing them from (delegitimized) critique and framing future discussion of the argument around how to study markets scientifically rather than the means by which the scientific study of markets is valorized in the first place.

Hayek and Friedman: remaking states and households *in the name of* free markets

As argued in the previous section, Hayek and Friedman use a range of author framing gestures in order to set the scene for the promotion of the free market as the ideal principle for organizing society. More specifically, they do so via a scepticism-modesty-proposal-foreclosure sequence which seeks simultaneously to entwine a science of economics with the valorization of free markets and to prevent critiques of their approach from untangling science from free markets. It is therefore unsurprising that (as noted above) critical engagements with neoliberalism have focused on how the abstract formalism of a science of free markets has yet to be realized in practice, with state empowerment, de-democratization and economization being the more likely outcomes. Yet this leaves outside the scope of critical analysis the foundational assumptions which underpin the putative science of free markets. It is to these that we now turn.

Hayek and Friedman's defence of a science of free markets leads them, in other works, to focus on how the 'real economy' should/could move closer to the abstract ideal of the market. This is often discussed in terms of distortions or obstacles which need eliminating – for example, trade union power and discretionary state intervention. On the surface, these are standard neoliberal claims about undesirable interference in potentially 'pure' market processes, meaning that the texts appear to be arguments for negation – that is, for the need to remove the artificial poison from the naturally occurring market. In contrast, we contend that a rather different case is being made: the texts argue for specific kinds of states and households *per se* rather than position them as obstacles on the road to market utopia. Hence, while neoliberal intellectuals valorize the free market as an abstract ideal, the crucial passages in their texts are those which discuss the sites in society – principally, states and households – which require remaking *in the name of* free markets. It is the apparent expulsion of states and households from markets which forces these texts into a strong dependence on states and households in order to make markets possible; without states and households, markets in capitalism have no foundation upon which they can be constructed and perpetuate.

To illustrate, we start by considering essays published in the same volumes as the 'science' texts. Hayek's 'The Economic Conditions of Interstate Federalism' (Hayek, 1948b) begins by stating that 'the main purpose of interstate federation is to secure peace' across borders (p. 255), between different individual nation-states as part of a larger political union. However, within a few pages he clarifies that the main means of achieving this is to create an economic union: otherwise, 'conflicts of interests tend to become conflicts between the same [national] groups of people, instead of conflicts between groups of constantly varying composition' (p. 257). As such, Hayek recommends a single, federation-wide monetary policy, the absence of tariffs within the union, and bans on state assistance for certain industries. The means of achieving these goals comes later in the text: the 'federation will have to possess the *negative* power of preventing individual states from interfering with economic activity ... there must be no substitution of day-to-day interference and regulation for the impersonal forces of the market' (p. 267, p. 268; emphasis added). Hence, through the federation 'providing a rational *permanent* framework' (p. 268; emphasis added) which insulates national states from popular participation in political life, Hayek attacks the idea of democracy itself, arguing that democracy 'will work only if we do not overload it' (p. 271). In other words, *economic union can be achieved* only *by the proactive, perpetual remaking of states in an anti-democratic manner.*

In 'The "Welfare" Effects of an Income Tax and an Excise Tax' (Friedman, 1953b), Friedman critiques the 'alleged' superiority of income compared to excise taxes in terms of the welfare outcomes they generate (p. 100). He discusses the effects of income and excise taxes on indifference curves – which are used in mainstream economics to model consumption preferences for given individuals and communities – to argue that the latter in fact have superior welfare effects than the former. However, as with Hayek the implications come later: Friedman builds on his analysis to argue explicitly against progressive income taxation – used by governments to reduce levels of socio-economic inequality – because it is likely to 'falsify [i.e. render inefficient] rates of substitution' of one good for another by members of the community when altering their consumption preferences (p. 112). Hence, through the claim that debates on taxation should be about potential allocative efficiency rather than putative distributional outcomes (p. 107), Friedman contends that the only optimal form of taxation is that which looks like an excise tax – levied on all members of the community at the same level (pp. 112–113). A key implication is that individuals and thus households (which are taken to be the same thing) ought to be held responsible for the waxing and waning of general economic fortunes – for example, if they consume in a sub-optimal manner – and not societal factors such as axes of inequality (for more on this, see Bruff, in press). When economic difficulties ensue, households thus need to bear the burden of adjustment towards an optimal use of resources, becoming more accurate in estimating future income and forming more appropriate consumption preferences. In other words, *economic efficiency can be achieved* only *by the proactive, perpetual remaking of households in a manner which denies social justice.*

Space prevents a more detailed discussion of these texts, but it is instructive to connect them to other canonical works authored by Hayek and Friedman, which can also be read and critiqued in the literary-theoretical manner outlined in this article. For instance, Hayek's (1941) *The Pure Theory of Capital* argues in detail that markets are inherently dynamic, meaning that the future is unknown and no market participant has full knowledge of their situation as a result. Nevertheless, he still contends that a *tendential* state of equilibrium and order in the economy is possible, but only if the market can operate unhindered by non-market forces (for more on this, see Bruff, in press). Towards the end of the book – which is ostensibly a critique of neoclassical forms of economics such as Friedman's – Hayek makes clear that the main obstacles to markets operating in this fluid and dynamically ordered way are monopolies as operated by trade unions and especially the state. Strikingly, private monopolies (i.e. by a dominant firm) are conspicuous by their absence, presumably because Hayek would claim that market processes would erode them naturally over time; hence, states need to be self-constraining, non-monopolistic entities in order to facilitate the unhindered market.

Moreover, in *The Constitution of Liberty* (1960) Hayek outlines an expanded conception of legitimate state coercion – which is legitimate insofar as it performs the anti-democratic duties discussed above – and discusses at length welfare states and progressive taxation, which are criticized heavily as illegitimate forms of coercion because they prevent individuals and households from being responsible for their own and for more general economic outcomes.

Regarding Friedman, *A Theory of the Consumption Function* (1957) outlined his famous Permanent Income Hypothesis (PIH). The PIH argues that individuals plan over the whole life cycle their expected incomes and therefore consumption patterns – for instance, if they foresee career progression which leads to a gradually increasing salary. However, this argument coheres only via the assumption that savings and income levels are unrelated phenomena; that is, a poor individual's savings decisions are as unconstrained by material circumstances as a rich individual's. As such, Friedman assumes inequality is not a factor in savings and consumption patterns, for they are borne out of individual life cycle calculations. A key implication is the conclusion (p. 234) that rising permanent income expectations are more economically optimal if they result from individuals investing in their own future rather than the outcome of external stimulus (for example, state spending in response to a recession). In other words, Friedman attacks the notion of *state* borrowing, but endorses *personal* borrowing; households ought to be remade as indebted societal sites, with clear implications for the reproduction of various axes of inequality. Moreover, as with Hayek the remaking of states as self-constraining entities emerges as a key goal, in the name of free markets, so they do not provide the external stimulus which distorts and undermines individual life cycle calculations. This is also the underlying rationale for the mammoth *A Monetary History of the United States, 1867–1960* (Friedman & Schwartz, 1963); indeed, it is striking that, for someone who is rhetorically hostile to the state, Friedman managed to co-author almost 1000 pages on how *precisely* the state should have acted in the sphere of monetary policy over the course of a century.

It is hopefully clear that the texts discussed in this article ought to be understood not just for *what* is written in them, but also for *how* they are written. This enables us to acknowledge how Hayek and Friedman utilize literary techniques of production in the attempt to constrain and limit the available grounds for critique of their position. Moreover, our analysis facilitates the decisive rejection of the notion that neoliberal texts are fundamentally about the valorization of free markets, because we can now recognize instead that they (re)produce highly specific images of states and households in service to the abstract principle of the free market. States and households need to be at the heart of analyses of neoliberalism, and thus of critiques of it – in theory and in practice.

Conclusion

Via a literary-theoretical approach to the reading of texts, this article has argued that neoliberal thought can be productively re-examined in order to bring something new to discussions of canonical texts in this tradition and also to debates and controversies about contemporary forms of neoliberalism. Utilizing Friedman and Hayek as exemplars, we have argued that their explicit project – the construction of a science of free markets – has served to mask an implicit yet more important agenda – the remaking of states and households. As such, we contend that it is time for critiques of neoliberalism to move beyond the 'pure' theory / 'messy' practices dichotomy, as productive as this has been over the last two decades. Instead, we ought to understand neoliberalism as the attempt to orchestrate societies in coercive, non-democratic and unequal ways. Furthermore, this attempt is not somehow an *effect* of projects to realize the vision of a free market utopia; *it is the project itself.*

It was noted earlier in the article that neoliberalism's genesis in the mid-twentieth century – in an era characterized by the growing role in capitalism for 'non-market' domains such as the state, trade unions, and welfare programmes – meant that from the beginning there was a recognition that such domains could not be eliminated or drastically reduced in scope and power overnight. For this reason, it is essential that we understand the current period of authoritarian neoliberalism as actually *closer* to the neoliberal vision than in the past. States are reconfiguring into increasingly authoritarian entities or are expanding already-existing forms of authoritarian practices, households have become increasingly weighed down by indebtedness, the expulsion of the poor and vulnerable from social programmes supposed to help them has become gradually normalized, and the 'solutions' on offer to continued low or non-existent economic growth – which frequently invoke the fiction of the 'free market' – are strongly reminiscent of the processes (such as the securitization of financial instruments) which catalyzed the emergence of serious crises in the late 2000s.

The analytical implications of our argument are hopefully clear by now. Regarding the implications for resisting neoliberalism on the basis of the critique that we offer, it is hoped that this article speaks to the growing recognition that the state is imbricated in and not protective against neoliberal practices. This might, in the longer-term, create more propitious conditions for the emergence of new, more equitable modes of living via a greater awareness of what needs to change (Bruff, 2016a). However, this is only possible if we engage in and also look beyond formal forms of politics and activism, towards households as being a potentially crucial site of politicization which 'provide[s] leverage for radical social critique' (Young, 2005, p. 146; see also Dowling, 2016; Federici, 2012). In other words, if the great power of the neoliberal project has been the attempted remaking of states and households in the name of the market, then what happens if we pursue an alternative endeavour, seeking to remake states and households in the name of equality, justice, dignity and solidarity?

Notes

1. Synonymic terms such as 'competitive markets' or simply 'the market' perform the same function as 'free markets' in neoliberal texts. As noted in the section 'Remaking states and households' in this article, neoliberal texts make their claims about 'free markets' in terms of negation – i.e. the need to eliminate undesirable interference in otherwise naturally occurring market processes. As such, the function performed by the literary device 'free markets' extends to similar terms invoked to make the same points about negating unnatural interferences. See also Bruff (in press).
2. An ostensibly similar argument has been made by Melinda Cooper. However, there are two key differences between her and our position: (i) Cooper argues that during the 1960s and 1970s neoliberal intellectuals 'refined and in some cases utterly revised their founding concepts' in response to various social upheavals (2017, p. 18), which skips over the canonical works we consider of such importance for neoliberalism's subsequent trajectory; (ii) while she is correct to point to the growing *political* alliance between (economic) neoliberalism and (social) neoconservatism from the 1970s onwards, the *intellectual* and *philosophical* basis for such an alliance had always been immanent to neoliberalism (as this article shows).
3. For reasons of space, this article does not address the ordoliberal strand of neoliberal thought. Nevertheless, the argument found in this article implicitly addresses a key thread within literatures on neoliberalism, namely ordoliberalism's possible incompatibilities with the Austrian and Chicago forms of neoliberalism due to its explicit recognition of the state's role in the constitution and functioning of markets. It is hopefully clear that, rather than asking whether ordoliberalism can be considered neoliberal or not, we ought to acknowledge that *all* significant strands of neoliberal thought envision crucial roles for states and households in the constitution of markets in capitalism. Ordoliberals are simply more explicit about states in particular compared to scholars such as Hayek and Friedman.

4. This includes the work of one of us, who has written extensively on neoliberalism. For instance, Bruff (2014) discusses 'social' institutions of governance such as collective bargaining in the workplace, political parties and welfare states, all of which could be understood as 'public' societal sites. While these institutions often have dense and multi-faceted connections with 'private' sites such as households – especially regarding workfarism – it is only more recently that an explicit discussion of households became visible in his work (Bruff & Wöhl, 2016). Nevertheless, the argument in the 2014 article 'non-market areas of social life took on a particularly important role in neoliberal ideology' (p. 114) facilitated the extension of the initial discussion to households. See also Koch (2018) on state coercion and localized forms of social struggle, especially around housing.
5. The reader will start to notice the repetition of a few key phrases and points. This is deliberate, for it maximizes the potential of our focus on the articulation and organization of language in neoliberal texts. It also permits the use of repetition in *our own* articulation and organization of language, as a means of showing what the implications are of our interrogation of neoliberal texts.

Acknowledgements

Previous versions of the article were presented at the 2017 conferences organized by the European Sociological Association in Athens and the European International Studies Association in Barcelona. Additionally, preliminary forms of the argument were presented as seminar talks in 2017 at the universities of Manchester and Nottingham. Many thanks to all of those who asked questions and provided feedback, especially Cemal Burak Tansel, and to the referees for their useful comments and suggestions.

Disclosure statement

No potential conflict of interest was reported by the authors.

References

Bakker, I., & Gill, S. (Eds.). (2003). *Power, production and social reproduction. Human in/security in the global political economy*. Basingstoke: Palgrave Macmillan.

Beck, M., & Germann, J. (2018). Managerial power in the German model: The case of bertelsmann and the antecedents of neoliberalism. *Globalizations*. doi:10.1080/14747731.2018.1502490

Benería, L., & Feldman, S. (Eds.). (1992). *Unequal burden: Economic crisis, persistent poverty, and women's work*. Boulder: Westview.

Benjamin, W. (1970). The author as producer. *New Left Review*, *1*(62), 83–96.

Brenner, N., & Theodore, N. (2002). Cities and the geographies of "actually existing neoliberalism". *Antipode*, *34*(3), 349–379.

Brown, W. (2015). *Undoing the demos: Neoliberalism's stealth revolution*. New York: Zone Books.

Bruff, I. (2011). Overcoming the state/market dichotomy. In S. Shields, I. Bruff, & H. Macartney (Eds.), *Critical international political economy: Dialogue, debate and dissensus* (pp. 80–98). Basingstoke: Palgrave Macmillan.

Bruff, I. (2014). The rise of authoritarian neoliberalism. *Rethinking Marxism*, *26*(1), 113–129.

Bruff, I. (2016a). Authoritarian neoliberalism and the myth of 'free markets'. *ROAR*, *4*, 14–27.

Bruff, I. (2016b). Neoliberalism and authoritarianism. In S. Springer, K. Birch, & J. MacLeavy (Eds.), *The handbook of neoliberalism* (pp. 107–117). New York: Routledge.

Bruff, I. (in press). Overcoming the allure of neoliberalism's market myth. *South Atlantic Quarterly*.

Bruff, I., & Wöhl, S. (2016). Constitutionalizing austerity, disciplining the household: Masculine norms of competitiveness and the crisis of social reproduction in the Eurozone. In A. Hozić & J. True (Eds.), *Scandalous economics: Gender and the politics of financial crises* (pp. 92–108). Oxford: Oxford University Press.

Cahill, D. (2014). *The end of laissez-faire? On the durability of embedded neoliberalism*. Cheltenham: Edward Elgar.

Cooper, M. (2017). *Family values: Between neoliberalism and the new social conservatism*. New York: Zone Books.

Dalla Costa, M., & James, S. (1975). *The power of women and the subversion of the community*. Bristol: Falling Wall Press.

Davies, W. (2014). *The limits of neoliberalism: Authority, sovereignty and the logic of competition*. London: Sage.

Dowling, E. (2016). Valorised but not valued? Affective remuneration, social reproduction and feminist politics beyond the crisis. *British Politics*, *11*(4), 452–468.

Federici, S. (2012). *Revolution at point zero: Housework, reproduction, and feminist struggle*. Oakland: PM Press.

Fraser, N. (2013). *Fortunes of feminism: From state-managed capitalism to neoliberal crisis*. London: Verso.

Friedman, M. (1953a). The methodology of positive economics. In M. Friedman (Ed.), *Essays in positive economics* (pp. 3–43). Chicago: University of Chicago Press.

Friedman, M. (1953b). The 'welfare' effects of an income tax and an excise tax. In M. Friedman (Ed.), *Essays in positive economics* (pp. 100–113). Chicago: University of Chicago Press.

Friedman, M. (1957). *A theory of the consumption function*. Princeton: Princeton University Press.

Friedman, M. (1962). *Capitalism and freedom*. Chicago: University of Chicago Press.

Friedman, M., & Schwartz, A. J. (1963). *A monetary history of the United States, 1867–1960*. Princeton: Princeton University Press.

Gramsci, A. (1985). *Selections from cultural writings* (D. Forgacs & G. Nowell-Smith (Eds.); W. Boelhower, Trans). London: Lawrence and Wishart.

Harcourt, W. (2017). Bodies in resistance: Conversations on gender, body politics and authoritarian neoliberalism. In C. B. Tansel (Ed.), *States of discipline: Authoritarian neoliberalism and the contested reproduction of capitalist order* (pp. 67–86). London: Rowman & Littlefield International.

Harries, E. W. (2001). *Twice upon a time: Women writers and the history of the fairy tale*. Princeton: Princeton University Press.

Harvey, D. (2005). *A brief history of neoliberalism*. Oxford: Oxford University Press.

Hayek, F. A. (1941). *The pure theory of capital*. London: Macmillan.

Hayek, F. A. (1944). *The road to serfdom*. Chicago: University of Chicago Press.

Hayek, F. A. (1948a). The use of knowledge in society. In F. A. Hayek (Ed.), *Individualism and economic order* (pp. 77–91). Chicago: University of Chicago Press.

Hayek, F. A. (1948b). The economic conditions of interstate federalism. In F. A. Hayek (Ed.), *Individualism and economic order* (pp. 255–272). Chicago: University of Chicago Press.

Hayek, F. A. (1960). *The constitution of liberty*. Chicago: University of Chicago Press.

Jessop, B. (2013). Putting neoliberalism in its time and place: A response to the debate. *Social Anthropology*, *21* (1), 65–74.

Kirzner, I. M. (1997). Entrepreneurial discovery and the competitive market process: An Austrian approach. *Journal of Economic Literature*, *35*(1), 60–85.

Koch, I. (2018). From welfare to lawfare: Environmental suffering, neighbour disputes and the law in UK social housing. *Critique of Anthropology*, *38*(2), 221–235.

Konings, M. (2012). Imagined double movements: Progressive thought and the specter of neoliberal populism. *Globalizations*, *9*(4), 609–622.

Mies, M. (1986). *Patriarchy and accumulation on a world scale: Women in the international division of labour.* London: Zed.

Mirowski, P. (2013). *Never let a serious crisis go to waste: How neoliberalism survived the financial meltdown.* London: Verso.

Morton, A. D. (2003). The social function of Carlos Fuentes: A critical intellectual or in the 'shadow of the state'? *Bulletin of Latin American Research*, *22*(1), 27–51.

Peck, J. (2010). *Constructions of neoliberal reason.* Oxford: Oxford University Press.

Peterson, V. S. (2010). Global householding amid global crises. *Politics & Gender*, *6*(2), 271–281.

Roberts, A. (2013). Financing social reproduction: The gendered relations of debt and mortgage finance in twenty-first-century America. *New Political Economy*, *18*(1), 21–42.

Soederberg, S. (2018). Evictions: A global capitalist phenomenon. *Development & Change*, 'Early View' section.

Springer, S. (2016). *The discourse of neoliberalism: An anatomy of a powerful idea.* London: Rowman & Littlefield International.

Starnes, K. (2016). *Fairy tales and international relations: A folklorist reading of international relations textbooks.* London: Routledge.

Starnes, K. (2018). Author framing in international relations: Understanding writing as disciplining political practice. Currently unpublished manuscript.

Tansel, C. B. (2017). Authoritarian neoliberalism: Towards a new research agenda. In C. B. Tansel (Ed.), *States of discipline: Authoritarian neoliberalism and the contested reproduction of capitalist order* (pp. 1–28). London: Rowman & Littlefield International.

Thompson, E. P. (1995). *The poverty of theory: Or an orrery of errors* (new ed.). London: Merlin Press.

Walby, S. (2009). *Globalizing inequalities: Complexity and contested modernities.* London: Sage.

Watson, M. (2017). Rousseau's Crusoe myth: The unlikely provenance of the neoclassical homo economicus. *Journal of Cultural Economy*, *10*(1), 81–96.

Wigger, A. (2018). The new EU industrial policy: Authoritarian neoliberal structural adjustment and the case for alternatives. *Globalizations*. doi:10.1080/14747731.2018.1502496

Young, I. M. (2005). House and home: Feminist variations on a theme. In I. M. Young (Ed.), *On female body experience: 'Throwing like a girl' and other essays* (pp. 123–154). Oxford: Oxford University Press.

3 Managerial power in the German model: the case of Bertelsmann and the antecedents of neoliberalism

Mareike Beck and Julian Germann

ABSTRACT

Our article extends research on authoritarian neoliberalism to Germany, through a history of the Bertelsmann media corporation – sponsor and namesake of Germany's most influential neoliberal think-tank. Our article makes three moves. Firstly, we argue that conceptualizing German neoliberalism in terms of an 'ordoliberal paradigm' is of limited use in explaining the rise and fall of Germany's distinctive socio-economic model (Modell Deutschland). Instead, we locate the origins of authoritarian tendencies in the corporate power exercised by managers rather than in the power of state-backed markets imagined by ordoliberals. Secondly, we focus on the managerial innovations of Bertelsmann as a key actor enmeshed with Modell Deutschland. We show that the adaptation of business management practices of an endogenous 'Cologne School' empowered Bertelsmann's postwar managers to overcome existential crises and financial constraints despite being excluded from Germany's corporate support network. Thirdly, we argue that their further development in the 1970s also enabled Bertelsmann to curtail and circumvent the forms of labour representation associated with Modell Deutschland. Inspired by cybernetic management theories that it used to limit and control rather than revive market competition among its workforce, Bertelsmann began to act and think outside the postwar settlement between capital and labour before the settlement's hotly-debated demise since the 1990s.

Introduction

Our article takes up the core concerns of the nascent scholarship on 'authoritarian neoliberalism' (AN). Mobilizing the work of Stuart Hall and Nicos Poulantzas, the major contribution of this literature has been to highlight the disciplinary, coercive and anti-democratic governance practices that political actors have used in the wake of the global and European financial crises to curtail opposition and close down alternatives (Bruff, 2014, 2016). Crucially for scholars of AN, it is these practices that make neoliberalism much more pernicious and persistent than the free market programmatic frequently attributed to it by both proponents and sceptics (Bruff, 2016, p. 107; Tansel, 2017). The emancipatory purpose of AN is to lift the veil of this liberal rhetoric to reveal new mechanisms and techniques of rule and potential points of resistance that are too often swallowed up by the master narrative of 'the market'.

Building on the recognition of the spatially and temporally variegated character of AN (e.g. Rioux, 2017), this article extends this line of investigation to Germany. The German experience is of interest for two reasons. First, it has been the focus of long-standing debates about the roles of state power and market forces in the constitution of a distinct but possibly fading German model (*Modell Deutschland*) of capitalism (e.g. Thelen, 2014). And second, the German state has assumed a domineering role in the eurocrisis that some have likened to 'an authoritarian mode of action' (Biebricher, 2013, p. 345).

The most prominent way to link the specificity of Germany to its dominance in the European Union (EU) has been to invoke an ordoliberal paradigm. Idolizing the strong state *and* free market, this variant of neoliberal thought is said to have shaped Germany's 'social market economy' after 1945 and to inform its contemporary crisis response (Blyth, 2013; Bonefeld, 2012; Young, 2014). This literature has revealed an intriguing correspondence between ordoliberal principles and EU governance practices (e.g. Wigger & Buch-Hansen, 2015) and the deleterious consequences of German crisis management (Ryner, 2015). And yet to us, the assumed fixity of ordoliberal dogma seems less able to explain either the specific social transformation of German capitalism after 1945 or the novel, if regressive, reforms that have undone these achievements since the 1990s. Thus, rather than search for continuity in the realm of ideas, our article proposes to examine the evolving socio-economic strategies and struggles of actors embedded in and yet reshaping the German social model. Building on contributions that examine the connections between business management and the rise of neoliberalism (Davies, 2014; Knafo, Dutta, Lane, & Wyn-Jones, 2018; Styhre, 2014), this article zooms in on the managerial innovations of the Bertelsmann AG – one of the world's largest media conglomerates.

The reasons for this choice are threefold. First, Bertelsmann is the corporate sponsor behind Germany's foremost think-tank, the Bertelsmann Foundation. In the eyes of many, the Foundation emerged as the key protagonist in the transformation of *Modell Deutschland* since the 1990s, most often in ways that have diminished its social and democratic features (Barth, 2006; Bauer, 2009; Biermann & Klönne, 2008; Böckelmann & Fischler, 2004; Schuler, 2010; Wernicke & Bultmann, 2007). There is, moreover, widespread agreement that the aims and methods of the Foundation have been shaped fundamentally by the corporate culture and management style of the Bertelsmann company (Schuler, 2010, pp. 14–21). In fact, the very *raison d'être* of the charity – created and headed by the firm's patriarch, Reinhard Mohn – has been to apply the approaches and achievements of his business to the German state and society (Fleishman, 2001, p. 133).

Second, while its social foundation is considered a neoliberal lodestar, the corporate history of Bertelsmann is deeply enmeshed in the preceding period of postwar reconstruction and the specificities of the *Modell Deutschland*. For many scholars, 'Bertelsmann epitomises the West German postwar economic miracle' (Fitzgerald, 2012, pp. 266–267), with Mohn representing a younger generation of managers who broke with the archaic forms of organization and leadership of the German business elite and transformed their businesses into multinationals (Berghahn, 1986; Ewing, 2014, p. 18). Among these corporations, thirdly and finally, Bertelsmann stands out by virtue of a uniquely adaptive management style. What set its corporate culture apart 'from nearly all other management concepts in the early Federal Republic of Germany was the "radicalness" with which it embraced the element of permanent change' (Wischermann, 2010, p. 262). Because it connects to both the rise of the German model after 1945 and its deconstruction in the 1990s, Bertelsmann's corporate history throws an innovative sidelight on the trajectory of German neoliberalism and its tendentially authoritarian characteristics.

Our argument proceeds in three steps. The next section identifies some of the promises and pitfalls of the ordoliberal narrative, and outlines an alternative account which locates elements of authoritarian rule within corporate strategies and the managerial innovations of Bertelsmann in particular. In keeping with the emphasis within AN on hierarchies and inequalities rather than markets, we argue that these practices represent instruments of control and empowerment rather than means of market rule. Against the image of an externally generated movement towards neoliberalism, the third section identifies the roots of a German management tradition of accounting practices and profit incentives pioneered at Cologne University in the interwar period. In the immediate postwar years, this helped Bertelsmann establish an operational basis for its growing business when facing an existential crisis of financial constraints and excessive growth. The third section shows how, facing the limits of these techniques in the 1970s, Bertelsmann turned to cybernetic management theories in order to limit, rather than revive, competition amongst its workforce. While introduced in the name of social progress, these practices were meant to curtail the more institutionalized versions of collective bargaining and co-determination of *Modell Deutschland* long before its hotly-debated demise. It is in this history that we can find the origins and complex objectives of the societal blueprint Bertelsmann introduced through its foundation in the 1990s. The conclusion situates our argument within the broader literature on neoliberalism and managerialism. It outlines the advantages of searching for their authoritarian features within changing corporate strategies rather than unchanging ordoliberal ideology.

German neoliberalism: an ordoliberal legacy?

The most popular approach to discerning the authoritarian tendencies of German neoliberalism zooms in on a peculiar economic doctrine called 'ordoliberalism'. This German variety of neoliberal thought was conceived in the interwar period by a circle of economists associated with the so-called Freiburg School as a 'third way' between *laissez-faire* capitalism and potentially totalitarian economic planning. To its advocates, ordoliberalism prescribes a central but legally demarcated role for the state in sustaining a competitive market order based on price stability, fiscal sobriety, and monetary restraint (Ptak, 2009, p. 100). Its critics, however, identify a latent authoritarianism that *combines* the tyranny of the market with that of the state. State power, in the ordoliberal imagination, is to be used to submit social actors to the logic of the market, to defend its price-finding function from popular 'interference', and to inculcate in the individual an ethos to contend with the forces of supply and demand (Biebricher, 2013, pp. 341–342; Bonefeld, 2012, pp. 5, 9). Political authority, in short, imposes an 'order of competition' at the expense of democratic participation, collective enterprise, and redistributive forms of welfare (cf. Wigger & Buch-Hansen, 2015, p. 85).

The corresponding narrative holds that Germany's postwar social market economy was built on the basis of this ordoliberal paradigm after 1945 (for a nuanced analysis, see Dyson, 2001). Although there is considerable disagreement over how much of ordoliberal thought was carried over into the postwar era (cf. Berghahn & Young, 2013; Bonefeld, 2012), many – though not all (cf. Hartmann, 2015, p. 125) – of its proponents suggest that since the crisis of Keynesianism of the 1970s, this paradigm has become a project that German state elites have aimed to realize at the European level (Art, 2015; Blyth, 2013, p. 101; Matthijs, 2016).

While focused on illuminating German-led austerity and the rigid surveillance and enforcement apparatus of post-crisis Europe (see Biebricher & Vogelmann, 2017), the principal advantage of this account lies in its potential to uncover an internally generated rather than externally imposed neoliberal trajectory (Dyson, 2001, p. 140). This corrects a line of reasoning which holds that Germany simply followed a global neoliberal transition in the 1990s. By drawing attention to a homegrown ideology of state-led and market-centred governance, the ordoliberal narrative goes some distance towards understanding the diverse sources, multiple trajectories, and varied forms of neoliberalism (cf. Bruff, 2008).

However, the key problem, as we see it, is that many ordoliberal accounts are so focused on the current crisis that they neglect the past. Because their explanatory value rests squarely on the presumed continuity of ordoliberal thought, they tend to exaggerate its original influence on Germany's postwar political economy. To be sure, ordoliberal arguments served as an important antidote to more far-reaching postwar plans for socialization and interventionism (Ptak, 2009). And yet in order to become acceptable again after 1945, capitalism had to be rendered 'social' in ways that marked a profound departure from ordoliberal precepts in several respects. In the place of the reactionary and proto-fascist exonerations of the state that shine through in key ordoliberal texts, a liberal-democratic, parliamentary and federal constitution was created (Berghahn & Young, 2013; Young, 2014). In like manner, the aversion to social policy within the ordoliberal canon was replaced by a redistributive welfare state (Manow, 2001). Additionally, from an ordoliberal standpoint, both the reconcentration of economic power in a tightly-knit network of big banks and industrial firms, and the inclusion of organized labour through corporatist arrangements would have to be judged as inadmissible 'conspiracies against the market' (Hien, 2013, p. 350). Lastly, the 'massification' of German culture and consumption, while part and parcel of the postwar economic miracle, was diametrically opposed to the social conservative ideal of a society of craftsmen and artisans that ordoliberal thinkers such as Wilhelm Röpke held on to (cf. Gööck, 1968, p. 184).

In our view, these and numerous other examples demonstrate the critical difference between ordoliberalism in theory and the social market economy in practice. Taking the former as a guide to Germany's postwar development risks missing out on some of its most distinctive features – especially the incorporation of organized labour – that have come under strain during the neoliberal era. Yet without a clear sense of what social institutions were established, we cannot fully understand how far, in what ways, and by whom they may have been eroded.

In sum, there is no shortcut which takes us from the Freiburg School writings in the interwar period to the present. If we are to understand the contours of German neoliberalism and its authoritarian features, we need to work our way through the postwar history of and social struggles over German capitalism (see also Cozzolino, 2018). Rather than debate the degree to which ordoliberal ideas were 'lost in translation' after 1945 (Hien & Joerges, 2017) or experienced an 'unlikely renaissance' (Biebricher, 2013, p. 339) some decades later, we propose to focus on actors that had to manoeuvre within the social market economy as it actually existed, while at the same time contributing significantly to its transformation. We believe that Bertelsmann offers a productive focal point not only due to its social foundation becoming extraordinarily influential since the early 1990s, but also because its business history is intimately connected with the postwar reconstruction of German capitalism and the contestations between capital and labour during its evolution (Schreyögg, Sydow, & Holtmann, 2011, p. 95).

The next section thus analyzes the corporate strategies associated with Bertelsmann's surge to power, as they played out within their concrete socio-economic context. We argue that the company's postwar success depended on managerial innovations which we trace back to a 'Cologne School' of business management, and which became vital because Bertelsmann lacked the corporate and financial support network that many established German firms enjoyed. Placed at one remove from the German model due to its newcomer status and peculiar business plan, these managerial practices enabled Bertelsmann to circumvent and fundamentally rethink its constitutive capital/labour compromise.

The Cologne roots of Bertelsmann's surge to power

Critical scholarship on Bertelsmann does much to dispel the rhetoric of its long-standing 'social mission' by revealing the corrosive impact of its reforms, the megalomania of its patriarch, and the complicity of his firm as propagandist of and profiteer from German fascism (e.g. Böckelmann & Fischler, 2004). And yet, quite where Bertelsmann's wider vision comes from, and what it seeks to accomplish, tends to be underspecified. Too often, the inquiry has been guided by some version of Berghahn's 'Americanization of German business' thesis. Accordingly, Mohn is portrayed as 'the Alfred P. Sloan of publishing' (Gershon, 1996; cf. 'Reinhard Mohn', 1987), modelling his firm on the business practices of General Motors (Wischermann, 2010, p. 261) and his think-tank on the Ford Foundation (Schuler, 2010, pp. 34–37). By contrast, this article takes up the ordoliberal proposition of *internal* impulses to reform along neoliberal lines, reaching further back into Germany's history than previously recognized. Rather than an exegesis of ordoliberal texts, however, we identify a German managerial tradition of 'ruling by numbers' that had developed independently from the US during the 1920s (Fear, 2005), and that came to define Bertelsmann's approach to capital-labour relations inside the firm and in German society at large (Bundesmann-Jansen & Pekruhl, 1992).

The engine of Bertelsmann's rapid postwar expansion is widely seen to be the mass-market book club. It offered its members a selection of titles at a considerable discount in exchange for a monthly subscription fee (Wössner, 1988, p. 150). Its secret of success lay in the innovative use of the door-to-door sales and mail-order publishing business which aggressively broadened its client base ('Die Bestsellerfabrik', 1957; Holtmann, 2008; Schreyögg et al., 2011, p. 89). Though critical to Bertelsmann's worldwide success, the exorbitant growth of its membership posed logistical and financial challenges that pushed the firm to the brink of collapse (Berghoff, 2013b, p. 859). Cut off from finance because book club subscriptions were not recognized as collateral (Gershon, 1996, p. 174; Tietz, 1985, p. 345; Wössner, 1988, p. 151), Bertelsmann lacked *Modell Deutschland's* distinctive bank-based support network, commonly credited for corporate Germany's postwar success.

Despite the often-repeated claims by Mohn to have been influenced by American business practices (e.g. Wischermann, 2010, pp. 260–261), our research suggests that in this moment of exponential growth and existential crisis, Bertelsmann instead searched for more immediate solutions that were much closer to home. Confirming the intuition of Berghoff (2013b, p. 866), our archival research reveals an as-of-yet unexplored connection to the German coal and steel industry via the person of Dr. Willi Schoess. Hired in April 1955 to oversee and control Bertelsmann's financial operations ('Die Bestsellerfabrik', 1957), what makes Schoess such a critically important figure is that he belongs to two influential and intersecting, distinctively German circles of business management theory and practice.

A student of business economics at the University of Cologne, Schoess was educated in the 'accounting and management tradition surrounding Eugen Schmalenbach' (Fear, 2005, p. 522). In the interwar period, Schmalenbach had pioneered a new standard of accounting that emphasized the profit/loss statement as the main device for assessing the commercial success of firms or divisions over time and against one another (Fear, 2005, p. 341). His key innovation was to elevate financial questions of profitability over technical questions of productivity, which gave managers a dynamic conception of a firm's capital use rather than a static understanding of its assets (Fear, 2005, pp. 342, 627).

Schoess recognized the managerial possibilities of these key innovations compared to the prevailing 'bureaucratic-conservative views' of corporate organization (Schoess, 1936, pp. 279, 280, 1953, pp. 2, 23). He soon applied these advances at the Vereinigte Stahlwerke, a major steel conglomerate, and the neuralgic centre of business management practice influenced by Schmalenbach and led by Heinrich Dinkelbach (Fear, 2005, p. 588). After serving in Germany's war of aggression, Schoess was rehired by Dinkelbach in 1947 to create 'the organizational preconditions' for the allied-mandated decartellization of the coal and steel industry (Bertelsmann Corporate Archive, 1954, p. 3).

Thus, Schoess brought with him a new set of financial accounting techniques that transformed the management of Bertelsmann and had far-reaching consequences for its future development into a multinational corporation and policy think-tank. His arrival in April 1955 started a process of corporate restructuring that began with the separation of the central firm from the publishing house and the newly created sales group (*Verlagsgemeinschaft*). The resulting two-level hierarchy was connected with a 'tighter organization of accounting' and intended to provide 'greater transparency of the numerical data necessary for executive decisions' (Bleicher, 1985, p. 62; Gööck, 1968, p. 161). Although he left the firm six months before this reorganization was completed in 1959, Schoess was commended by Mohn for his 'accomplishments in the construction of the accounting system of the publishing house and its subsidiary firms' (Bertelsmann Corporate Archive, 1958, p. 1).

This reform was critical to solving Bertelsmann's most pressing problem: the rampant growth of its book club exceeded the organizational capacities of the firm and jeopardized its financial and strategic planning. For a long time 'the absence of proper budgeting techniques and profit and loss statements rendered the enterprise a risky venture' (Tietz, 1985, p. 345). In this respect, the centralized accounting system Schoess introduced allowed Bertelsmann, for the first time, to take stock of its intangible assets of membership subscriptions and to explore what a company report from 1957 called 'the still wide open frontier of an unknown market' (quoted in Langenbucher, 1985, p. 41).

This new computational and managerial ability was also crucial in helping Bertelsmann manage the thousands of firms that acquired customers for its books. Initially tasked to recruit new and service existing customers on their own account, the marketing firms soon felt overburdened and underpaid and pushed for higher commissions and better conditions (Böckelmann & Fischler, 2004, p. 122; Tietz, 1985, p. 346). Under a new division of labour enabled by the accounting innovations, Bertelsmann reached a compromise: the sales companies not only received rent for each member they transferred to the sales group; the annual profits of the company were also divided up (Schaper, 1977, pp. 444–445). Though potentially more lucrative, this meant that the marketing agencies submitted to a centralized system of financial reporting that calculated and rewarded their relative performance (Berghoff, 2010, p. 29). This allowed Bertelsmann to gain the upper hand over an unruly but indispensable bunch of sales companies, whose intense and often dysfunctional competition with one another could now be organized, monitored, and fine-tuned in ways that would serve the interests of Bertelsmann (Lokatis, 2010).

Lastly, the new managerial tools also provided a platform for the divisionalization and subsequent diversification of Bertelsmann. Between 1955 and 1959, the company embarked on a systematic strategy of operative decentralization (Langenbucher, 1985, p. 41) that followed Schmalenbach's prescriptions. Based on his principle of 'delegate but supervise' (Fear, 2005, pp. 704, 706–707), Bertelsmann transformed its subsidiaries into independent 'profit centres' while centralizing administrative functions such as finance, accounting, and budgeting (Bleicher, 1985, p. 62; Gööck, 1968, p. 188). This meant that their chief executives were now solely responsible for their domain while remaining subject to central supervision through financial accounting techniques (Berghoff, 2010, p. 28). One of Mohn's close advisors recalled the 'famous monthly enterprise statistic, developed over years according to Reinhard Mohn's conceptions', comprising 'the financial benchmark data of the enterprise, its divisions, and the profit centres, amended by specific indicators of the factors of success of the individual operations' and providing Mohn 'with a comprehensive overview of the state of business in a very short time' (Luther, 1985, pp. 289–299; Bleicher, 1985, p. 62). The underlying power relationship was summarized by one manager, who noted '[i]f they meet their financial obligation to the company, they will have autonomy' (Berghoff, 2013a, p. 186).

Overall, an enduring, if continually evolving, system of management was built on the basis of financial accounting techniques from the Dinkenbach/Schmalenbach school, which 'remained largely exceptional until the late 1950s' (Fear, 2005, p. 737) and in the mid-1990s still set Bertelsmann apart in Germany's business world (Albers, 1995, pp. 2, 3, 4 fn. 18; Göttert, 2002; Palaß, 1992, pp. 316, 322). Compared to Germany's industrial giants, which had used these managerial techniques in order to reintroduce a measure of competition and raise productivity, Bertelsmann was a medium-sized company that was only beginning to diversify its operations and expand internationally (Berghoff, 2010, p. 28). Crucially, these techniques enabled Bertelsmann to manage a still untapped consumer market based on a business model of intangible assets that few people at the time knew how to value and that put it outside the bank/industry nexus of the German model. While the toolkit has since evolved, it had a lasting impact on the corporate strategy and social orientation of Bertelsmann. Because these financial accounting tools were so vital to the ability of Mohn and his chief executives to 'read' their firm and plan its expansion, they rendered Bertelsmann particularly receptive to future innovations in the field of management theory and practice. Transplanted into a nascent media corporation engaged in the mass-marketization of literary consumption, moreover, this new programmatic of 'ruling by numbers' would also enter into the image of corporate responsibility Bertelsmann developed in the face of public scrutiny and cultural criticism.

In sum, we believe to have found in these managerial forms of power the seeds of an endogenous branch of neoliberalism that originates in Cologne and which – through Bertelsmann's corporate success and a mandate to 'educate' German society – connects to the transformation of the German socio-economic model since the 1990s. How Mohn and his executives further developed this management system and defined their vision of society in response to the unruly 1970s is the subject of the next section.

Beyond profit incentives and competition: cybernetics and managerial power

Bertelsmann was not only one of the first companies in Germany to repurpose managerial techniques for a sustained growth offensive; it also innovated with regards to the ultimate object of management, that is the discretionary power over the labour of others. Many established German businesses only reluctantly parted with patriarchal modes of corporate governance and workplace control (Berghahn, 1986; Hilger, 2008). A large number of them fought tooth and claw against the extension of work council rights and parity co-determination that were enacted during the turbulent 1970s. Bertelsmann differed not in its opposition to these reforms, but in the managerial solutions it provided. Because it had depended on its workers as a vital source of funding, Bertelsmann had long sought new ways to incorporate, incentivize and control labour and to circumvent the institutions that defined its postwar settlement with capital in Germany. In the heated class context of the 1970s, the forms of profit-sharing and workers 'participation' Bertelsmann had pioneered to manage a mushrooming conglomerate and its workforce took on a wider significance.

Ostensibly, the 'social model Bertelsmann' promised to interpose modern management as a mediating force between capital and labour, anticipating the reforms and rhetoric Mohn would promote through his Foundation in the following years. And yet a closer look reveals that it was premised on techniques that empowered managers at the expense of the representation and self-organization of labour. While part of a broader trend across the advanced capitalist world (cf. Duménil & Lévy, 2011, p. 78), our research reveals the specific challenges that Bertelsmann addressed, and that led to a more disciplinary way out of the temporary settlement between capitalism and democracy. Thus, while shifting the geographical focus away from the Anglo-Saxon area, we also highlight the emerging gaps and cracks underneath *Modell Deutschland*, details that are sometimes obscured by common assumptions about its social and economic progress.

The material reasons for why Bertelsmann became 'the first big company in Germany which gave its employees a share in profits' (Schuler, 2010, p. 26) have been intimated above: Bertelsmann suffered from a chronic shortage of capital and the state levied a high tax of 60% on corporate profits. Cleverly, Mohn distributed Bertelsmann's profits equally amongst his employees in the years from 1951 to 1955, on condition that they return them as a loan for an interest payment of 2%. This allowed Mohn to evade taxation and reinvest all of Bertelsmann's profits (Berghoff, 2013b, p. 86). In 1955, Mohn introduced a pension scheme that followed the same principle (Hagemann-Wilholt, 2016, p. 248). At risk of missing out on the postwar boom and excluded from the established networks of German business, Mohn had to tap into his labour force in order to generate the funds necessary to sustain the expansion of his book club.

More than a tax-saving trick, the profit-sharing scheme served as a continual source of Bertelsmann's corporate expansion well into the 2000s (Berghoff, 2013b, p. 862; Jungblut, 1972). This not only spurred workers' motivation, as Mohn liked to claim (Bundesmann-Jansen & Pekruhl, 1992, p. 180). As early as 1970 – two decades before the arrival of the neoliberal ideology of 'shareholder value' – these financial strategies also established profit maximization as a legitimate corporate goal (Hagemann-Wilholt, 2016, p. 251) and engaged employees as shareholders. If one took Mohn's rhetoric at the time at face value, one could think of these strategies as replacing 'order' with self-management, creativity and individualism (Lehning, 2004, p. 278), supplemented by communitarian values (for a discussion of neoliberalism and communitarianism, see Bieling, 2007). Indeed, we encounter these tropes in the 1990s with respect to the entrepreneurial subject and market-based governance that his Foundation is said to have introduced into Germany (Barth, 2007). In our view, however, these managerial innovations were born out of immediate concerns with the success of the firm rather than an intention to restore market rule. Hence, rather than ingrain a shareholder or market mentality in the individual, the main aim of the new managerial techniques was to cut it back to size.

The problem was that the growing expansion and diversification of Bertelsmann in the 1960s and 1970s had rendered the management of the organization increasingly imprecise. Indeed, insofar as greater competition between the profit centres had been introduced, it had detrimental results for the overall coherence and profitability of the company. Mohn and his successor at the firm and Foundation, Mark Wössner, argued that profit centres might run astray from the overall corporate objective precisely because the individual might prioritize their own profits over the goals of central management (Hagemann-Wilholt, 2016, p. 262). The development of carefully calibrated and regularly audited profit and risk-sharing schemes for employees and managers were not enough (Bundesmann-Jansen & Pekruhl, 1992, p. 34–35; Lehning, 2004, p. 278). To bring workers in line with the needs and wants of the firm, new management techniques were needed.

A trained engineer, Wössner found a possible solution in cybernetic management theories (Glißmann & Peters, 2001, p. 95; Hagemann-Wilholt, 2016, p. 262), which had originated in the USA but undergone a parallel and distinct development in German scientific and public debates after 1945 (Aumann, 2011). The core idea, as Wössner explained, was to 'create a constantly reproducing and evolving *Regelkreis* [closed loop control]' (cited in Hagemann-Wilholt, 2016, p. 261) that would continuously synchronize the goals of individual workers and subsidiary profit centres with an overall corporate objective and regularly adjust that objective to a rapidly changing environment (Hagemann-Wilholt, 2016, p. 263).

The overarching tool generated for that purpose was the *Sozialbilanz* ('social stock taking'), a report that was first published in 1978 but prepared throughout the 1970s. The *Sozialbilanz* was supposed to measure how closely corporate objectives were followed in Bertelsmann's daily operations and how far they accomplished the intended results. In cases of failure, managers could adjust the various profit-sharing schemes and means for workers participation. The aim was to establish an overall management system that could 'learn' from the actual operations of the company, address deficits as they occurred, and thus close any loopholes within Bertelsmann's corporate universe (Hagemann-Wilholt, 2016, p. 261). In the eyes of its proponents, this provided a more 'objective' tool for setting company goals and making management decisions based on what was learned – according to Knafo et al. (2018), a core objective of new managerial strategies. Thus, we have a clear adaptation of the old, more rigid 'ruling by numbers' towards an evolving and decentralized 'feedback' system. Workers' participation became a tool of systematic surveillance where the market incentive failed to ensure that the individual parts of the company worked as a whole.

While the *Sozialbilanz* lost its central significance in the late 1980s (Hagemann-Wilholt, 2016, p. 263), Bertelsmann has retained to this date its more traditional employee 'suggestion system' (*Vorschlagswesen*), which German corporations introduced at the turn of the nineteenth century but largely phased out in the 1960s. It enlisted individual workers in monitoring everyday operations as a way of controlling and optimizing their labour power and rewarded them for any corresponding cost savings (Wischermann, 2010, p. 242). Enshrined in a corporate constitution that promises social coherence and individual fulfilment, Bertelsmann's corporate culture has become a 'measuring instrument' for upper management (Bundesmann-Jansen & Pekruhl, 1992, p. 175; Lehning, 2004, p. 278).

In sum, we argue that under the guise of increased participation, a new managerial form of continuous data collection, feedback and improvement was established which sought to ensure that new business objectives could be found and realized in a complex environment. For us, the real significance of Bertelsmann's seemingly more 'social' workers' policies lies in equipping its managers with extended powers to control labour in the interest of the firm so that competition would not be counterproductive. At the same time, the accompanying discourse about self-fulfillment and self-responsibility provided a neat answer to public debates about labour alienation and workplace democracy in the contentious 1970s (Glißmann & Peters, 2001, pp. 94–95). It was on the basis of his unique model of worker participation that Mohn argued publicly against parity co-determination and the influence of unions in business operations (Hagemann-Wilholt, 2016, p. 252).

Management, in the vision of Mohn and sympathetic social reformers, was posited as a 'third factor' between capital and labour (Biedenkopf, 1985, p. 382; Glißmann & Peters, 2001, pp. 94–95). The expansion of its influence was justified by this mediating role, which appeared increasingly important the more the postwar social partnership came under strain. Internally, however, Mohn left no doubt about where he stood, rejecting even modest steps towards a democratization of the economy as giving undue weight to labour. Bertelsmann's income sharing and participatory schemes explicitly eschewed any legally enshrined, institutionalized, and collective decision-making power in favour of a vague and unenforceable employee 'voice', valued for their 'harmonising effect at the expense of trade unions' (quoted in Wischermann, 2015, p. 173). Rather than simply defend the prerogatives of capital, however, Mohn went on the offensive. By virtue of their managerial innovations, he explained, corporations like Bertelsmann presented a superior form of organization to the slow, cumbersome, and ineffective executive of democracy (Wischermann, 2015, p. 172). Thus, by 1980 already, Mohn advocated that the techniques his firm had crafted to organize power over subordinates and their participation in the enterprise could serve as a model for redefining the role of organized labour and restructuring the state apparatus of liberal democracies.

It is from this point on that our story of Bertelsmann intersects with wider debates on managerialism as a form of neoliberal governance (Davies, 2014; Knafo et al., 2018; Styhre, 2014). With Mohn's transition from the top of the company to the Foundation, Bertelsmann joined the ranks of consultancies and companies elsewhere that – on the back of the systematic assault on the welfare state and organized labour in the USA and UK – aimed to disseminate new ideas and techniques into public governance that were drawn from business management (Bislev, Salskov-Iversen, & Hansen, 2002). Future research will need to investigate Bertelsmann's precise influence on the implementation in Germany of what has come to be known as 'new public management'. Here, our contribution to this literature is to highlight the need to understand how managerial answers to labour and social struggles can show the twists and turns in corporate management and its implications for (state-led) authoritarian rule. For the principal objective of Bertelsmann's managerial innovations was never simply to introduce market competition, because it had often proved damaging to the strategies of the firm. On the contrary, the question for Mohn and his associates was about how to ensure compliance precisely because 'market-based' governance could not be trusted to lead to the desired results (see Hagemann-Wilholt, 2016, p. 262; Knafo et al., 2018).

Conclusion

This article has outlined the contours of a contribution that Bertelsmann has made to the neoliberal transformation of the German political economy. We find that due to its postwar expansion being difficult to finance, plan and steer, and because workers had to be brought into the firm's financial strategies from the beginning in order to ensure its survival, from early on Bertelsmann's executives came to see managerial innovations in the exercise of corporate power as the font and matrix of their success. These new techniques link back to an endogenous school of German financial accounting and, complemented by American cybernetics from the 1970s, forged a management system that emphasizes continuous control of its labour force and organizations in the name of social responsibility, workplace participation and income distribution. Long before the neoliberal turn under Thatcher and Reagan, Bertelsmann sought to retool capital-labour relations outside of the corporatist structures of *Modell Deutschland.* Thus, without denying the importance of the new management know-how which American consultancies brought to Germany (Hilger, 2000), our research has revealed an independent line of development that links Bertelsmann to a long-standing tradition of German business management. In this respect, our work goes some length in questioning the image of a global diffusion of neoliberalism, with its often implicit and sometimes explicit assumption that the USA and UK were the major centres of innovation (see also Bruff & Tansel, 2018; Harrison, 2018).

Unlike the putative Anglo-American emphasis on the entrepreneurial subject and the shareholder society often assumed in this literature, we argue that market-based governance was never the primary objective of Bertelsmann's managerial innovations. Instead, Bertelsmann's managers found profit incentives and competition to be counterproductive to the overall objectives of the firm and thus had to be reined in. In its own ways, Bertelsmann's corresponding managerial innovations empowered it, on the one hand, to understand and manage the conglomerate and its labour force; on the other, they served to undercut the power of unions and work councils. It is this specific management system rather than a market model that we believe anchors both Mohn's blueprint for German society and his influential Foundation, singularly shaped by 'the leadership style and the approaches of business' (Fleishman, 2001, p. 133).

Emphasizing the specific corporate challenges of Bertelsmann, our search for the antecedents of its contribution has led us to Cologne rather than to Freiburg and yields an account that, while still requiring future research and elaboration, differs in important respects from the ordoliberal optic. First, our article approaches AN as a project to reshape German society in the image of corporate hierarchies rather than a state-imposed market order. This shift in focus not only dislodges the market as the be-all and end-all of neoliberal reform; it can also recast the capitalist state itself – including its executive and coercive apparatus – as an object of managerial reconstruction rather than a supreme authority towering above society. Most importantly in this regard, our study helps understand what state elites might have found appealing in managerial practices such as 'new public management'. If Bertelsmann's experience is anything to go by, it is the ability to exercise power in new ways rather than the dogma of the free market that is attractive. Future research along these lines ought to focus on how and why Bertelsmann's managerial innovations have made inroads into German public administration since the 1990s, a fact often stated but rarely historically analyzed.

Second, our analysis yields a more dynamic view than a narrative which conceives of the development of the German political economy in terms of an unchanging ordoliberal paradigm. Although our story also begins in the interwar period, it does not rule out that critical innovations and adaptations of the techniques handed down to Bertelsmann from this period have since occurred. As mentioned above, the types of managerial practices we identify have undergone further modifications, developing nominally 'participatory' and 'inclusive' elements that conceal the corporate hierarchies from which they flow. But while certainly more flexible and difficult to track than an ordoliberal doctrine, we believe they are no less at odds with the ideal of a society governed by and for the people and thus – from the progressive outlook of AN – it is just as vital to comprehend and contest them as well as ordoliberalism.

Acknowledgements

We would like to thank Ian Bruff and Cemal Burak Tansel for organizing and facilitating this special issue, as well as two anonymous reviewers for helping to improve our argument. Ian Bruff, Sam Knafo and Ian Lovering provided useful comments on earlier versions of our paper, for which we are very grateful.

Disclosure statement

No potential conflict of interest was reported by the authors.

References

Albers, S. (1995). Dezentralisierte Führung von Unternehmen mit Hilfe eines internen Beteiligungsmarktes. *Manuskripte aus den Instituten für Betriebswirtschaftslehre der Universität Kiel*, 377. Retrieved from https://www.econstor.eu/bitstream/10419/149835/1/manuskript_377.pdf

Art, D. (2015). The German rescue of the eurozone: How Germany is getting the Europe it always wanted. *Political Science Quarterly*, *130*(2), 181–212.

Aumann, P. (2011). The distinctiveness of a unifying science: Cybernetics' way to West Germany. *IEEE Annals of the History of Computing*, *33*(4), 17–27.

Barth, T. (2006). *Bertelsmann: Ein globales Medienimperium macht Politik: Expansion als Bildungsdienstleister und politische Einflussnahme - internationale Perspektive*. Hamburg: Anders Verlag.

Barth, T. (2007). Gütersloher Reform-Vollstrecker und ihr deutscher Sonderweg in den Neoliberalismus. In J. Wernicke & T. Bultmann (Eds.), *Netzwerk der Macht - Bertelsmann. Der medial-politische Komplex aus Gütersloh* (pp. 57–76). Marburg: Bund demokratischer Wissenschaftler.

Bauer, R. (2009). Bürgergesellschaft als Bertelsmann-Project. Ein kritischer Bericht. In I. Bode, A. Evers, & A. Klein (Eds.), *Bürgergesellschaft als Projekt* (pp. 265–291). Wiesbaden: VS Verlag für Sozialwissenschaften.

Berghahn, V. (1986). *The Americanisation of West German industry, 1945-1973*. Leamington Spa: Berg.

Berghahn, V., & Young, B. (2013). Reflections on Werner Bonefeld's 'freedom and the strong state: On German ordoliberalism' and the continuing importance of the ideas of ordoliberalism to understand Germany's (contested) role in resolving the eurozone crisis. *New Political Economy*, *18*(5), 768–778.

Berghoff, H. (2010). From small publisher to global media and services company: Outline of the history of Bertelsmann, 1835-2010. In U. Engelen & H. Berghoff (Eds.), *175 years of Bertelsmann: The legacy for our future* (pp. 6–83). Munich: C. Bertelsmann.

Berghoff, H. (2013a). Becoming global, staying local: The internationalisation of Bertelsmann, 1962-2010. In C. Lubinski, J. Fear, & P. Fernández Pérez (Eds.), *Family multinationals: Entrepreneurship, governance, and pathways to internationalization* (pp. 169–190). London: Routledge.

Berghoff, H. (2013b). Blending personal and managerial capitalism: Bertelsmann's rise from medium-sized publisher to global media corporation and service provider, 1950–2010. *Business History*, *55*(6), 855–874.

Bertelsmann Corporate Archive. (1954). Curriculum vitae, Dr. Willi Schoess, November 1954. 0017.PA/1511.

Bertelsmann Corporate Archive. (1958). Letter from Reinhard Mohn to Dr. Willi Schoess, 30 July 1958. 0017.PA/1511.

Biebricher, T. (2013). Europe and the political philosophy of neoliberalism. *Contemporary Political Theory*, *12* (4), 338–375.

Biebricher, T., & Vogelmann, F. (Eds.). (2017). *The birth of austerity: German ordoliberalism and contemporary neoliberalism*. London: Rowman & Littlefield International.

Biedenkopf, K. (1985). Im Dienst der Gemeinschaft: Das Sozialmodell Bertelsmann. In G. Hadding & G. Schukies (Eds.), *150 Jahre Bertelsmann: 1835–1985* (pp. 380–400). München: C. Bertelsmann.

Bieling, H.-J. (2007). Neoliberalism and communitarianism: Social conditions, discourses and politics. In D. Plehwe, B. J. A. Walpen, & G. Neunhöffer (Eds.), *Neoliberal hegemony: A global critique* (pp. 207–221). New York: Routledge.

Biermann, W., & Klönne, A. (2008). *Agenda Bertelsmann: Ein Konzern stiftet Politik*. Köln: Papyrossa.

Bislev, S., Salskov-Iversen, D., & Hansen, H. K. (2002). The global diffusion of managerialism: Transnational discourse communities at work. *Global Society*, *16*(2), 199–212.

Bleicher, K. (1985). Führung durch Vorbild: Management und Mitarbeiter in einer Unternehmenskultur. In Bertelsmann AG (plc) (Ed.), *150 Jahre Bertelsmann: Die Geschichte des Verlagsunternehmens in Texten, Bildern und Dokumenten* (pp. 59–82). München: C. Bertelsmann.

Blyth, M. (2013). *Austerity: The history of a dangerous idea*. New York: Oxford University Press.

Böckelmann, F., & Fischler, H. (2004). *Bertelsmann: Hinter der Fassade des Medienimperiums*. Frankfurt: Eichborn.

Bonefeld, W. (2012). Freedom and the strong state: On German ordoliberalism. *New Political Economy*, *17*(5), 633–656.

Bruff, I. (2008). *Culture and consensus in European varieties of capitalism: A 'common sense' analysis*. London: Palgrave Macmillan.

Bruff, I. (2014). The rise of authoritarian neoliberalism. *Rethinking Marxism*, *26*(1), 113–129.

Bruff, I. (2016). Neoliberalism and authoritarianism. In S. Springer, K. Birch, & J. MacLeavy (Eds.), *The handbook of neoliberalism* (pp. 107–117). New York: Routledge.

Bruff, I., & Tansel, C. B. (2018). Authoritarian neoliberalism: Trajectories of knowledge production and praxis. *Globalizations.* doi:10.1080/14747731.2018.1502497

Bundesmann-Jansen, J., & Pekruhl, U. (1992). *Der Medienkonzern Bertelsmann: Neues Management und gewerkschaftliche Betriebspolitik.* Köln: Bund-Verlag.

Cozzolino, A. (2018). Reconfiguring the state: Executive powers, emergency legislation, and neoliberalization in Italy. *Globalizations.* doi:/10.1080/14747731.2018.1502495

Davies, W. (2014). *The limits of neoliberalism: Authority, sovereignty and the logic of competition.* London: Sage.

Die Bestsellerfabrik. (1957, July 24). *Der Spiegel 30/1957.* Retrieved from http://www.spiegel.de/spiegel/print/d-41758081.html

Duménil, G., & Lévy, D. (2011). *The crisis of neoliberalism.* Cambridge: Harvard University Press.

Dyson, K. (2001). The German model revisited: From Schmidt to Schröder. *German Politics, 10*(2), 135–154.

Ewing, J. (2014). *Germany's economic renaissance.* New York: Palgrave Macmillan.

Fear, J. (2005). *Organizing control: August Thyssen and the construction of German corporate management.* New York: Harvard University Press.

Fitzgerald, S. (2012). *Corporations and cultural industries: Time Warner, Bertelsmann, and News Corporation.* Lanham: Lexington.

Fleishman, J. (2001). Die operative Stiftung: Reinhard Mohn und Andrew Carnegie: Zwei große Philanthropen im Vergleich. In T. Middelhoff, G. Schulte-Hillen, & G. Thielen (Eds.), *Reinhard Mohn: Unternehmer, Stifter, Bürger* (pp. 129–137). Gütersloh: Verlag Bertelsmann Stiftung.

Gershon, R. (1996). *The transnational media corporation: Global messages and free market competition.* London: Routledge.

Glißmann, W., & Peters, K. (2001). *Mehr Druck durch mehr Freiheit: Die neue Autonomie in der Arbeit und ihre paradoxen Folgen.* Hamburg: VSA-Verlag.

Gööck, R. (1968). *Bücher für Millionen.* Gütersloh: Bertelsmann.

Göttert, J.-M. (2002). *Die Bertelsmann Methode.* Frankfurt: Ueberreuter Wirtschaftsverlag.

Hagemann-Wilholt, S. (2016). *Das 'gute' Unternehmen: Zur Geschichte der Unternehmenskommunikation.* Bielefeld: Transcript Verlag.

Harrison, G. (2018). Authoritarian neoliberalism and capitalist transformation in Africa: All pain, no gain. *Globalizations.* doi:10.1080/14747731.2018.1502491

Hartmann, E. (2015). European social policy: Social cohesion through competition? In E. Hartmann & P. Kjaer (Eds.), *The evolution of intermediary institutions in Europe: From corporatism to governance* (pp. 121–138). London: Palgrave Macmillan.

Hien, J. (2013). The ordoliberalism that never was. *Contemporary Political Theory, 12*(4), 349–358.

Hien, J., & Joerges, C. (2017). *Ordoliberalism, law and the rule of economics.* Oxford: Hart Publishing.

Hilger, S. (2000). American consultants in the German consumer chemical industry: The Stanford Research Institute at Henkel in the 1960s and 1970s. *Entreprises et histoire, 25*, 46–64.

Hilger, S. (2008). 'Globalisation by Americanisation': American companies and the internationalisation of German industry after the Second World War. *European Review of History: Revue Europeenne d'histoire, 15*(4), 375–401.

Holtmann, J. P. (2008). *Pfadabhängigkeit strategischer Entscheidungen: Eine Fallstudie am Beispiel des Bertelsmann Buchclubs Deutschland.* Cologne: Kölner Wissenschaftsverlag.

Jungblut, M. (1972, January 14). Wie Arbeitnehmer am Gewinn beteiligt werden: Börse für Bertelsmänner. *Die Zeit.* Retrieved from http://www.zeit.de/1972/02/boerse-fuer-bertelsmaenner/komplettansicht

Knafo, S., Dutta, S., Lane, R., & Wyn-Jones, S. (2018). The managerial lineages of neoliberalism. *New Political Economy*, 'Latest Articles' section.

Langenbucher, W. (1985). Bertelsmann nach 1945: Ein Kapitel deutscher Verlags- und Unternehmensgeschichte. In Bertelsmann AG (plc) (Ed.), *150 Jahre Bertelsmann: Die Geschichte des Verlagsunternehmens in Texten, Bildern und Dokumenten* (pp. 38–58). München: C. Bertelsmann.

Lehning, T. (2004). *Das Medienhaus. Geschichte und Gegenwart des Bertelsmann-Konzerns.* Munich: Beck.

Lokatis, S. (2010). A concept circles the world: From the Lesering to the internationalization of the club business. In H. Berghoff & U. Engelen (Eds.), *175 years of Bertelsmann: The legacy for our future* (pp. 130–171). Munich: C. Bertelsmann.

Luther, S. (1985). Corporate governance als Lebensaufgabe. In G. Hadding & G. Schukies (Eds.), *150 Jahre Bertelsmann: 1835-1985* (pp. 293–303). München: C. Bertelsmann.

Manow, P. (2001). Ordoliberalismus als ökonomische Ordnungstheologie. *Leviathan*, *29*(2), 179–198.

Matthijs, M. (2016). Powerful rules governing the Euro: The perverse logic of German ideas. *Journal of European Public Policy*, *23*(3), 375–391.

Palaß, B. (1992). Genuß ohne Reue. *Manager Magazin*, *12*, 314–322.

Ptak, R. (2009). Neoliberalism in Germany: Revisiting the ordoliberal foundations of the social market economy. In P. Mirowski & D. Plehwe (Eds.), *The road from Mont Pèlerin: The making of the neoliberal thought collective* (pp. 98–138). Cambridge: Harvard University Press.

Reinhard Mohn: The Alfred P Sloan of Publishing. (1987, October 5). *Forbes*, p. 124.

Rioux, S. (2017). The right to starve: Hunger, discipline and labour market restructuring under authoritarian neoliberalism. In C. B. Tansel (Ed.), *States of discipline: Authoritarian neoliberalism and the contested reproduction of capitalist order* (pp. 87–106). London: Rowman & Littlefield International.

Ryner, M. (2015). Europe's ordoliberal iron cage: Critical political economy, the euro area crisis and its management. *Journal of European Public Policy*, *22*(2), 275–294.

Schaper, F.-W. (1977). *Handbuch des Buchhandels Band IV: Übrige Formen des Bucheinzelhandels - Zwischenbuchhandel und Buchgemeinschaft*. Gütersloh: Verlagsgruppe Bertelsmann GmbH.

Schoess, W. (1936). Die Arbeitsverteilung in Maschinenfabriken. *Zeitschrift Für Organisation*, *10*(11), 458–459.

Schoess, W. (1953). Geschäftsbuchhaltung in einem Hüttenwerk mit IBM Lochkarten. *IBM-Nachrichten*, *115*, 1–25.

Schreyögg, G., Sydow, J., & Holtmann, P. (2011). How history matters in organisations: The case of path dependence. *Management & Organizational History*, *6*(1), 81–100.

Schuler, T. (2010). *Bertelsmannrepublik Deutschland: Eine Stiftung macht Politik*. Frankfurt: Campus Verlag.

Styhre, A. (2014). *Management and neoliberalism: Connecting policies and practices*. London: Routledge.

Tansel, C. B. (Ed.). (2017). *States of discipline: Authoritarian neoliberalism and the contested reproduction of capitalist order*. London: Rowman & Littlefield International.

Thelen, K. (2014). *Varieties of liberalization and the new politics of social solidarity*. Cambridge: Cambridge University Press.

Tietz, B. (1985). Königsidee Buchgemeinschaft: Neue Leser durch eine neue Marktpolitik. In Bertelsmann AG (plc) (Ed.), *150 Jahre Bertelsmann: Die Geschichte des Verlagsunternehmens in Texten, Bildern und Dokumenten* (pp. 339–356). München: C. Bertelsmann.

Wernicke, J., & Bultmann, T. (Eds.). (2007). *Netzwerk der Macht – Bertelsmann: Der medial-politische Komplex aus Gütersloh*. Marburg: Bund demokratischer Wissenschaftler.

Wigger, A., & Buch-Hansen, H. (2015). EU competition regulation: A case of authoritarian neoliberalism? In E. Hartmann & P. Kjaer (Eds.), *The evolution of intermediary institutions in Europe: From corporatism to governance* (pp. 81–98). London: Palgrave Macmillan.

Wischermann, C. (2010). Corporate culture at Bertelsmann in the second half of the 20th century. In H. Berghoff & U. Engelen (Eds.), *175 years of Bertelsmann: The legacy for our future* (pp. 238–281). Munich: C. Bertelsmann.

Wischermann, C. (2015). Kultur: Unternehmenskultur des Medienkonzerns Bertelsmann in den 1970/80er Jahren. In C. Wischermann, K. Patzel-Mattern, L. Martin, & T. Jungkind (Eds.), *Studienbuch institutionelle Wirtschafts- und Unternehmensgeschichte* (pp. 166–179). Stuttgart: Steiner.

Wössner, M. (1988). Wachstumsstrategien im Medienbereich. In H. Henzler (Ed.), *Handbuch Strategische Führung* (pp. 147–163). Wiesbaden: Springer.

Young, B. (2014). German ordoliberalism as agenda setter for the Euro crisis: Myth trumps reality. *Journal of Contemporary European Studies*, *22*(3), 276–287.

4 Authoritarian neoliberalism and capitalist transformation in Africa: all pain, no gain

Graham Harrison

ABSTRACT

As a region of the world capitalist political economy, Africa has been the epitome of neoliberalism as a universal project to remake societies in its image. In Africa, the neoliberal project encountered a region already ensconced in state-forms that were authoritarian, albeit very often weaker than their analogues in Latin America or Southern Europe. In these circumstances, neoliberalism both reconstructed and relied upon authoritarian state practices: reassertions of law and order, rising technocracy, re-built bureaucracies, and 'choiceless democracy'. Liberal advocates of neoliberalism indulged authoritarian governance in the belief that economic liberalization would generate economic growth and transformation. Reviewing these authoritarian neoliberal constructions, one is struck by how poorly they performed as vehicles for market-based capitalist transformation. In a phrase, the pain of neoliberal adjustment was accompanied by no palliative of sustained economic 'gain'. Liberalization, executed by top-down and undemocratic governance, has generated fragile growth, instability, some enrichment and no economic transformation. This conjuncture is pivotal to an understanding of moves by some governing elites to explore and at times implement non-neoliberal development strategies. The article concludes by suggesting that neoliberalism is currently a somewhat besieged orthodoxy. However, the exploration of unorthodox development strategies has taken place within an authoritarian political shell.

Introduction

This article argues that authoritarian neoliberalism in Africa is a failed strategy of capitalist transformation. Aspiring to combine an administrative and technocratic governance with economic liberalism, authoritarian neoliberalism has not generated a sustained process of accumulation, investment, and sectoral change away from low-productivity economies. As such, neoliberalism combines both a normatively troubling mode of governance with a useless economic model. Conceptualizing authoritarianism as a state form historically generated by the absence of a socially-dominant bourgeoisie, we pose the question whether the neoliberal project effectively infuses this state form with the wherewithal to promote capitalist development, which is its fundamental claim to legitimacy. Finally, we identify how the neoliberal project is currently weakened in Africa, and that some African governments and intellectuals are constructing possible alternatives to it, albeit still within the authoritarian mode of governance.

The neoliberal social project and the authoritarian state

Neoliberalism

It is now well-recognized that the term neoliberalism is in danger of losing its identity, or at least having successfully developed through conceptual diffusion rather than focus (Venugopal, 2015). Beyond its signification of a 'critical' approach to the study of the 'free market', it is difficult to pin down a conceptual definition that is workable between writers who commonly have different theoretical concerns and methodologies. Neoliberalism has been used to identify a reinvigorated neoclassical/laissez-faire ideology of the market society (Stedman Jones, 2012; Turner, 2011); to focus on the shift in the political economy of capitalism towards finance-based attacks on labour and regulation (Crouch, 2011; Dumènil & Lèvy, 2004; Harvey, 2005); to express concern with the changes in state form that involve technical and depoliticizing institutions and discourse (Demmers, Fernandez, & Hogenboom, 2004); to characterize governmentalities based in the rationalities of individualism and responsibility (Joseph, 2013; Larner, 2000; Ong, 2006); to criticize a wide range of actions by capital and international financial institutions (Cammack, 2002; Owusu, 2003); and to announce new global regimes (Gill, 1995), new ideologies of 'common sense', new social-psychologies, and affects (Brown, 2015). It is also the case that writers have been wont to see neoliberalism in recombinant, 'rolled out', and 'inclusive' forms – present in many places and in many guises – a move that improves the concept's ability to engage with diverse social realities but which also renders it potentially less distinct (Ong, 2007; Peck & Tickell, 2002; Porter & Craig, 2004).

There is, of course, a simple core premise within this expansive literature, which is expressed by Giroux as well as anyone: a 'belief that the market should be the organizing principle for all political, social, and economic decisions' (Giroux, 2004, p. xii). It is just that the subsequent analytical and methodological move that this definition suggests is radically unfixed. Thus, it is important to set out as clear a conceptualization of the term as we can here before proceeding any further. In this article, neoliberalism is understood to be a global social project to realize an ideology of the free market into as many aspects of the political economy as possible (Gill & Cutler, 2014, p. 9; Harrison, 2010). It is based on the core neoclassical tenet that free markets are socially-optimal, efficient, and tend towards equilibrium (Shaikh, 2004), and it is animated by a desire to realize this particular market ontology principally through states. This allocates to the state a strong predisposition towards the enforcement of privatized and marketized social relations, not as a prelude to capitalist development but rather as a structural property of its political economy.

Neoliberalism as a social project is realized through classes, cadres, and epistemic communities dedicated to the universal realization of a more or less coherent neoliberal world. This is as utopian or millenarian a project as any in modern political ideology (Clarke, 2005, p. 51; Comaroff & Comaroff, 2000). It is ambitious, expansive, and combative. It is unrealized, but it possesses enough faith, evidence, resource, power, and legitimacy to render it a component of almost every political institution in the world. It has amply demonstrated its tenacity (Mirowski, 2013; Streeck, 2014). The social project of neoliberalism is expansive; it is about the creation of regulations, habits, disciplines and incentives, and norms in the name of free markets. The *telos* of these practices is a universal condition in which neoliberalism is understood as a natural phenomenon, not a political one.

The literature on neoliberalism is more than sufficiently diverse and contentious to expect that this brief definitional standpoint might be subjected to all manner to criticisms. That makes our definition unexceptional. The framing of neoliberalism as a social project does however, allow us to focus on the empirical and material nature of neoliberalism (cf. Tansel, 2017). Hence, it is possible to maintain a relatively clear sense of neoliberalism's ideological core without slipping into the ideationalist trap in which neoliberalism has its own agency (see also Bruff & Tansel, 2018). It also allows us to accept neoliberalism as, *ab initio*, a 'dirty' and incomplete phenomenon without getting tied up in sometimes overly-complex discussions about hybridity, contextualization, and contestation (Ong, 2006). As a social project, neoliberalism is intrinsically and constitutively hybrid and compromised by all manner of socio-political institutions which 'corrupt' the ideal, economistic or technically pure abstractions that might be used to theorize neoliberalism (Fine, 2015).

Authoritarianism

There is a rough and stylized way of seeing authoritarianism as statist, centralized and undemocratic political governance. Used descriptively, authoritarianism is defined by the removal of popular accountability or participation in the decisions of the state and a substantial centralization of executive power in a bureaucracy. It associates itself with states that are disposed to use heavy mixtures of bureaucratic fiat and coercion. From these co-ordinates, we have the wherewithal to develop a descriptive categorization of coercive and pervasive bureaucratic governance and to call this authoritarianism. But, from a Marxist tradition of political economy, it is difficult to discern the salient ways in which authoritarian state practices relate specifically to the social relations of capitalism. There is a need for a logic of articulation between authoritarianism and neoliberalism to provide a means to generate a conceptualization of authoritarian neoliberalism (see also Tansel, 2018). This logic needs to move beyond the recognition that all capitalist states contain 'moments' or tendencies of authoritarian practice because this renders the coupling of authoritarianism and neoliberalism largely descriptive.

This article will treat authoritarianism as a distinct state form that derives from national political economies in which there is no universally-dominant bourgeoisie. In these countries, property relations are not near-universally based in private property; the social relations of labour are significantly varied and not based on a near-universal proletarianization; the capitalist class remains heavily dependent on state power or limited in its social domination; and processes of accumulation are weak and halting.

These broad conditions prevail throughout Africa. Land tenure is sustained through combinations of collective, lineage, and freehold forms, and small- and medium-sized businesses typically enjoy formal and informal entitlements to their assets and property. African capitalist classes remain strongly intertwined with the factional dynamics that contest access to state power, and they are also dominated by international capital in those sectors where there is global interest. Class relations are commonly interstitial: combinations of wage work, trading, agriculture, frequent migration, good and bad years, debt and credit, legality and illegality. People's labour is organized around 'multiplex' labour: small-scale farming, entrepreneurship, wage employment (casual and formal, temporary and permanent), trading and craft production. The social relations of labour are defined by complex differentiations and a not inconsiderable contingency in which sustained and large-scale employment by capital is absent. And, within African bourgeoisies, accumulation is defined by low-technology and low-productivity forms of production that do not generate strong processes of transformative change. As such, it is possible to understand authoritarianism as a political response to these socio-economic circumstances that prevail in post-colonial African countries, an historically-specific state form that coalesces around the major-order political challenge of developing a strong capitalist class that might drive a process of accumulation and transformation (see also de Smet & Bogaert, 2017). And, we can see this authoritarian state-form within a global historical context.

Mouzelis' (1986) and Thomas's (1984) conceptualizations of authoritarianism are a useful starting point here.[1] In Mouzelis's analysis of post-oligarchic 'semi-peripheral' states, he sets out a nuanced account of the rise of authoritarianism in southern Europe and Latin America in the 1920s. Authoritarianism is a mode of governance that aims to deploy centralized and purposeful state power to promote the structural transformation of the economy in situations where existing classes and property regimes seem unable to do so (1986, pp. 184–196). Thomas analyzes 'peripheral' states in similar ways, but from a *Marxisant* dependency perspective. He recognizes the weakness of national bourgeoisies and the absence of a process of capitalist development, and relates this to a state-form in which capitalist classes and the state develop authoritarian modes of governance to shore up their power against popular discontent (1984, pp. 82–88). Thus, in both analyses, authoritarianism is a mode of rule based in a particular historical circumstance which can be shorthanded as capitalist transition, analogous to the general patterns of Africa's post-colonial condition (see also Jenss, 2018, on Latin America).

We have defined neoliberalism as a universal social project pursued in the name of free markets, and authoritarianism as a specific state-form that emerges in countries in which the bourgeoisie is weak and capitalist development requires centralized and forcible state action. We need now to connect these two together in order to set out a workable definition of authoritarian neoliberalism. This is not entirely straightforward. Authoritarianism, in our conceptualization, is not simply those facets and tendencies of states to act undemocratically by deploying bureaucratic and police compulsion to aspects of social life. In this more descriptive rendering, *all* states are in some degree authoritarian. The condition of the authoritarian state is one of diverse social relations that are partially subjected to the domination of capital which poses a major political-strategic question about capitalist transformation (in mainstream social science, the more anodyne term 'development' is used). It is this condition that generates systemically – not contingently – states that aim to use force and fiat to support capitalist classes and reorder complex social relations in the image of the market.

But, the socio-economic doctrine of neoliberalism is one means to this aspirational end. There is no perfect comity between authoritarianism and neoliberalism. Indeed, in Mouzelis and Thomas, the authoritarianism of the (semi) periphery is distinctly *dirigiste* in ways that would be anathema to many neoliberals (although see Bruff & Starnes, 2018). Nevertheless, it remains the case that a fundamental legitimacy claim asserted by advocates of neoliberalism is its ability to generate capitalist transformation. Thus, we define authoritarian neoliberalism as a 'subspecies' of authoritarianism, distinguished by a bundle of practices and institutions that construct states that use bureaucracy and coercion in the attempt to construct, enforce and discipline societies into marketized forms in the faith that, by doing so, competition and entrepreneurship will generate capitalist transformation.

This definition orients an analysis of authoritarian neoliberalism in Africa in a certain direction. It asks questions about the wherewithal of authoritarian neoliberalism to promote capitalist transformation; and it remains open to the possibility that other kinds of authoritarianism – other subspecies – are also historically possible.

Neoliberalism in/and Africa

Yes it hurt, yes it didn't work

Neoliberalism was, *ab initio*, a global project, not a 'western' one. The clearest example of this is the introduction of structural adjustment programmes (SAPs) in Africa from 1979 onwards (van de Walle, 2001, p. 215). SAPs were credit packages designed by the World Bank and International Monetary Fund, disbursed to debt-distressed African countries and conditioned on the adoption of a set of policies which had as their overarching aim the neoliberalization of development strategy. Policy changes included central bank independence, the removal of exchange rate controls, the introduction of technologies to promote fiscal discipline and the reduction of budget deficits, the abolition of quotas and lowering of tariffs on international trade, the opening up of economies to foreign direct investment, the elimination of price controls, the removal of state-owned trading agencies, and the privatization of state-owned enterprises.

This is not the place to recall the misfortunes of structural adjustment in Africa. There is a very large literature that does this.[2] But, the fact that over 200 SAPs were (in some degree) implemented in Africa during the 1980s and hundreds more agreements with 'social' and 'poverty reduction' components followed in the 1990s shows very clearly how Africa was at the forefront of the neoliberal project from the latter's very origins. The first neoliberal crises occurred in Africa as currencies went into freefall, low rates of growth dipped further, commodity price spikes scoured real disposable income levels, and more generally people's livelihoods became even less stable (Mkandawire & Olukoshi, 1995).

Food riots generated violent police responses (Lawrence, 1986; Walton & Seddon, 1994), drastic policy measures were imposed by increasingly centralized cabals focused on the Ministry of Finance and/or the Presidency, and new or revived forms of struggle over new opportunities for enrichment by factionalized elites rendered governance partial, incoherent, violent, and unpredictable. Accountability of the government to citizens was constantly undermined by accountability of the government to the World Bank, IMF, and aligned bilateral donors. Formal constitutional and legal measures to introduce multi-party politics made little difference to these substantively authoritarian practices, a condition described by Mkandawire as choiceless democracy (Mkandawire, 1999).

In a nutshell, for Africa, neoliberalism has largely been realized through centralized and undemocratic state practices that resemble authoritarianism. Not only did it generate massive amounts of social harm and instability, but it also generated at best weak responses in terms of economic recovery, reduced debt, or a recovered inflow of foreign direct investment (Bond, 2006; Bush, 2004).

Welcome to the desert of the neoliberal real

Reem Koolhass asserted that 'Lagos is not catching up with us. Rather, we may be catching up with Lagos.'[3] This stylized provocation has some insight that we can bring to bear on our interest in the interplay of neoliberalism and authoritarianism. It suggests that Africa's especially intense and protracted subjection to the neoliberal project offers possible meanings to the fortunes of the project in other places. We can identify three cardinal examples of this.

(1) The neoliberal project is intrinsically crisis-ridden (Harvey, 2007). Indeed, the notion of 'crisis' is something of a misnomer for what are often more akin to permanent and severe instabilities. Neoliberalism *is* crisis. The currency crashes, recessions, turbulent governance, and civil instability that visited African countries throughout the 1980s are examples of phenomena that might now properly be understood as global and immanent to the neoliberal project. Analogous neoliberal crises have taken place in Latin American economies in the mid-1980s, Russia and the former Soviet Union in the early 1990s, South-east Asian countries in the late 1990s, Latin American countries (again) in the early 2000s, in the US in 2001 (dot com), and of course pretty much

everywhere since 2007.[4] No sensible economist is arguing that the causes and conditions of the 2008 crisis have been resolved. Crisis and austerity are a way of life (Evans & McBride, 2017). The specifics of these crises are hardly all the same but they are underpinned by *laissez-faire* macroeconomics, the rising power of finance capital, and global deregulation. The neoliberal project has bequeathed the world an era of uneven and combined permanent crisis management (McNally, 2009). It is no exaggeration to say that the neoliberal project generates a systemic intensification of economic crisis in order to survive those crises, and in the process creates the possibility of more forceful realizations of its worldview (Crouch, 2011; Mirowski, 2013).

(2) The implementation of neoliberalism involves impositions and coercions by the state. These vary widely in form and intensity but the impositional and coercive reflex is immanent to the neoliberal project, not incidental or momentary trait. It might involve the removal of policies from public accountability, the creation of neoliberal cabals (sometimes labelled as 'champions' and 'change agents' in neoliberal Doublespeak) to propound reforms, the deployment of the police to enforce policies that generate social protest, the recourse to global regulatory change in order to present policies as inevitable fate rather than political decision, and the creation of 'shadow elites' who straddle think-tanks, universities, private capital and governments to shore up the power of the neoliberal project. And it might involve bare dispossession (Harvey, 2004).

In the 1980s, issuing out of the general anti-statism which was galvanized by the 'Berg Report' (World Bank, 1981), structurally adjusting African states underwent a forcible 'roll-back' in their activities and material base (Woodehouse, 2003). The emaciation of (often already weak and unstable) African states tended to exacerbate deeper governance crises in which the core authority and institutional coherence of state seemed uncertain. 'Roll back' generated forms of governance that were evacuated even of the minimal and procedural accountabilities embedded within single-party states. As a result, subsequently, those who designed and enforced neoliberalism through the IFIs steered lending strategies towards a reconstruction of the state. This reconstruction facilitated two things. Firstly, a stronger infrastructure for capitalist rule of law: more censuses and surveys, more effective tax-raising administration, and more coherent and transparent investment and property law, an increasingly powerful technocratic mode of governance (Harrison, 2007). Secondly, a more proactive bundle of institutions to incentivize and enhance private investment and entrepreneurialism: investment promotion centres, support for the development of information communication technologies and training to socialize an entrepreneurial sociability amongst small- and medium-sized enterprises, the creation of special economic zones (near ports or along corridors) that become subsidized 'hotbeds' for new investment, and the development of myriad public-private partnerships in which services are contracted to private businesses (Mawdsley, 2015). Some references by IFIs and Western donors to democracy, civil society, and participation were in reality very much second-order concerns compared with the principal objectives of creating a Hayekian strong state (cf. Gamble, 1996) and a governance regime to promote market societies. These two objectives – a leaner and stronger state purposed with the social engineering of a market society – easily resided in a centralized project of statebuilding, prosecuted by centralized and technocratic governing elites (see also Kreitmeyr, 2018).

The neoliberal realities of permanent crisis and a tendential authoritarian response by the state were Africa's realities from the 1980s and are now the world's reality. Africa endured an early and distinctly intense iteration of the neoliberal project's authoritarian statecraft.

(3) The neoliberal project is unstable and expansive. The foundational motivation of neoliberalism's advocates draws focus onto fundamental changes in the state and the economy, but the focus hardly remains there. As a form of social engineering, it might be that neoliberalism projects itself

through instruments such as education (Brown, 2015), training and the promotion of human capital and resilience (Joseph, 2013), techniques of incarceration (Wacquant, 2009), the provision of certain kinds of social support which either generate entrepreneurial behaviours through microfinance (Bateman, 2010) or intensified labour through 'workfare' (Perelman, 2011; Standing, 2011), and the deployment of psychosocial 'nudges' which have as their target the brain's cognitive functions. There is no necessary sequencing of these facets of intervention: they are likely to be prosecuted in varied and partially-coherent combinations depending on all manner of contextual circumstances. What they represent is neoliberalism's universal scope of ambition. As this totalizing project endures and expands, its frontiers are extensive (all countries, all societies) and intensive (all facets, every individual).

Africa offers long-standing and striking examples of this expansiveness. The initial focus on currency liberalization, international trade deregulation, and budgetary austerity has hardly disappeared but has been overlain with what might be characterized as increasingly ambitious remits. This has involved remaking state institutions, legal reform, encouraging a certain kind of civil society, promoting customer-like attitudes towards public services, putting more development practice into the hands of private companies, and promoting entrepreneurial behaviour through IT, training and microfinance. African countries that have endured neoliberal social engineering for decades have witnessed a shift from macroeconomic, through institutional and social, and into individual change. Africa is the world-regional best exemplar of neoliberalism's dark rendering of Samuel Beckett's well-known aphorism: try again, fail better.

In summary, Africa shows clearly three constitutive features of the neoliberal project: its proclivity for crisis, its authoritarian tendencies, and its desire to expand from core macroeconomic strategy into as many aspects of socio-political life as possible. Not only does Africa demonstrate these properties in neoliberalism, it also provides important insights as to how well the project fares, not least because Africa has endured an exceptionally long-lasting and virulently implemented version of neoliberalism.

What Africa shows to the rest of the world is a state of affairs in which protracted neoliberal reform generates short intervals of growth usually concentrated on narrow bases such as an export price change, large investment, or specific and largely isolated economic sectors (Bracking, 2016). This has generated some material improvements in people's well-being and a reduction in extreme poverty. But, it has also generated sporadic economic decline; a continued uncertainty in livelihoods accompanied by processes of social differentiation; intensified work; a rise in fraudulent, corrupt and get-rich-quick strategies which often lead to wealth being taken out of country (Ndikumana & Boyce, 2011); growing depletion of natural resources (Woodehouse, 2003); and a continued dependence on international resources and validation to sustain basic budgetary and expenditure processes. This has also generated its own social resistances (Branch & Mampilly, 2015; Harrison, 2002). Taking these patterns together, it is clearly the case that authoritarian neoliberalism in Africa has most definitively not generated any evidence of a capitalist development (Bush, 2007; Rowden, 2013; Wengraf, 2018).

The loosening grip of neoliberalism?

African countries are clearly not rapidly forging ahead in the way that Latin American countries did in the 1960s, North-east Asian countries did in the 1970s, or East Asian countries did in the 1990s. Africa, the quintessential neoliberal region, is also the world-region most starkly defined by major-order problems of mass poverty and faltering economic transformation. The major sites of mass poverty reduction, industrialization, and growth throughout the era of neoliberalism have been outside Africa (Henley, 2007). They have, not incidentally, also been in places where the neoliberal project has been relatively weak and where governments have innovated and experimented with the regulation of prices and capital.

Neoliberalism in Africa has been authoritarian in the sense that states have used top-down, centralized and coercive measures to attempt to impose the market society, but this has generated fragile and limited success and little evidence of sustained economic transformation. In other words, it has not only failed a 'neoliberal test' of generating progress through market liberalization; it has also failed the 'authoritarianism test' within which centralized and coercive governance works to promote the capitalist development and the conditions of possibility for the ascent of a national bourgeoisie. Authoritarian neoliberalism in Africa has been in this sense an absolute failure, neither mitigated by a process of economic development nor an account of successful developmental governance.

This historical lesson has fed into the politics of some African countries. Since the late 1990s, African governments have sought ways to reduce the influence of external neoliberal advocates and to explore developmental unorthodoxies. Some scholars cursorily explain this as largely a result of the rise of China or the Beijing Consensus, but it is surely more profoundly based in a concern amongst African states and some intellectuals to find better ways to generate economic transformation in countries with mass poverty. This 'unorthodox turn' is presently nothing more than a set of embryonic challenges to neoliberalism. There is not a 'model' that one can set out in categorical form. Furthermore, neoliberalism is hardly in decline. Zambia is a good example of how attempts to generate economically-nationalist state strategies can falter and lead to a return to the neoliberal agenda (Fraser, 2009; Larmer, 2005). But, generally, this turn is significant. It represents a potentially systemic attempt to move away from neoliberalism and to do so in a way that offers a more purposeful authoritarianism than that which realized/realizes itself under neoliberal hegemony. For as long as neoliberalism maintains its domineering globalization, unorthodoxies such as these constitute a kind of resistance, albeit a normatively complex one.

Towards a developmental authoritarianism?

We are using the term authoritarianism here to identify a state form in which centralized and coercive power is deployed systemically and purposefully to generate capitalist transformation in societies in which a capitalist class is present but hardly dominant or possessing the wherewithal to accumulate in a rapidly expanding fashion, drawing in larger numbers of wage labourers. Authoritarian neoliberalism displays the markings of centralized and top-down power, but its strategic orientation towards a free-market society renders it unable to countenance the historic necessities of capitalist transformation, a transformation that can take many forms but will always involve *dirigiste* reallocations of property, strong support for emerging capitals, the disciplining of labour, and a nationalist attitude towards the global political economy.

Let us start by returning to Zambia. In 2011 the Zambian government introduced subsidies on fertilizers through a Farming Input Support Programme (Whitworth, 2015). This shift was articulated through a revived sense of national development purpose, explicitly identified as against the grain of global neoliberalism (Larmer & Fraser, 2007). The use of price subsidies on fertilizer or improved seeds against IFI advice commenced in Malawi in 2005, during a period of malnutrition and near-famine and in response to political pressures to move beyond neoliberal agricultural policy (Chinsinga, 2007; Mpesi & Muriaas, 2012). The subsidies generated a positive production response, although the modalities of the subsidies and their longer-term impact have been less clear and less positive (Chirwa & Dorward, 2013). The premise of these interventions is that agriculture will not develop without state regulatory intervention in agricultural markets, interventions that include 'getting the prices wrong' (cf. Amsden, 1992).

One might add to the evidence regarding regulatory innovation in agricultural development. There has been a push back against foreign investment in which a 'national interest' of one kind of another takes political priority. There are examples of this in relation to Mozambique and Tanzania (Monson, 2006; Pitcher, 2003). In Tanzania, particularly since the presidency of John Magufuli, FDI contracts have been renegotiated (especially within the mining sector), although there remain substantial reservations concerning the extent to which the Tanzanian state is able to promote capitalist transformation (Gray, 2015). There are other examples. One of Kenya's cash transfer schemes does not follow normal donor approaches and is set up to avoid dependence on external sources, largely as a result of concerns with state legitimacy and social stability (McCord, 2010, p. 16). Mali's decentralization plans and their financial management involved a rejection of World Bank programme advice and a strongly-defended national programme which donors eventually bought into (Bergamaschi, 2007). Cameroon and Senegal re-introduced tariffs on chicken imports to protect their own poultry industries (Johnson, 2011). These policies are clearly not in keeping with the neoliberal worldview. However, these kinds of unorthodoxy can only be seen as specific and unsystemic: reactions to especially difficult aspects of neoliberal reform. They do not offer a clear alternative model to neoliberalism; far less evidence of resistance of the kind that advocates of global social justice might wish to see. But, this is not the whole story.

In his work on political settlements, Khan (2010) identifies a set of key diagnostic concepts that relate closely to the ability of the state to act in non-liberal ways in pursuit of capitalist transformation. The core point is that the state's allocation of resources will vary in stability and efficacy according to how it maps onto the relative power of different social groups. Within this general terrain, a strategic meta-question emerges: how to promote transformative growth within a set of social relations that potentially destabilize the power of the elite group/coalition that controls government? This is the growth-stability trade-off. It relates closely to the strategic pressure that generates authoritarian governance in African economies and it offers an articulated analytical framework through which to evaluate the emergence of unorthodox development policies.

In an African context, this framing has been used to identify in some states a 'developmental patrimonialism', in which the opaque and strategic allocation of rights to accumulate are conditioned on the achievement of medium-term performance goals (Kelsall, 2013; Whitfield, Therkildsen, Buur, & Kjaer, 2015). In essence, the allocation of credit, subsidy, protection, or a more general political support is actioned in the expectation that the recipients – part client and part private business – will innovate, invest, access new markets, or increase output. Ethiopia (Gagliardone, 2014; Lefort, 2012; Oqubay, 2017; Vaughan & Gebremichael, 2011) and Rwanda (Booth & Golooba-Mutebi, 2012) are key examples of this, although one can also identify less clear versions of this in Angola (Croese, 2016; Wolf, 2017), Nigeria (Ovadia, 2016), and Ghana (Chalfin, 2010). Another broader example is Uganda's National Development Plan (Hickey, 2013).

These are not randomly-chosen country cases from the region. In each example, some structural change has taken place and it has done so in part as a result of strategic and authoritative state action. What matters most within the political dynamics of these policies is the extent to which the rights to accumulate, allocated or confirmed by the state, generate strong investment and growth responses from capital. This is centrally dependent on the incentive structures integrated into the patrimonial relationship. In Rwanda, Ethiopia, and Uganda, these practices have been integrated into a strong politics of security and national interest; in Nigeria, Ghana, and Angola one finds a politics of resource nationalism, although it would be a stretch to characterize this politics as anything more than emergent.

Let us take one country case in a little more detail. Rwanda has negotiated an uneasily positive relation with the IFIs in which it both cleaves to core neoliberal macroeconomic directives and maintains a strong sense of national interest and a willingness to deploy other development strategies. The Rwandan government seems more akin to developmental rather than neoliberal forms of authoritarianism, where development is itself a means to consolidate state power (Harrison, 2017; Mann & Berry, 2016). Most centrally, the government has constructed a complex and opaque network of political support and discipline in connection with a set of diversified companies. This pattern of ownership is defined by ultimate ruling party control but legally by private ownership and management. These companies are politically tasked with generating investment in new areas, exporting, and finding ways to grow rapidly (Booth & Golooba-Mutebi, 2012). In agriculture, the government has maintained subsidies on fertilizers and seeds at considerable cost and in the face of the anxieties of donors. It has done this as part of a concerted project to improve the productivity of smallholder agriculture, a project that has involved broader and deeper efforts to transform productivity as well (Harrison, 2016). The government has also tried to find non-neoliberal ways of generating some financial depth using compulsory contribution mechanisms (Behuria, 2016, p. 640). More recently, the government has introduced a Made in Rwanda strategy, which has involved a ban on the importation of second-hand clothing and a stronger remit for the government (especially through the Rwanda Development Board) to push for local content in FDI and growth in national manufacture.

In relation to Rwanda and related cases, it is important not to overstretch the evidence. None of these authors are suggesting that their cases are definitive examples of a systemic alternative to neoliberalism, let alone a wide-ranging developmentalism. But, there is in each case both unorthodox strategy-making and a salient politics of developmental transformation, even if buried within or against other discourses. This is historically significant; these kinds of formations would have been unthinkable in the late 1980s. And, there is evidence in all of these countries of sustained economic growth, even if not structural transformation.

What these examples do show is how unconvincing the neoliberal form of authoritarianism is for the purposes of generating sustained transformative growth. Even with such immense inputs of resource, technical assistance and knowledge generation, African governments which achieve a modicum of stability and growth tend to explore ways out of the neoliberal grip.

Conclusion

Let us summarize the argument. We have used the concept of authoritarianism within a Marxist political economy framework to identify a state form that derives from the social relations of a capitalist economy in which the bourgeoisie is weak and there is a prevailing and complex productive economy based on small-scale and low-productivity livelihoods. In these circumstances, there is a disposition for states to seek top-down and forceful ways to generate growth and accumulation through political support for capital. This is what underpins the more descriptive accounts of authoritarianism in their condemnation of undemocratic and centralized modes of governance. We have conceptualized neoliberalism as a universal project to (re)make the world in the image of a free-market society, best understood through the practices of those who champion the project. We have argued that the African experience with neoliberalism is long-lasting, highly developed, and based within authoritarian co-ordinates of governance. In this sense, Africa offers us a worrying image of where authoritarian neoliberalism leads: systemic social repression, low growth and instability, and insubstantial performances of participation and accountability. If other regions are beginning to see these dynamics, it is important to bear in mind that they are long-standing in Africa and in this sense, darkly, Africa is a world-leader. Taking this dour audit into account, we moved on to demonstrate how the core purposes of authoritarianism are not inextricably wedded to a marketizing project and that some African governments and intellectuals are pushing to move into more developmental modes of development strategy-making.

It would be erroneous to offer this evidence as an embryonic new model. There has been for some time a desire – partly ideological – to identify an African developmental state, but the substance of these arguments is usually rather fragile. What the evidence does suggest is that the authoritarian state form is more developmentally effective when uncoupled from the demonstrably weak marketizing project of neoliberalism. In a sense, authoritarian neoliberalism is the worst of both worlds for African countries which have small economies, mass poverty, and small industrial sectors. It is all of the pain and little gain beyond the pockets of upper middle-class estates and shopping malls.

Making this argument implies a rejection of neoliberalism but a more relativized approach to authoritarianism. The suggestion is that authoritarian states might be effective development actors when untied from neoliberal doctrine. This point-of-view contrasts with the increasing concern with the depoliticization, surveillance, securitization, and centralization of politics in Western countries. But, this contrast is more apparent than real. Concerns with undemocratic and centralized governance in developed capitalist states are entirely valid, but they also rely on a more descriptive – perhaps even neo-Weberian – categorization. The social relations of production in Western states are not like those that prevail in African countries. If we are to derive conceptions of the state from the Marxist tradition, there must be clear conceptual distinctions between the kinds of social formations within which the state resides. In spaces where the major political question beyond the basic stability of rule is economic transformation, authoritarianism occupies an indeterminate position. It is a mode of governance integrated into a country's social relations, a coercive and centralized set of practices, and potentially the best hope for countries with mass poverty to create the conditions of possibility for mass poverty reduction.

Notes

1. For the purposes of analytical transparency, I should note that Thomas writes within a broadly Marxist framework, but Mouzelis a more pluralized and Weberian fashion. This is a conflation of the two for my own purposes.
2. For example Campbell and Loxley (1989); Mohan, Brown, Milward, and Zack-Williams (2000); SAPRIN (2004).
3. Accessed from http://icarusfilms.com/if-lag, February 2018.
4. I am starting in 2007, because this is when sudden spikes in food prices generated extreme urban livelihood stress amongst the poor throughout the world.

Acknowledgements

I would like to thank the referees and issue editors for their insightful and helpful comments.

Disclosure statement

No potential conflict of interest was reported by the author.

References

Amsden, A. (1992). *Asia's next giant: South Korea and late industrialization*. Oxford: Oxford University Press.

Bateman, M. (2010). *Why doesn't microfinance work? The destructive rise of local neoliberalism*. London: Zed.

Behuria, P. (2016). Centralising rents and dispersing power while pursuing development? Exploring the strategic uses of military firms in Rwanda. *Review of African Political Economy, 43*(150), 630–647.

Bergamaschi, I. (2007). *Mali: Patterns and limits of donor-driven ownership* (GEG Working Paper 2008/41).

Bond, P. (2006). *Looting Africa: The economics of exploitation*. London: Zed.

Booth, D., & Golooba-Mutebi, F. (2012). Developmental patrimonialism? The case of Rwanda. *African Affairs, 111*(444), 379–403.

Bracking, S. (2016). *The financialisation of power: How financiers rule Africa*. London: Routledge.

Branch, A., & Mampilly, Z. (2015). *Africa uprising: Popular protest and political change*. London: Zed.

Brown, W. (2015). *Undoing the demos: Neoliberalism's stealth revolution*. New York: Zone Books.

Bruff, I., & Starnes, K. (2018). Framing the neoliberal canon: Resisting the market myth via literary enquiry. *Globalizations*. doi:10.1080/14747731.2018.1502489

Bruff, I., & Tansell, C. B (2018). Authoritarian neoliberalism: Trajectories of knowledge production and praxis. *Globalizations*. doi:10.1080/14747731.2018.1502497

Bush, R. (2004). Undermining Africa. *Historical Materialism, 12*(4), 173–201.

Bush, R. (2007). *Poverty and neoliberalism: Persistence and reproduction in the Global South*. London: Pluto.

Cammack, P. (2002). Neoliberalism, the World Bank and the new politics of development. In U. Kothari & M. Minogue (Eds.), *Development theory and practice: Critical perspectives* (pp. 157–178). Basingstoke: Palgrave Macmillan.

Campbell, B. K., & Loxley, J. (1989). *Structural adjustment in Africa*. Basingstoke: Macmillan.

Chalfin, B. (2010). Recasting maritime governance in Ghana: The neo-developmental state and the port of Tema. *The Journal of Modern African Studies, 48*(4), 573–598.

Chinsinga, B. (2007, August). *Resurrecting the vestiges of a developmental state in Malawi? Reflections and lessons from the 2005/2006 fertilizer subsidy programme*. Presented at Guy Mhone memorial conference on development, Zomba, Malawi.

Chirwa, E., & Dorward, A. (2013). *Agricultural input subsidies: The recent Malawi experience*. Oxford: Oxford University Press.

Clarke, S. (2005). The neoliberal theory of society. In A. Saad-Filho & D. Johnston (Eds.), *Neoliberalism: A critical reader* (pp. 50–59). London: Pluto Press.

Comaroff, J., & Comaroff, J. L. (2000). Millennial capitalism: First thoughts on a second coming. *Public Culture, 12*(2), 291–343.

Croese, S. (2016). State-led housing delivery as an instrument of developmental patrimonialism: The case of post-war Angola. *African Affairs, 116*(462), 80–100.

Crouch, C. (2011). *The strange non-death of neoliberalism*. Cambridge: Polity.

Demmers, J., Fernandez, A., & Hogenboom, B. (Eds.). (2004). *Good governance in the era of global neoliberalism*. London: Routledge.

de Smet, B., & Bogaert, K. (2017). Resistance and passive revolution in Egypt and Morocco. In C. B. Tansel (Ed.), *States of discipline: Authoritarian neoliberalism and the contested reproduction of capitalist order* (pp. 211–233). London: Rowman & Littlefield International.

Dumènil, G., & Lèvy, D. (2004). *Capital resurgent: Roots of the neoliberal revolution*. Massachusetts: Harvard University Press.

Evans, B., & McBride, S. (Eds.). (2017). *Austerity: The lived experience*. Toronto: University of Toronto Press.

Fine, B. (2015). Development as zombieconomics in the age of neoliberalism. *Third World Quarterly, 30*(5), 885–904.

Fraser, A. (2009). Zambia: Back to the future? In L. Whitfield (Ed.), *The politics of aid: African strategies for dealing with donors* (pp. 299–328). Oxford: Oxford University Press.

Gagliardone, I. (2014). New media and the developmental state in Ethiopia. *African Affairs, 113*(451), 279–299.

Gamble, A. (1996). *Hayek: The iron cage of liberty*. Cambridge: Polity.

Gill, S. (1995). Globalisation, market civilisation, and disciplinary neoliberalism. *Millennium: Journal of International Studies, 24*(3), 399–423.

Gill, S., & Cutler, A. C. (2014). New constitutionalism and world order. In S. Gill & A. C. Cutler (Eds.), *New constitutionalism and world order.* (pp. 1–21). Cambridge: Cambridge University Press.

Giroux, H. (2004). *The terror of neoliberalism: Authoritarianism and the eclipse of democracy*. London: Paradigm.

Gray, H. (2015). The political economy of grand corruption in Tanzania. *African Affairs, 114*(456), 382–403.

Harrison, G. (2002). *Issues in the contemporary politics of sub-Saharan Africa: The dynamics of struggle and resistance*. Basingstoke: Palgrave Macmillan.

Harrison, G. (2007). *The World Bank and Africa: The construction of governance states*. London: Routledge.

Harrison, G. (2010). *Neoliberal Africa: The impact of global social engineering*. London: Zed.

Harrison, G. (2016). Rwanda: An agrarian developmental state? *Third World Quarterly, 37*(2), 354–370.

Harrison, G. (2017). Rwanda and the difficult business of capitalist development. *Development and Change, 48* (5), 873–898.

Harvey, D. (2004). The 'new' imperialism: Accumulation by dispossession. *Socialist Register, 2004*, 63–87.

Harvey, D. (2005). *A brief history of neoliberalism*. Oxford: Oxford University Press.

Harvey, D. (2007). Neoliberalism as creative destruction. *The Annals of the American Academy of Political and Social Science, 610*(1), 21–44.

Henley, D. (2007). *Asia-Africa development divergence: A question of intent*. London: Zed.

Hickey, S. (2013). Beyond the poverty agenda? Insights from the new politics of development in Uganda. *World Development, 43*(1), 194–206.

Jenss, A. (2018). Authoritarian neoliberal rescaling in Latin America: Urban in/security and austerity in Oaxaca. *Globalizations*. doi:10.1080/14747731.2018.1502493

Johnson, M. (2011). Lobbying for trade barriers: A comparison of poultry producers' success in Cameroon, Senegal and Ghana. *The Journal of Modern African Studies, 49*(4), 575–599.

Joseph, J. (2013). Resilience as embedded neoliberalism: A governmentality approach. *Resilience: International Policies, Practices and Discourses, 1*(1), 38–52.

Kelsall, T. (2013). *Business, politics, and the state in Africa*. London: Zed Press.

Khan, M. (2010). Political settlements and the governance of growth-enhancing institutions. Retrieved from http://eprints.soas.ac.uk/9968/

Kreitmeyr, N. (2018). Neoliberal co-optation and authoritarian renewal: Social entrepreneurship networks in Jordan and Morocco. *Globalizations*. doi:10.1080/14747731.2018.1502492

Larmer, M. (2005). Reaction and resistance to neo-liberalism in Zambia. *Review of African Political Economy, 32*(103), 29–45.

Larmer, M., & Fraser, A. (2007). Of cabbages and King Cobra: Populist politics and Zambia's 2006 election. *African Affairs, 106*(425), 611–637.

Larner, W. (2000). Neo-liberalismi policy, ideology, governmentality. *Studies in Political Economy, 63*(1), 5–25.

Lawrence, P. (Ed.). (1986). *World recession and the food crisis in Africa*. London: James Currey.

Lefort, R. (2012). Free market economy, 'developmental state' and partystate hegemony in Ethiopia: The case of the 'model farmers'. *The Journal of Modern African Studies, 50*(4), 681–706.

Mann, L., & Berry, M. (2016). Understanding the political motivations that shape Rwanda's emergent developmental state. *New Political Economy, 21*(1), 119–144.

Mawdsley, E. (2015). DFID, the private sector and the re-centring of an economic growth agenda in international development. *Global Society, 29*(3), 339–358.

McCord, A. (2010). *Differing government and donor perspectives on cash transfer based social protection in sub-Saharan Africa: The implications for EU social protection programming paper*. Overseas Development Institute.

McNally, D. (2009). From financial crisis to world-slump: Accumulation, financialisation, and the global slowdown. *Historical Materialism, 17*(1), 35–83.

Mirowski, P. (2013). *Never let a serious crisis go to waste: How neoliberalism survived the financial meltdown*. London: Verso.

Mkandawire, T. (1999). Crisis management and the making of 'choiceless democracies'. In R. Joseph (Ed.), *State, conflict, and democracy in Africa* (pp. 119–136). London: Lynne Rienner.

Mkandawire, T., & Olukoshi, A. (Eds.). (1995). *Between liberalization and oppression: The politics of structural adjustment in Africa*. Dakar: CODESRIA.
Mohan, G., Brown, E., Milward, B., & Zack-Williams, A. (2000). *Structural adjustment: Theory, practice, and impacts*. London: Routledge.
Monson, J. (2006). Defending the people's railway in the era of liberalization: TAZARA in Southern Tanzania. *Africa, 76*(1), 113–130.
Mouzelis, N. (1986). *Politics in the semi-periphery: Early parliamentarism and late industrialisation in the Balkans and Latin America*. Houndmills: Macmillan.
Mpesi, A., & Muriaas, R. (2012). Food security as a political issue: The 2009 elections in Malawi. *Journal of Contemporary African Studies, 30*(3), 377–393.
Ndikumana, L., & Boyce, J. (2011). *Africa's odious debts: How foreign loans and capital flight bled a continent*. London: Zed.
Ong, A. (2006). *Neoliberalism as exception: Mutations in citizenship and sovereignty*. Durham: Duke University Press.
Ong, A. (2007). Neoliberalism as a mobile technology. *Transactions of the Institute of British Geographers, 32* (1), 3–8.
Oqubay, A. (2017). *Made in Africa: Industrial policy in Ethiopia*. Oxford: Oxford University Press.
Ovadia, J. (2016). *The petro-developmental state in Africa: Making oil work in Angola, Nigeria, and the Gulf of Guinea*. London: Hurst.
Owusu, F. (2003). Pragmatism and the gradual shift from dependency to neoliberalism: The World Bank, African leaders, and development policy in Africa. *World Development, 31*(10), 1655–1672.
Peck, J., & Tickell, A. (2002). Neoliberalizing space. *Antipode, 34*(3), 380–404.
Perelman, M. (2011). *The invisible handcuffs of capitalism: How market tyranny stifles the economy by stunting workers*. New York: Monthly Review Press.
Pitcher, M. A. (2003). *Transforming Mozambique*. Cambridge: Cambridge University Press.
Porter, D., & Craig, D. (2004). The third way and the third world: Poverty reduction and social inclusion in the rise of 'inclusive' liberalism. *Review of International Political Economy, 11*(2), 387–423.
Rowden, R. (2013). The myth of Africa's rise. *Foreign Policy*, Retrieved from http://foreignpolicy.com/2013/01/04/the-myth-of-africas-rise/
SAPRIN. (2004). *Structural adjustment: The policy roots of economic crisis, poverty, and inequality*. London: Zed Books.
Shaikh, A. (2004). The economic mythology of neoliberalism. In A. Saad-Filho & D. Johnston (Eds.), *Neoliberalism: A critical reader* (pp. 41–50). London: Pluto Press.
Standing, G. (2011). *The precariat: The new dangerous classes*. London: Bloomsbury.
Stedman Jones, D. (2012). *Masters of the universe: Hayek, Friedman, and the birth of neoliberal politics*. Princeton: Princeton University Press.
Streeck, W. (2014). *Buying time: The delayed crisis of democratic capitalism*. London: Verso.
Tansel, C. B. (Ed.). (2017). *States of discipline: Authoritarian neoliberalism and the contested reproduction of capitalist order*. London: Rowman & Littlefield International.
Tansel, C. B. (2018). Reproducing authoritarian neoliberalism in Turkey: Urban governance and state restructuring in the shadow of executive centralization. *Globalizations*. doi:10.1080/14747731.2018.1502494
Thomas, C. (1984). *The rise of the authoritarian state in peripheral societies*. New York: Monthly Review Press.
Turner, R. (2011). *Neo-liberal ideology: History, concepts and policies*. Edinburgh: Edinburgh University Press.
van de Walle, N. (2001). *African economies and the politics of permanent crisis, 1979–1999*. Cambridge: Cambridge University Press.
Vaughan, S., & Gebremichael, M. (2011). *Rethinking business and politics in Ethiopia: The role of effort, the Endowment Fund for the Rehabilitation of Tigray* (Africa Power and Politics Research Report 02).
Venugopal, R. (2015). Neoliberalism as concept. *Economy and Society, 44*(2), 165–187.
Wacquant, L. (2009). *Punishing the poor: The neoliberal government of social insecurity*. Durham: Duke University Press.
Walton, J., & Seddon, D. (Eds.). (1994). *Free markets and food riots: The politics of global adjustment*. Oxford: Blackwell.
Wengraf, L. (2018). *Extracting profit: Imperialism, neoliberalism, and the new scramble for Africa*. Chicago: Haymarket Books.

Whitfield, L., Therkildsen, O., Buur, L., & Kjaer, M. (2015). *The politics of African industrial policy*. Cambridge: Cambridge University Press.

Whitworth, A. (2015). Explaining Zambian poverty: A history of (nonagriculture) economic policy since independence. *Journal of International Development*, *27*(7), 953–986.

Wolf, C. (2017). Industrialization in times of China: Domestic-market formation in Angola. *African Affairs*, *116*(464), 435–461.

Woodehouse, P. (2003). African enclosures: A default mode of development. *World Development*, *31*(10), 1705–1720.

World Bank. (1981). *Accelerated development in sub-Saharan Africa: An agenda to action*. Washington, DC: World Bank.

5 Neoliberal co-optation and authoritarian renewal: social entrepreneurship networks in Jordan and Morocco

Nadine Kreitmeyr

ABSTRACT

This paper analyzes social entrepreneurship networks (SENs) – composed of social entrepreneurs, business and political elites, and international actors – in Jordan and Morocco and how they foster processes of authoritarian renewal through neoliberal forms of co-optation. I argue that these new neoliberal networks and pre-existing patterns of social interaction complement each other, fostering linkages between well-established elites and hand-picked social entrepreneurs as well as societal groups. The two case studies illustrate different trajectories of the development of SENs and their embeddedness in the respective political, social and economic contexts. Importantly, such trajectories indicate a similar direction of travel: social entrepreneurship, rather than acting as a driver of progressive change, has been aligned with the authoritarian regimes and cements neoliberalism as a mode of governance. This mutation of neoliberal tactics towards more inclusionary and consensual patterns seeks to ensure the survival of both neoliberalism and of authoritarian governance. Thus, the article brings to light repertoires of authoritarian neoliberalism that have hitherto been understudied. Moreover, it offers a critical perspective on social entrepreneurship as an increasingly popular phenomenon that, in academia and beyond, has all too often been approached from an uncritical and apolitical perspective.

Introduction

Social entrepreneurship, or the efforts to address socio-economic issues via business means, is a relatively recent phenomenon in the Middle East and North Africa (MENA). Social entrepreneurs emphasize innovation, sustainable development and active citizenship, and seek cross-sector partnerships with the state, business sector and donors (Alvord, Brown, & Letts, 2004; Dacin, Dacin, & Tracey, 2011). Although social entrepreneurship in MENA countries dates back to the early 2000s, it is only after the Arab uprisings of 2011 that an 'entrepreneurship boom' has swept the region. Entrepreneurship promises solutions to many of those socio-economic issues that have been cited during the uprisings, such as employability and job creation, economic and social development – including the education and health care systems – as well as the integration of marginalized societal groups (Abdou, Fahmy, Greenwald, & Nelson, 2010; Jamali & Lanteri, 2015; Schroeder, 2013). In addition to societal actors – especially the youth – authoritarian elites in business and politics as well as international actors economically, politically and socially exploit social entrepreneurship as a new neoliberal phenomenon (Angeles, 2015; Qayyum, 2012). The aim is to engineer and control the capitalist market as a means of preserving their privileges, and thus, also to maintain authoritarian rule (e.g. de Smet & Bogaert, 2017; Hertog, Luciani, & Valeri, 2013; Heydemann, 2004).

In his elaborations on authoritarian neoliberalism, Cemal Burak Tansel (2017) describes this phenomenon with regard to the global South as a symbiosis of neoliberal economic management and authoritarian statism (p. 19). The state, policy-makers, ruling and economic elites constitute the key actors in the maintenance of this order. In addition to state coercion and control, these actors draw on non-coercive practices such as consent-making activities and co-optation to neutralize opposition (Bank, 2004; Gerschewski, 2013; Wong, 2012). Although the literature on authoritarianism and neoliberalism addresses the restructuring of state-business-society relations and the prevalence of divide-and-rule politics and co-optation, the emergence of novel mechanisms and patterns of co-optation is largely under-theorized. In addition, little research has been conducted on (social) entrepreneurship in authoritarian systems (e.g. Horn, 2013; Jamali & Lanteri, 2015; Mair & Marti, 2009; Sukarieh, 2016). This can be explained by the fact that the literature on social entrepreneurship is largely uncritical and apolitical, and has been shaped around a commitment to a 'utopian' image of social entrepreneurship (for exceptions, see Dey, 2014; Dey & Steyaert, 2012; Horn, 2013).

This paper explores the social entrepreneurship networks (SENs) composed of social entrepreneurs, business and political elites and international actors in the MENA region. It analyses how the local actors in SENs actually join up and foster the renewal of authoritarianism via neoliberal means. The paper addresses the relationship between authoritarian statisms and neoliberalism with a particular focus on the interplay of tried-and-tested and new patterns and mechanisms of co-optation that emerged from SENs in Jordan and Morocco between 2006 and 2014. I argue that new neoliberal networks and pre-existing patterns of social interaction complement each other, fostering linkages between well-established elites and hand-picked social entrepreneurs as well as societal groups. Social entrepreneurship, thus, has been aligned with the authoritarian regimes, and it potentially serves to cement neoliberalism as a mode of governance. As such, this article brings to light repertoires of authoritarian neoliberalism that have hitherto been understudied (see also Beck & Germann, 2018; Jenss, 2018; Tansel, 2018).

The two cases presented below are taken from a comprehensive mixed-methods social network analysis of SENs in Jordan and Morocco, which is based on primary empirical data (semi-structured interviews, reports, news articles) gathered during field research in both countries in 2012 and 2013 (see also Kreitmeyr-Koska, 2016). In this analysis, I examine questions of position and power – understood in relational terms as the exercise of power (control, domination) and access to power (inclusion and participation) at the network and at the actor level – as proxies for co-optation through the social network concepts of *centrality* (degree, eigenvector and betweenness) and *coreness* (Bono, 2007; Borgatti, Everett, & Freeman, 2013).[1] In particular, this study focuses on the Jordanian King Abdullah II Award for Youth Innovation and Achievement (KAAYIA) and the Office Chérifien des Phosphates Entrepreneurship Network (OCPEN) in Morocco, as the key royal initiatives and vehicles for co-optation in these two SENs. References to the role of other actors in the SENs are made in order to give insights into the broader dynamics in Jordan and Morocco. Nevertheless, this does not mean that all actors in the SENs follow the same strategies. International actors may unintentionally, rather than actively, contribute to co-optation and authoritarian renewal.

The Jordanian and Moroccan SENs illustrate different trajectories of the development of social entrepreneurship and its alignment to the political agendas of the regimes, while also indicating a similar direction of travel. The kings in both monarchies came to power at approximately the same time and are neo-patrimonial rulers who strongly rely on a small group of loyal elites and co-optation strategies. Moreover, they have initiated similar neoliberal reforms. However, I highlight that the development of SENs and the purpose of neoliberal co-optation differ. While the Jordanian case shows how social entrepreneurship facilitates the co-optation and creation of a new generation of socio-economic elites, the Moroccan case highlights that social entrepreneurship also facilitates the co-optation of the broader society and functions as a problem-fixing tool to address particular socio-economic challenges.

Authoritarian renewal, neoliberalism, and co-optation

Authoritarianism in MENA countries has mutated noticeably since the 1990s. Reforms in the political, economic and social spheres, *inter alia* economic and political liberalization and new modes of political participation, led to opposing interpretations of these changes. While some have analyzed these developments as indicators of political transformation – i.e. democratization – more recently, transformations in authoritarian governance strategies have been regarded as changes *within* regimes and not changes *of* regimes. In consequence, such developments are interpreted as survival strategies of regime elites to preserve the status quo of authoritarian rule, and thus, indicate authoritarian resilience and renewal instead of democratization (Cavatorta, 2013; Heydemann, 2004, 2007; Valbjorn & Bank, 2010).[2] As Heydemann (2007, p. 3) notes:

> What is emerging in the Arab world, therefore, is a hybrid form of authoritarianism. It combines tried-and-true strategies of the past – coercion, surveillance, patronage, corruption, and personalism – with innovations that reflect the determination of authoritarian élites to respond aggressively to the triple threat of globalization, markets, and democratization.

In this context, neoliberalism has played a crucial role. De Smet and Bogaert (2017, p. 212) contend that 'pre-existing forms of authoritarianism are transformed in relation to and converged with structural shifts in global capitalism'. From this perspective, neoliberalism cannot be reduced to a set of economic and political policies and reforms that aim to liberalize and integrate Arab countries into the global economy. On the contrary, neoliberalism appears at the same time as a socio-political project that aims at restructuring social relations and state power, economy and society (see also Bruff & Tansel, 2018; Harrison, 2018). This manifests in class or elite struggles in and among these three spheres, including, *inter alia*, the selective inclusion and exclusion of actors, their marginalization and resistance as well as a transfer of social responsibility from the state to private actors (Bergh, 2014; Cammett, 2007; Henry & Springborg, 2010; Hertog et al., 2013; Heydemann, 2004; Schlumberger, 2004). The promotion and formation of neoliberal entrepreneurial subjects which internalize 'market' ideas such as competition, responsibility, self-management and self-empowerment is another manifestation of these restructuring processes. In this understanding, entrepreneurship is not merely a profession but a way of life. Sukarieh (2016), in particular, has shown that, in the case of Jordan, entrepreneurship constitutes an elite project that appeals to elite youth and adults who, together with international actors, engage in the promotion of entrepreneurship among the lower-middle class and poor youth. The latter, however, are aware of the differences in opportunities and perspectives in terms of financial access and personal ties, and, therefore, do not uncritically participate in these entrepreneurial networks.

Non-coercive practices such as co-optation are key practices in the above-described restructuring processes. As opposed to repression, co-optation signals a non-coercive regime strategy to generate support, or as Gerschewski (2013, p. 22) expresses it, 'the capacity to tie strategically-relevant actors (or a group of actors) to the regime'. The mechanisms to do so include *inter alia* resource allocation, privileges and concessions as well as patronage and clientelism (Cavatorta, 2007; Gerschewski, 2013;

Wong, 2012). Co-optation is embedded in specific temporal and spatial contexts. Consequently, the recent trajectory of authoritarian renewal via neoliberal means has produced new patterns and mechanisms of co-optation. Albrecht and Schlumberger (2004) and Bank (2004) demonstrate how these mechanisms have evolved since the 1980s, from resource allocation towards inclusionary mechanisms and the 'economization' of discourses, participation and action. These mechanisms affect the co-optation of hand-picked actors and serve to broaden the regime's social base. In addition, the 'economized' discourses and neoliberal ideas link local regime elites with global actors, and highlight the interplay of universal neoliberal elements with the local political, economic and social contexts (De Smet & Bogaert, 2017; Tansel, 2017).

Despite the global and the MENA entrepreneurship boom, few scholars have explicitly addressed how the respective political system impacts on social entrepreneurship or how neoliberalism and social entrepreneurship relate to each other (Craig & Porter, 2006; Dey, 2014; Horn, 2013). It is commonly assumed that social entrepreneurs address problems that have been caused by a mix of state withdrawal from social provisions and the implementation of neoliberal policies. Dey (2014, pp. 55–56), however, demonstrates that social entrepreneurship itself is a neoliberal phenomenon as it is a 'tactic of neoliberal governmentality' that 'turns the social into a space of competition, individual responsibility and self-organization by demanding entrepreneurial virtues and behaviours from people who until recently were not envisioned as entrepreneurs'. Moreover, the strong involvement of local and global elites – who have already capitalized on neoliberal reforms – underlines the need to link social entrepreneurship to class struggles and to elite political projects. In contrast to established conceptions of social entrepreneurship, I contend that SENs are inherently political and should be perceived as important components of new modes of neoliberal governance. Research on social entrepreneurship in the MENA region is still an emerging field and, with only a few exceptions, comprises studies that focus on mapping SENs (Abdou et al., 2010; Jamali & Lanteri, 2015; Sukarieh, 2016). The case studies of SENs in Jordan and Morocco, therefore, contribute to a better understanding of social entrepreneurship as a new phenomenon in the MENA region and its linkages to the questions of neoliberalism, authoritarian renewal and co-optation.

The development of social entrepreneurship networks in the Middle East and North Africa

Social entrepreneurship as a phenomenon and concept dates back to the 1970s. International organizations exclusively supporting social entrepreneurs include Ashoka (founded in 1980 in the USA), Synergos (founded in 1986 in the USA), the Schwab Foundation (founded in 1998 in Switzerland) as well as the Skoll Foundation (founded in 1999 in the UK); these are the major actors in the field of social entrepreneurship.[3] They have been active in the MENA region since 2003 and recognized around 200 social entrepreneurs in 10 MENA countries between 2003 and 2014.[4] Significant numbers of internationally recognized social entrepreneurs are based in Egypt, Jordan, Morocco, Lebanon and the Palestinian Territories whereas Tunisia, Saudi Arabia, Kuwait, the United Arab Emirates and Libya only have one or two recognized social entrepreneurs and enterprises each. However, since 2011 their numbers have been increasing and other international actors, such as the World Bank, have started to engage in social entrepreneurship. In several cases, social enterprises operate across the MENA region, i.e. they were founded in one country and opened branches or franchises in several more. The most prominent examples are Injaz, Education for Employment (EFE) and Endeavor.

Analysis of these international organizations shows that they differ from other types of support organizations with regard to the types of linkages they have with social enterprises and entrepreneurs. They provide a combination of financial support, advice and skill development through fellowships and awards. They cultivate novel types of relations and are based on a selection process that includes personal recommendations or nominations, documentation, interviews and field visits. Although the terms of these fellowships and awards vary from support organization to support organization (e.g. duration, selection process, extent of support), they share several commonalities. Instead of merely applying for and receiving project grants, social entrepreneurs get stipends for a specific period of time (2–3 years) or a cash prize and become fellows for life who can attend meetings and training sessions. Equally, social entrepreneurs benefit from international and local exposure, recognition and access to global networks of actors from the private sector, state and civil society. Local support organizations focusing exclusively on social entrepreneurship follow similar approaches. However, as we will see in the following sections, they rely more heavily on local business actors as members of their selection committees, sponsors and mentors.

Both international and local support organizations strongly rely on personal ties in their selection processes. Ashoka, for instance, underlines the importance of networks of nominators; in 2012, more than 60% of applicants were nominated for a fellowship even though applicants can apply directly without a prior nomination (Ashoka, 2012, p. 25).[5] This often results in the collection of multiple local and international fellowships by a small number of social entrepreneurs. In so doing, the actors in the SENs foster the development of exclusive and elitist SENs in the MENA region which disseminate neoliberalism and the notion of entrepreneurship as the means to achieve sustainable socio-economic change. As the representative of one of the international organizations said in this context, '[t]he social entrepreneurship field is a bit of a club. Everybody knows each other.'[6]

Joining this club opens up a variety of opportunities for engagement with authoritarian elites and social entrepreneurs in the MENA region. As we will see in the analysis of the SENs in Jordan and Morocco, authoritarian elites play a decisive role in terms of the development and management of the SENs. Each SEN is strongly embedded in the respective local political context, even though state institutions play a minimal role in the institutionalization of these networks. The state institutions have not created supportive regulatory frameworks for social entrepreneurship, let alone becoming directly involved in their supervision. Although the actors in the SENs criticize the lack of institutionalized support, they do not generally question the outsourcing of social responsibility. On the contrary, in line with neoliberal notions such as self-responsibility, active citizenship as well as corporate social responsibility and private-led development, they promote a stronger engagement with private actors.[7]

The CEO king, the 'Generation Abdullah' and the creation of a new socio-economic elite in Jordan

The Jordanian King Abdullah II, and the new generation of loyal entrepreneurs he appointed upon his accession to the throne, have explored the potential of entrepreneurship and its compatibility with their political agenda early on.[8] Abdullah II has initiated a large-scale neoliberal restructuring process aiming at the transformation of Jordan into an economic success story and role model within the MENA region. In this context, he launched multiple initiatives, particularly in the field of human capital formation and information and communication technologies (ICT). However, the preservation of the status quo of power relations and elite interests have taken precedence over regime change or transformation (Bank, 2004; Bank & Schlumberger, 2004; Knowles, 2005; Wils, 2003).

Jordan is among the strongholds of social entrepreneurship in the MENA region. The first internationally recognized social entrepreneurs were awarded fellowships between 2006 and 2008; since then, the SEN has grown steadily and incorporated in its body a plethora of actors (Ashoka, 2008, 2011, 2013, 2014; Schwab Foundation, 2012; Skoll Foundation, 2009; Synergos, 2009, 2011, 2013). Moreover, local support organizations and initiatives were established and have also contributed to the development of the SEN. Taking account of international as well as local initiatives, such as the KAAYIA (King Abdullah II Award for Youth Innovation and Achievement), the total number of recognized Jordanian social entrepreneurs amounted to 79 individuals in 2014. Analysis of the Jordanian SEN demonstrates that the Jordanian King and loyal business elites dominate the SEN and are closely controlling and managing its development. They exploit the SEN to create a new generation of socio-economic elites, and thus, target the co-optation of hand-picked social entrepreneurs and their alignment to the political and economic agenda. The launch of an award for social entrepreneurs by the King as well as the focus on the entrepreneurs themselves, rather than the enterprise more broadly, facilitate this purpose.

The King Abdullah II Fund for Development (KAFD) was founded by royal decree in 2001 and functions as an umbrella for a multitude of youth initiatives that are related to the King's agenda. Among them is the KAAYIA, an award for social entrepreneurs in the MENA region launched by the King at the WEF-MENA (World Economic Forum on the Middle East and North Africa) in 2007.[9] Through this award, the Jordanian regime became more strategically involved in the SEN. The KAAYIA is one of the few cases of the active involvement of a ruler – and not solely the political and business elites – in a SEN in the MENA region. This also explains why among Jordanians the KAAYIA is better-known and more prestigious than the international recognition by Ashoka or Synergos, as receiving the award constitutes a 'royally certified entrepreneurship'.[10] The combination of having a chance to personally meet the King and to receive the support of the elites creates an appeal and mitigates the barrier against co-optation. For the elites, then, the explicit engagement of the King, the increasing local and international popularity of social entrepreneurship and its adaptability to the local context directly plays into the strategies of voluntary and inclusionary co-optation. Having said this, in many cases the KAAYIA finalists or winners subsequently have been recognized by Synergos and Ashoka. Thus, the KAAYIA also functions as a stepping stone into the regional social entrepreneurship community.[11]

Jordanian business elites are engaged in the SEN in several functions. In addition to the KAAYIA, they are partners, mentors, sponsors, jury members or board members. Moreover, many of these business actors have established social foundations or departments for corporate social responsibility (CSR) within their companies, through which they establish support and advice ties with social entrepreneurs.[12] Fadi Ghandour (Aramex/Wamda), Ghassan Nuqul (Nuqul Group) and Maher Kaddoura (Accenture Middle East) as well as a younger generation of high-ranking business actors such as Dina Shoman (Arab Bank) are worth mentioning in this regard. They are omnipresent actors in the Jordanian SEN, who support and influence hand-picked social entrepreneurs and also consider themselves as socially responsible entrepreneurs who invest in Jordan's development through private-led initiatives. Owing to their powerful position and linkages, these dominant actors have established themselves as decision-makers in the Jordanian SEN and, thus, play a decisive role in defining (social) entrepreneurship and appraising which ideas are worth supporting. As no formal procedures are in place for the establishment of ties, the selection process is based on pre-existing personal connections to actors in the SEN. In the absence of possessing such ties, social entrepreneurs face challenges establishing themselves in the SEN.

As opposed to this crucial role of the business elites, state institutions and representatives show only a very limited interest in the SEN and consequently play a minor role. While actors in the Jordanian SEN criticize the state's disinterest in creating an enabling environment for entrepreneurs, they nevertheless embrace the increasing responsibility of private actors for social provisions with reference to active citizenship, i.e. the responsibility to engage as active citizens in their communities and countries.[13] This means that the Jordanian SEN, despite the apparent distance from the regime, is part of the reproduction of the local capitalist order and thus one aspect of a broader strategy of co-optation. Co-optation also serves to create a new generation of socio-economic elites closely managed by the 'Generation Abdullah'. A closer look at this elite generation reveals that it is a small and, by now, ageing group of politically influential business actors who are mostly over the age of 50.[14] Therefore, the recruitment of new, younger actors who share the socio-economic and political agenda of the King and the 'Generation Abdullah' seems crucial. The socio-economic background of the recent social entrepreneurs plays a crucial role in entrenching this orientation. Most of Jordan's new social entrepreneurs are in their late 20s to early 30s, part of the well-educated middle-class with experience of living abroad, and reside in metropolitan cities. Although tribal affiliations and whether an entrepreneur is Palestinian or Transjordanian clearly mark social entrepreneurs, they do not play a decisive role in the SEN (contrary to their importance in many other domains of Jordanian life). In short, the new social entrepreneurs seek to resemble and emulate the King's business elite in many aspects, and can easily be mobilized in support of the regime.[15]

One case in particular exemplifies this dynamic within the Jordanian SEN. 'Entrepreneur X'[16] (early 30s) is a KAAIYA finalist and was awarded several international and local fellowships and prizes between 2009 and 2014. Starting out with only a few ties to business actors in the SEN, mainly friends from university and school, and the dream to one day personally meet the King and the Queen, this entrepreneur now proudly claims that there is not a single actor in the Jordanian SEN with whom X does not have ties.[17] 'Entrepreneur X' is involved in nearly every event on or for social entrepreneurs that has taken place in Jordan since 2010, and has become one of the key actors who introduce new social entrepreneurs to the networks and the elites. In fact, ties extend beyond Jordan, and 'Entrepreneur X' is one of the key social entrepreneurs and mentors in the MENA region. Many of the above-named members of the social and economic elites, *inter alia* the representatives of Aramex, Shoman Foundation/Arab Bank, Nuqul Group, Wamda and the KAFD, have been supporting the said entrepreneur for several years. As 'Entrepreneur X' explained, '[The CEO] decided that if I need anything from [the company] I just need to write an email to anyone in that company and they have to immediately do it'.[18]

In all these different functions, the social entrepreneur acts as an individual, i.e. the social *enterprise* receives much less emphasis and attention than the *entrepreneur*. This is a widespread phenomenon in the Jordanian SEN, independent of which international or local support organization recognizes an entrepreneur. It clearly shows that individualism and co-optation are not necessarily regarded as negative traits within the SEN. On the contrary, both established elites and social entrepreneurs seem to share the interest in forming exclusive and elitist ties and to create, present and celebrate a new generation of socio-economic elites.

The Moroccan *makhzen* & the SEN as a problem-solving tool

Upon his accession to the throne, King Mohammad VI announced the beginning of a new era of political change and socio-economic development in Morocco. In this context, the King gave the ongoing neoliberal restructuring process a 'social' touch by emphasizing human development, social inclusion, poverty reduction, and civic participation. Owing to this change of agenda, Mohammad VI was called 'King of the Poor' during the first couple of years of his reign. Hand-picked members of the Moroccan elite families who have been aligned to the Moroccan regime (*makhzen*) since Morocco's independence and a few newcomers, mainly technocrats, comprise the King's circle of cronies who are influential actors in the economy and politics.[19] However, similar to Jordan, the overriding interest to preserve the *makhzen* and the status quo of power relations resulted in authoritarian renewal rather than change (Benhaddou, 2009; Boukhars, 2011; Catusse, 2011; Vermeren, 2011).

Morocco is not a social entrepreneurship stronghold and the SEN developed slowly between 2007 and 2014. Despite the selection of nine Moroccan fellows, Ashoka, Synergos and the Schwab Foundation have not established themselves in Morocco (Ashoka, 2013, 2014; Chung & Jonsdottir, 2014; Schwab Foundation, 2012; Synergos, 2009). Having said this, Moroccan social entrepreneurs have been supported by numerous international actors who do not exclusively focus on social entrepreneurship, such as the British Council or the US Department of State. Numerous local support organizations and initiatives have also emerged since 2011. Thus, international support is much more dispersed than in Jordan, and the development of the Moroccan SEN has to be attributed predominantly to local support. Considering the local recognition of social entrepreneurs, the total number of internationally and nationally recognized Moroccan fellows amounted to 32 in 2014.

As this analysis will demonstrate, instead of constraining the Moroccan SEN, the weak presence of international actors has created opportunities for the *makhzen*, elites and a small number of actors closely aligned to the *makhzen* to dominate the SEN. These groups are actively controlling and managing the development of the SEN. Contrary to the Jordanian case, however, the focus is not on co-opting a new elite generation. Instead, they have engineered the SEN as a problem-solving tool to outsource social responsibility from the state to the SEN and to address particular socio-economic issues that pose challenges to them. Thus, in the Moroccan case, co-optation predominantly targets the broader society. The activities in the field of social entrepreneurship on the local level have been flourishing since the Arab uprisings when, *inter alia*, Startup Maroc (2011) and the Moroccan Center for Innovation and Social Entrepreneurship (MCISE, 2012) were founded by young Moroccan professionals who possess similar characteristics as the Jordanian social entrepreneurs. The MCISE has become one of the most prominent organizations in the Moroccan SEN in a short amount of time, and it has established ties with some of the most important elites and institutions linked to the *makhzen*. Social enterprises such as Enactus, EFE and Injaz, who became active in the Moroccan SEN between 2004 and 2007, have also intensified their engagement with entrepreneurship education and promotion.[20]

Actors in the Moroccan SEN, like the Jordanian ones, rely on tried-and-tested strategies of co-optation as well as more innovative ones that emerged with the spread of entrepreneurship. These manifest in the form of support and advice ties – namely sponsoring/CSR, board membership, competitions, awards/prizes, volunteering and mentoring – and aim at mobilizing the youth from the broader society as well as initiating a controlled competition among (hand-picked) social enterprises and entrepreneurs. As is the case in the Jordanian SEN, state institutions do not play a major role in the Moroccan SEN. Through the active engagement of the business elites in the SEN, the responsibility of citizens to become active entrepreneurial agents of socio-economic change is transmitted from the state to the elites and (social) entrepreneurs. The example of the royal phosphate company Office Chérifien des Phosphates (OCP Group) lucidly illustrates this trend.

The OCP Group is one of the key royal, political and economic institutions for the generation of rents, elite co-optation and the exercise of control in Morocco. Similar to the royal holding Société Nationale d'Investissement (SNI), the King and the royal family hold major stakes in the OCP Group

(Vermeren, 2011). Since 2011, OCP has developed into a major business actor in the Moroccan SEN and is involved in practically every event and initiative in the field of entrepreneurship. This includes not only the support on the local level but also the mentoring and international exposure of social entrepreneurs. Several factors explain this development. In 2011, over a period of several months, OCP faced demonstrations and demolitions at several of its mining sites across the country (e.g. in Youssoufia, Safi and Khouribga) by local unemployed youth who demanded employment by the OCP. These protests caused considerable financial losses and damage (for details, see Bogaert, 2015). Presumably to contain these challenges, the OCP initiated several programmes in the field of employability, entrepreneurship/self-employment and social development such as the OCP Skills programme (launched in 2011) and the OCP Entrepreneurship Network (OCPEN, established in 2013). While the OCP Skills focuses on employment training of youth and their recruitment, the OCPEN focuses on entrepreneurship promotion as a means to create employment and self-employment opportunities (OCP Foundation, 2013, 2014; OCP Group, 2013a, 2013b). Especially during the crisis of 2011, the OCP approached individual actors, among them several social entrepreneurs, to conduct trainings as part of the OCP Skills programme. These hand-picked actors operated as role models and experts on entrepreneurship, and were loyal regime supporters who had the task of presenting alternative employment opportunities to the protesting unemployed youth – and convincing them to end their protest.

In general, however, the OCP announces specific calls for application and also accepts project proposals on an ongoing basis that target issues and communities across the country – thus, not exclusively the regions in which OCP operates factories and mines (OCP Foundation, 2013). Having said this, the OCP has predominantly supported social enterprises in the regions where it operates, and the most prominent social enterprises in the Moroccan SEN. With a few exceptions, mainly in 2011, OCP has focused on the *enterprise* rather than the *entrepreneur*, reaching out to the youth in the broader society.[21] This tendency underlines how offering solutions to specific issues is a major concern for the OCP, and directly touches upon the personal interests of the King. Since entrepreneurship is increasingly popular among the youth and international organizations and institutions, it is seen as a relatively easily exploitable tool of co-optation by the Moroccan elite. In contrast to the Jordanian King, Mohammad VI did not personally launch an entrepreneurship initiative but decided to act through the OCP, thus aiming to reach out to a large segment of unemployed youth.[22] Moreover, as Cammett (2004) suggests, the King and the elites do not aim to create a new elite generation as their Jordanian counterparts, but are actively trying to prevent such a scenario on the grounds that such a new elite might challenge the existing status quo.

Social entrepreneurs and local support organizations alike make use of these opportunities and receive support and advice by the OCP. They consider the interest and support of the OCP for (social) entrepreneurship as an important achievement for the Moroccan SEN and 'happily' seek to be co-opted by this crucial and powerful actor. In fact, while they proudly state that the OCP supports them, they also seem to fear the OCP and are reluctant to talk about details of this relation or to openly object to OCPs engagement in the SEN.[23]

Generating new resources for co-optation and authoritarian renewal

The development of social entrepreneurship and SENs in the MENA region has been accompanied by new patterns of co-optation. As the cases of the SENs in Jordan and Morocco demonstrate, this process has brought together business and social interests that accepted and embodied neoliberal practices, and provided them new resources with which to expand the scope of co-optation.

While many of these patterns and resources were already in place, there are also novel ones that materialized with the growing pervasiveness of neoliberalism and of the logics of entrepreneurship in particular. Moreover, innovation does not necessarily mean novelty *per se*. Patterns and resources can be borrowed from a different context and adapted to entrepreneurship (e.g. fellowships). They can also constitute new 'labels' for tried-and-tested patterns and resources, as is the case with mentoring which, in the case of the SENs studied, predominantly describes existing patron-client relations.

As has been demonstrated in the above analysis, resources of neoliberal co-optation within the SENs can be grouped into two interrelated categories that combine tried-and-tested forms with innovative ones: (I) co-optation through material incentives and support; and (II) co-optation through immaterial support. Material incentives and support are provided in several forms. Co-optation takes place through, *inter alia*, grants, donations, cash prizes and stipends provided by international or local support organizations and business elites to social entrepreneurs. Immaterial support, however, manifests itself in the establishment of new social ties (e.g. strategic partnerships, jury or board membership), human capital formation (e.g. training, mentoring) and the generation of symbolic capital (e.g. recognition, prestige). Thus, we can observe a diversification of patterns of co-optation and resources and a strong reliance on immaterial support.

Furthermore, resources can be differentiated into direct and indirect ones, depending on whether the regime elites actively engage with actors whom they seek to co-opt and provide specific resources to, or whether they are merely facilitators of socio-economic action. Direct resources can take many different forms, and they are predominantly provided to hand-picked actors. Indirect resources, by contrast, facilitate spaces and opportunities to take socio-economic action and build on the fact that entrepreneurship is popular among young Arabs and, therefore, is relatively easy to deploy as a tool of mobilization. The examples from Jordan and Morocco underline that the creation of entrepreneurship initiatives by the monarchy are considered 'royally certified entrepreneurship' and encourage voluntary co-optation. This reminds us that both sides, those who co-opt and those who are co-opted, benefit from this arrangement, which strengthens the role the SENs as new components of a broader neoliberal governance that co-exists and interweaves with authoritarian state practices.

Conclusion: neoliberal co-optation and authoritarian renewal

This article has argued that social entrepreneurship in the MENA region constitutes a novel approach that enables the rulers and elites, here Jordan and Morocco, to entrench both authoritarian rule and neoliberal forms of governance. The neoliberal ideas and practices promoted by international and local actors have led to the emergence of new patterns of interaction between state, business and society, and thus novel forms of co-optation. The SENs mobilized resources for co-optation not only of a material kind or inclusionary in character; they can also have symbolic value, e.g. prestige and recognition. As the example of the KAAYIA highlights, the ruler's engagement in entrepreneurship justifies and legitimizes a logic of entrepreneurial selfhood that is expected to overcome socio-economic challenges through individual ingenuity. As can hopefully be seen, this is highly depoliticizing because people are steered towards societal participation via non-disruptive activities.

The comparison of the Jordanian and the Moroccan SENs underlines the embeddedness of neoliberal networks and patterns of co-optation in their respective local political, economic and social contexts. In the case of Jordan, the regime and business elites around King Abdullah II exploit social entrepreneurship for the co-optation of hand-picked social entrepreneurs. These entrepreneurs are formed as a new generation of socio-economic elites. In Morocco, by contrast, social entrepreneurship functions as a problem-solving tool to outsource social responsibility and to address particular socio-economic issues that pose challenges to the regime. While this process also includes the co-optation of hand-picked social entrepreneurs, in general co-optation targets the broader society. Contrary to cases of authoritarian neoliberalism in representative democratic systems, where we observe a move towards more authoritarian patterns in enforcing neoliberal rules, the findings of this article demonstrate that neoliberalism can mutate its survival tactics by adopting seemingly more 'consensual' practices which, nevertheless, coexist with and potentially reinforce authoritarian governance. Finally, I have demonstrated that critical research on social entrepreneurship in authoritarian regimes contributes to a deeper understanding of social entrepreneurship itself, and also offers new perspectives that point to a broader research agenda which could generate new resources for critique of authoritarian neoliberalism in MENA countries, and thus for genuinely progressive change.

Notes

1. Details of the complete social network analysis are available upon request. In total, 44 interviews were conducted with social entrepreneurs, representatives of international and local support organizations, business actors and experts. The names of all interview partners were anonymized. For further details, see Kreitmeyr-Koska (2016).
2. For a discussion of the literatures on democratization and authoritarian resilience with regard to the Arab uprisings, see Valbjorn (2014).
3. Ashoka and Synergos have country representatives in the MENA region; the others are based abroad and occasionally travel to the region.
4. This calculation is based on the annual reports and announcements published by Ashoka, Synergos, the Schwab Foundation and the Skoll Foundation between 2003 and 2014.
5. Among the social entrepreneurs interviewed in Jordan and Morocco, every single one reported that s/he was encouraged to apply, or was nominated, for a fellowship by an actor from inside the SEN (representatives of international/local organizations, business actors, entrepreneurs).
6. Personal interviews with social entrepreneurs, representatives of local and international support organizations and business actors; see also Ashoka (2013); KAAYIA (2015); OCP Foundation (2014); Schwab Foundation (2008); Skoll Foundation (2009); Synergos (2014).
7. Personal interviews with social entrepreneurs, support organizations, representatives of the private sector and experts, 2011–2013; see also the contributions in Jamali and Lanteri (2015) and Kreitmeyr (2017).
8. Bank and Schlumberger (2004) describe these actors as the 'Generation Abdullah' (p. 41). Examples are Fadi Ghandour (founder of Aramex and Yahoo Maktoob) and Ghassan Nuqul (Nuqul Group).
9. Personal interviews with finalists, winners and project managers of KAFD/KAAYIA, Amman, March/April 2013; see also KAAYIA (2009, 2011, 2013, 2015).
10. I thank one of the reviewers for suggesting this term.
11. Personal interviews with social entrepreneurs and representatives of international and local support organizations, 2012–2013; see also the annual reports of the KAAYIA, Ashoka and Synergos.
12. See for example the annually published sustainability reports by Aramex (2006, 2010, 2011, 2012, 2013, 2014), the Nuqul Group (2009, 2011, 2012, 2013, 2014) and the Arab Bank (2010, 2011, 2012, 2013, 2014); see also Bailey et al. (2011).
13. Personal interviews, Amman, March/April 2013.
14. On these elites and elite change in Jordan, see Bank and Schlumberger (2004) and Wils (2003). The Moroccan elites, by contrast, are more numerous and their lineages reach back to the nineteenth century (Waterbury, 1970; Benhaddou, 2009).
15. There are cases of entrepreneurs who do not possess these characteristics, but they tend to come from the lower middle-class and/or from smaller towns or refugee camps. They are often presented as the

exceptional cases that underline that everyone can be a successful (social) entrepreneur. Personal interviews, Amman, March/April 2013; see also Abdou et al. (2010) and Jamali and Lanteri (2015).

16. In order to respect the wish for anonymity, the author calls this entrepreneur 'Entrepreneur X' instead of providing his/her name.
17. Personal interview with 'Entrepreneur X', Amman, March 2013.
18. Personal interview with 'Entrepreneur X', Amman, March 2013.
19. Examples are the Kettani (Wafa Bank/Attijariwafa) and the Benjelloun (Banque Marocaine de Commerce Extérieur) families as well as the technocrats Mostafa Terrab and Hassan Bouhemou, who direct the OCP and the SNI respectively.
20. The oldest recognized Moroccan social enterprises date back to the 1980s; the most famous ones are the Association Solidarité Féminine (founded 1985), l'Amicale Marocaine des Handicapés (founded 1992), and Al-Jisr (founded 1999). Although they are also well-connected in the SEN, they do not actively foster the promotion and growth of the SEN. Personal interviews, Casablanca, May 2012/September 2013.
21. Personal interviews with social entrepreneurs, Casablanca/Rabat, September 2013.
22. The SNI complements this approach and supports social enterprises that promote entrepreneurship and offer entrepreneurship education (e.g. Injaz, EFE, Al Jisr). It is the second major business actor in the Moroccan SEN. Personal interviews, Rabat/Casablanca, May 2012/September 2013.
23. Personal interviews with social entrepreneurs, Rabat/Casablanca, September 2013.

Acknowledgements

I would like to thank Mohammad Yaghi and the participants of the workshop 'Networks of Dependency' which was organized by the research network 'Reconfigurations' in the Centre for Near and Middle Eastern Studies at Phillips University Marburg in July 2015 for their insightful comments on an earlier draft of this paper. Furthermore, I would like to thank Cemal Burak Tansel and the anonymous reviewers for their constructive feedback and suggestions for improvement.

Disclosure statement

No potential conflict of interest was reported by the authors.

References

Abdou, E., Fahmy, A., Greenwald, D., & Nelson, J. (2010). *Social entrepreneurship in the Middle East: Toward sustainable development for the next generation*. Wolfensohn Center for Development, Brookings/Dubai School of Government/Silatech.

Albrecht, H., & Schlumberger, O. (2004). 'Waiting for Godot': Regime change without democratization in the Middle East. *International Political Science Review, 25*(4), 371–392.

Alvord, S., Brown, L., & Letts, C. (2004). Social entrepreneurship and societal transformation: An exploratory study. *Journal of Applied Behavioral Science, 40*(3), 260–282.

Angeles, N. (2015). The Middle East's rising social enterprise sphere. *The NU Social Enterprise Review, 2*, 15–18.

Arab Bank. (2010). *Sustainability report 2010*. Amman: Arab Bank.

Arab Bank. (2011). *Sustainability report 2011*. Amman: Arab Bank.

Arab Bank. (2012). *Sustainability report 2012*. Amman: Arab Bank.

Arab Bank. (2013). *Sustainability report 2013*. Amman: Arab Bank.

Arab Bank. (2014). *Sustainability report 2014*. Amman: Arab Bank.

Aramex. (2006). *Sustainability report 2006*. Amman: Aramex.

Aramex. (2010). *Annual report 2010*. Amman: Aramex.

Aramex. (2011). *Annual report 2011*. Amman: Aramex.

Aramex. (2012). *Annual report 2012*. Amman: Aramex.

Aramex. (2013). *Annual report 2013*. Amman: Aramex.

Aramex. (2014). *Annual report 2014*. Amman: Aramex.

Ashoka Arab World. (2008). *2003 to 2008: A report on our first five years*. Cairo: Ashoka.

Ashoka Arab World. (2011). *2011 annual report*. Cairo: Ashoka.

Ashoka Arab World. (2012). *2012 annual report*. Cairo: Ashoka.

Ashoka Arab World. (2013). *2013 annual report: 10 years*. Cairo: Ashoka.

Ashoka Arab World. (2014). *2014 annual report*. Cairo: Ashoka.

Bailey, J., Gallegos, J., Kumar, S., Lemaitre, R., Longley, S., Luppino, R., ... Seekins, C. (2011). *Global social entrepreneurship: Final report*. Milan: New School University – GPIA/Synergos.

Bank, A. (2004). Rents, cooptation, and economized discourse: Three dimensions of political rule in Jordan, Morocco and Syria. *Journal of Mediterranean Studies, 14*(1/2), 155–180.

Bank, A., & Schlumberger, O. (2004). Jordan: Between regime survival and economic reform. In V. Perthes (Ed.), *Arab elites: Negotiating the politics of change* (pp. 35–60). Boulder: Lynne Rienner.

Beck, M., & Germann, J. (2018). Managerial power in the German model: The case of bertelsmann and the antecedents of neoliberalism. *Globalizations*. doi:10.1080/14747731.2018.1502490

Benhaddou, A. (2009). *Les Élites du Royaume. Enquête sur l'Organisation du Pouvoir au Maroc*. Paris: Riveneuve Édition.

Bergh, S. (Ed.). (2014). *The redeployment of state power in the Southern Mediterranean*. London: Routledge.

Bogaert, K. (2015). The revolt of small towns: The meaning of Morocco's history and the geography of social protest. *Review of African Political Economy, 42*(143), 124–140.

Bono, I. (2007). *Power in networks and power networks: Some notes towards a two-level network approach to power* (Working Paper No. 8). Torino: Dipartimento Di Studi Politici, Universita di Torino.

Borgatti, S., Everett, M., & Freeman, L. (2013). *Analyzing social networks*. London: Sage.

Boukhars, A. (2011). *Politics in Morocco: Executive monarchy and enlightened authoritarianism*. London: Routledge.

Bruff, I., & Tansel, C. B. (2018). Authoritarian neoliberalism: Trajectories of knowledge production and praxis. *Globalizations*. doi:10.1080/14747731.2018.1502497

Cammett, M. (2004). Challenges to networks of privilege in Morocco: Implications for network analysis. In S. Heydemann (Ed.), *Networks of privilege in the Middle East: The politics of economic reform revisited* (pp. 245–279). New York: Palgrave Macmillan.

Cammett, M. (2007). *Globalization and business politics in Arab North Africa: A comparative perspective*. Cambridge: Cambridge University Press.

Catusse, M. (2011). Le «Social»: Une Affaire d'Etat dans le Maroc de Mohammed VI. *Confluences Méditerranée, 2011/3*(78), 63–76.

Cavatorta, F. (2007). More than repression: The significance of Divide et Impera in the Middle East and North Africa – The case of Morocco. *Journal of Contemporary African Studies, 25*(2), 187–203.

Cavatorta, F. (Ed.). (2013). *Civil society activism under authoritarian rule: A comparative perspective*. London: Routledge.

Chung, C., & Jonsdottir, O. (2014). *Lighting the way: A report on the social enterprise landscape in Morocco*. London: Social Enterprise UK.

Craig, D., & Porter, D. (2006). *Development beyond neoliberalism? Governance, poverty reduction and political economy*. London: Routledge.

Dacin, T., Dacin, P., & Tracey, P. (2011). Social entrepreneurship: A critique and future directions. *Organization Studies, 22*(5), 1203–1213.

De Smet, B., & Bogaert, K. (2017). Resistance and passive revolution in Egypt and Morocco. In C. B. Tansel (Ed.), *States of discipline: Authoritarian neoliberalism and the contested reproduction of capitalist order* (pp. 211–233). London: Rowman & Littlefield International.

Dey, P. (2014). Governing the social through 'social entrepreneurship': A Foucauldian view of 'the art of governing' in advanced liberalism. In H. Douglas & S. Grant (Eds.), *Social entrepreneurship and enterprise: Concepts in context* (pp. 55–72). Melbourne: Tilde University Press.

Dey, P., & Steyaert, C. (2012). Social entrepreneurship: Critique and the radical enactment of the social. *Social Enterprise Journal*, *8*(2), 90–107.

Gerschewski, J. (2013). The three pillars of stability: Legitimation, repression, and co-optation in autocratic regimes. *Democratization*, *20*(1), 13–38.

Harrison, G. (2018). Authoritarian neoliberalism and capitalist transformation in Africa: All pain, no gain. *Globalizations*. doi:10.1080/14747731.2018.1502491

Henry, C., & Springborg, R. (2010). *Globalization and the politics of development in the Middle East* (2nd ed.). Cambridge: Cambridge University Press.

Hertog, S., Luciani, G., & Valeri, M. (Eds.). (2013). *Business politics in the Middle East*. London: Hurst.

Heydemann, S. (Ed.). (2004). *Networks of privilege in the Middle East: The politics of economic reform revisited*. Basingstoke: Palgrave Macmillan.

Heydemann, S. (2007). *Upgrading authoritarianism in the Arab world*. Analysis Paper 13. Washington, DC: The Saban Center for Middle East Policy, Brookings Institution.

Horn, D. (2013). *Democratic governance and social entrepreneurship: Civic participation and the future of democracy*. London: Routledge.

Jamali, D., & Lanteri, A. (Eds.). (2015). *Social entrepreneurship in the Middle East* (Vol. I and II). Basingstoke: Palgrave Macmillan.

Jenss, A. (2018). Authoritarian neoliberal rescaling in Latin America: Urban in/security and austerity in Oaxaca. *Globalizations*. doi:10.1080/14747731.2018.1502493

King Abdullah II Award for Youth Innovation and Achievement (KAAYIA). (2009). *Report 2009*. Amman: KAAYIA.

King Abdullah II Award for Youth Innovation and Achievement (KAAYIA). (2011). *Report 2011*. Amman: KAAYIA.

King Abdullah II Award for Youth Innovation and Achievement (KAAYIA). (2013). *Report 2013*. Amman: KAAYIA.

King Abdullah II Award for Youth Innovation and Achievement (KAAYIA). (2015). *Report 2015*. Amman: KAAYIA.

Knowles, W. M. (2005). *Jordan since 1989: A study in political economy*. London: I. B. Tauris.

Kreitmeyr, N. (2017). Entrepreneurship, crisis and socio-economic development in the Mediterranean: Formal and informal institutions and entrepreneurial activity. *Mediterranean Politics*, *22*(3), 432–438.

Kreitmeyr-Koska, N. (2016). *Neoliberal networks & authoritarian renewal: A diverse case study of Egypt, Jordan & Morocco* (PhD thesis). University of Tübingen, Tübingen.

Mair, J., & Marti, I. (2009). Entrepreneurship in and around institutional voids: A case study from Bangladesh. *Journal of Business Venturing*, *24*(4), 419–435.

Nuqul Group. (2009). *Sustainability report 2009*. Amman: Nuqul Group.

Nuqul Group. (2011). *Sustainability report 2011*. Amman: Nuqul Group.

Nuqul Group. (2012). *Sustainability report 2012*. Amman: Nuqul Group.

Nuqul Group. (2013). *Sustainability report 2013*. Amman: Nuqul Group.

Nuqul Group. (2014). *Sustainability report 2014*. Amman: Nuqul Group.

Office Chérifien des Phosphates Fondation (OCP Foundation). (2013). *Rapport d'Activité 2013: Penser & Agir pour le Développement Citoyen*. Rabat: OCP Foundation.

Office Chérifien des Phosphates Fondation (OCP Foundation). (2014). *Rapport d'Activité 2014: S'Engager, Parager, Agir*. Rabat: OCP Foundation.

Office Chérifien des Phosphates (OCP Group). (2013a). *Feeding the soil to feed the planet*. Casablanca: OCP Group.

Office Chérifien des Phosphates (OCP Group). (2013b). *Sustainability report 2013: People, planet, phosphate*. Casablanca: OCP Group.

Qayyum, M. (2012). *The latest way to solve poverty in the Middle East*. Carnegie Endowment for International Peace: Sada. Retrieved from http://carnegieendowment.org/sada/2012/12/18/latest-way-to-solve-poverty-in-middle-east/fcli

Schlumberger, O. (2004). *Patrimonial capitalism: Economic reform and economic order in the Arab World* (PhD thesis). University of Tübingen, Tübingen.
Schroeder, C. (2013). *Startup rising: The entrepreneurial revolution remaking the Middle East.* Basingstoke: Palgrave Macmillan.
Schwab Foundation. (2008). *Activity report 2006-2008.* Geneva: Schwab Foundation for Social Entrepreneurship.
Schwab Foundation. (2012). *Outstanding social entrepreneurs 2012.* Geneva: Schwab Foundation for Social Entrepreneurship.
Skoll Foundation. (2009). *Annual report 2009.* Palo Alto: Skoll Foundation.
Sukarieh, M. (2016). On class, culture, and the creation of the neoliberal subject: The case of Jordan. *Anthropological Quarterly*, *89*(4), 1201–1225.
Synergos. (2009). *Arab world social innovators program: Class of 2009.* New York: Synergos.
Synergos. (2011). *2011 report of activities.* New York: Synergos.
Synergos. (2013). *2013 report of activities.* New York: Synergos.
Synergos. (2014). *The Synergos approach to social problems.* New York: Synergos.
Tansel, C. B. (2017). Authoritarian neoliberalism: Towards a new research agenda. In C. B. Tansel (Ed.), *States of discipline: Authoritarian neoliberalism and the contested reproduction of capitalist order* (pp. 1–28). London: Rowman & Littlefield International.
Tansel, C. B. (2018). Reproducing authoritarian neoliberalism in Turkey: Urban governance and state restructuring in the shadow of executive centralization. *Globalizations.* doi:10.1080/14747731.2018.1502494
Valbjorn, M. (2014). Three ways of revisiting the (post-) democratization debate after the Arab Uprisings. *Mediterranean Politics*, *19*(1), 157–160.
Valbjorn, M., & Bank, A. (2010). Examining the 'post' in post-democratization: The future of Middle Eastern political rule through lenses of the past. *Middle East Critique*, *19*(3), 183–200.
Vermeren, P. (2011). *Le Maroc de Mohammed VI: La Transition Inachevée.* Paris: La Découverte.
Waterbury, J. (1970). *The commander of the faithful: The Moroccan political elite. A study in segmented politics.* New York: Columbia University Press.
Wils, O. (2003). *Wirtschaftseliten und Reform in Jordanien. Zur Relevanz von Unternehmer-Bürokraten-Netzwerken in Entwicklungsprozessen.* Hamburg: Deutsches Orient-Institut.
Wong, S. H.-W. (2012). Authoritarian co-optation in the age of globalisation: Evidence from Hong Kong. *Journal of Contemporary Asia*, *42*(2), 182–209.

6 Authoritarian neoliberal rescaling in Latin America: urban in/security and austerity in Oaxaca

Alke Jenss

ABSTRACT

There is an increasing consensus that, across the globe, austerity policies have often relegated fiscal pressures from the state to the urban scale. These are sometimes discussed under the label 'austerity urbanism'. This article explores urban authoritarian neoliberalism through an examination of spatial and scalar manifestations of neoliberal restructuring. It asks how austerity urbanism's rescaling takes effect in spatially variegated ways in the intermediate city of Oaxaca in Southern Mexico. I argue that Oaxaca's austerity programmes and its rescaling of security provision are two intertwined, rather than parallel, processes. The paper builds on and aims to advance the authoritarian neoliberalism literature by linking it to literatures on the postcolonial Latin American state and urban studies. The article makes two contributions: first, it identifies and carves out multi-scalar aspects of authoritarian neoliberalism (by speaking to the urban realm); second, it contributes to the authoritarian neoliberalism literature on the 'South'. Hence, the aim is to reveal the multi-scalar aspects of authoritarian neoliberalism and to illustrate its explanatory power in the global South.

Setting the scene

Federal Police came to the rescue of Municipal and State Police on 7 September 2017. In Oaxaca, an intermediate city of 500,000 in Southern Mexico, the teachers union's local branch had blocked roads with makeshift barricades, set buses on fire and shown their disgust at President Pena Nieto's visit (Matías, 2017). In their eyes, the Convention Centre he inaugurated that day could only bring more investors, and thus, conflict, to Oaxaca. The government of Oaxaca state in turn declared the Centre necessary to make Oaxaca competitive in the global economy (El Universal, 2017a). The involvement of Federal Police in urban security in moments of political crisis, and the pressure on Oaxaca to become a 'competitive city', are not coincidental. There is a consensus that austerity policies, which relegate fiscal pressures from the state to the urban scale and are sometimes discussed under the label 'austerity urbanism' (Peck, 2015), are increasingly backed by coercive state measures. This article asks how austerity urbanism's rescaling takes effect in spatially variegated ways, in the intermediate city of Oaxaca. How do contradictions in these rescaling processes create authoritarian responses on the one hand, and opportunities for contestation on the other? I argue that neoliberal policies, and specifically, austerity programmes and the rescaling of security provision in Oaxaca are two intertwined, rather than parallel, processes. The paper builds on and expands the conceptual reach of the authoritarian neoliberalism (AN) literature, bringing it into dialogue with a case from the global South. I reveal the multi-scalar aspects of AN (by speaking to the urban realm), and link AN to existing literature on the postcolonial Latin American state.

Oaxaca is an emblematic Latin American case for several reasons. First, while megacities are studied in their own right (as category and unit of analysis), research often by-passes mid-sized cities such as Oaxaca. This is surprising, because institutions such as UN Habitat III (2015, p. 4) suggest that these 'emerging cities' are the hubs of contemporary planetary urbanization. More than half of the world's urban population now lives in intermediate cities (UN Habitat III, 2015, p. 5). Second, Oaxaca's local austerity plans are discursively and materially linked to disciplining dissenters. Central claims in the AN literature, such as the legal fixing of fiscal policies out of reach of political contestation (Oberndorfer, 2015), are found in its competitive cities programme and budget plans. Third, choosing Oaxaca as a case is based on demands by a 'post-colonial field of urban studies' (see the seminal work by Robinson, 2005), to give 'greater profile to lesser-known cities' (Parnell & Oldfield, 2014, p. 2). Fourth, authoritarian elements of government are by no means new to Oaxaca's already deeply unequal social relations. Yet, it has been the site of emerging, particularly authoritarian and violent government mechanisms since 2006. These actually prefigure some of the disciplinary constellations which in Europe only became more visible in the crisis years after 2008. Oaxaca's history of political struggle, coercion and spaces of resistance (Hesketh, 2017) make it an excellent example of wider processes of enclosure across Latin America.

The article's first section briefly links AN to debates on the local and Latin American state. Next, I discuss continuities and changes over time in Oaxaca as a history of struggles. This enables us to better understand the third and fourth sections, which discuss the scalar restructuring implicit in recent austerity and competitiveness programmes and the attempts to fix and secure these. The fifth section focuses on the spatial effects of austerity within Oaxaca's urban authoritarian neoliberalism, and the ensuing production of spatially variegated (in)security. The conclusion ties the empirical discussions back to the main argument.

Authoritarian neoliberalism in postcolonial Latin American states

On a conceptual level, the article explores scalar and spatial aspects of urban AN, based on an understanding of austerity[1] and security rescaling as intertwined processes. It makes two contributions: first, it identifies and carves out multi-scalar aspects of AN (by speaking to the urban realm); second, it links AN to existing literatures on the postcolonial Latin American state.

Taking AN to the urban is based on a puzzle. There is a wealth of valuable studies on urban disciplining and policing, often combining concerns for public space and democratic governance in the urban 'punitive turn' (Müller, 2016). They focus on surveillance (Graham, 2011), the grounding of violence in urban planning (Davis, 2016b) or on the production of patterns of safe and unsafe spaces (Amar, 2013; Rosales, Garay Reyna, & Pedrazzani, 2016), navigated according to markers of class, race and gender (i.e. Guimarães, 2017; Moncada, 2009; Monroe, 2016; Vásquez Duplat, 2016). Another body of scholarship emphasizes how urban (re)development projects and/or zero tolerance policies of street space are imbued with racialized discourses (Mele, 2017; Picker, Murji, & Boatcă, 2018; Swanson, 2007).

The state at this local level often seems to retreat, as if the city did not relate to other scales (yet, see Boudreau, 2016; Müller, 2016; Tulumello, 2017). This is why the AN literature's focus on the state 'as the key organizational structure through which the authoritarian enshrinement of neoliberal accumulation regimes is facilitated' (Tansel, 2017, p. 4) is central to this article, which is interested in the *constitutive* role of the local state. AN enables us to see how the state, based on a 'historically specific set of capitalist accumulation strategies that both exacerbates the existing, structural trends in the political organization of capitalism and embodies distinct practices geared towards unshackling accumulation at the expense of democratic politics and popular participation' (ibid., p. 5), devises a spectrum of disciplinary strategies for the city, based on relations of forces converging in the urban. Various institutional levels with varying scalar reach participate in these. Individuals and collectives are subjected to increasingly pre-emptive economic, financial and corporeal discipline 'in the name of necessity' (Bruff, 2014, p. 123; see Poulantzas, 2002; Jenss, 2016). Yet, research which explicitly links municipal fiscal restraints experienced in the global North and South to contested notions of security and authoritarian developments, is still scarce.

Taking AN to the urban means exploring the reconceptualization of the state 'as increasingly non-democratic through its subordination to constitutional and legal rules that are deemed necessary' (Bruff, 2014, p. 116) via its local expressions. This does not oppose local to global, but implies multi-scalar processes: urban austerity in Latin America is thus linked to 'intelligent austerity' programmes in vogue on a continent-wide scale. Their reasoning is the perceived necessity to confront the structural reduction of growth in the region at the 'end of the super cycle of raw commodities' – 'intelligent' meaning that they theoretically avoid excessive cuts that would affect growth and thus taxes (i.e. they are selective) (ECLAC, 2016, pp. 5, 24).

Hence, the article contributes to the AN literature on the 'South' (see also Harrison, 2018; Kreitmeyr, 2018; Tansel, 2018) and explicitly links it to literature on the Latin American state. This implies some conceptual adaptation. The notion of coloniality of power (Quijano, 2000) is helpful here. What does coloniality of power in the local state imply for AN? First and foremost, the relations of social forces stressed by Poulantzas (2002) as the basis for understanding the state, are not only shaped by class. Racial and gendered hierarchies, articulated in different ways in time and space, also shape the local state, and their intersections form an urban coloniality of power (see also Laó-Montes & Dávila, 2012). Second, city histories such as Oaxaca's 'prefigure' those of the 'North', as the selectivity of social services and authoritarian elements have long been normalized (even in post-revolutionary Mexico: see Morton, 2018), and the coloniality of global power relations partly explains this. Latin American states and cities 'simply have not previously enjoyed much of the public provision of elements of life portrayed' in stories of European deregulation (Mabin, 2014, p. 30). Third, the historical condition of postcoloniality is in conjunction with a particular form of integration into the global economy that is often based on the export orientation of raw materials and capital dependency (see, for a new discussion of dependency approaches, Pimmer & Schmidt, 2015). Oaxaca does not attract the kind of capital New York does, to put it bluntly. Fourth, informality may well be the norm in economic and political organization (Helmke & Levitsky, 2006). Decolonial perspectives on urban informality question the binary view on formality and (criminalized) informality, *inter alia* to unsettle the assumption that the formal economic sector serves as the only base for the reproduction of statehood by tax revenue (Goldstein, 2016; Varley, 2013). The ambiguity of informality is not a preserve of the 'South' (Parnell & Oldfield, 2014, p. 2); this is another reminder that austerity measures do not imply less regulation, but qualitative differences in state practices (see also Peck, 2015).

My argument is based on three data packages. A small number of qualitative interviews were conducted during a pilot trip in 2017 for a project on security production in the urban (cited as 'IV0#'). Social and economic indicators by official agencies (Coneval, Inegi, IMCO) provide context. Additional document analysis is based on local media and legally binding documents from different scales of political negotiation that converge in shaping neoliberal policies in Oaxaca (the National

Urban Development Programme, the State Development Plan 2011–2016, and the Oaxaca Municipal Development Plans 2014–2016, 2017–2018).

A history of struggles

This section provides a brief history of local struggles through the lens of (local) state theory, which enables us to account for the historical dynamics of social relations, urban socio-economic structures and multi-scalar influences in Oaxaca. Postcolonial Oaxaca has continuously exposed the coloniality of power relations (Quijano, 2000), particularly in the limited possibilities of political participation in urban politics (1), in the city's economic base in surrounding mining and agricultural sectors (2), in its organization of coercion (3), and in the city's spatial layout (4).

(1) Political participation is necessarily selective in the heterogeneous postcolonial society, and the state's relation to local forms of political organization has been contradictory. These local forms, often self-identified as indigenous, are not *per se* non-authoritarian, yet they implied an active political subjectivity for lower-class and indigenous communities. Imbued with racialized attributions, city and state officials continuously presented these *usos y costumbres* as rural, outside the urban (Overmyer-Velázquez, 2007, p. 68). (2) Despite persisting communal land holdings in the surrounding mountains (on the survival of non-capitalist formations, see Hesketh, 2016), the owners of cocoa and coffee plantations and mining investors (many were European immigrants) shaped the state's urban expression. These small dominant fractions in Oaxaca, often mocked as *vallistocracia*,[2] strived to control dissenters, even when, during the radical socio-economic changes at the start of the twentieth century, they attempted to reshape the urban as 'modern'. (3) Coloniality is tangible in Oaxaca's history of political violence, even though peasant rebels and disenchanted lower middle classes repeatedly contested authoritarian mechanisms of rule. Police-like, but rather autonomous *jefaturas políticas* complemented the state's military, particularly during the 1877–1915 Porfirian dictatorship.[3] (4) The city's spatial stratification is clearly based on power relations co-defined by coloniality: dominant fractions that combined political and economic power owned the city centre. Historically, colonial/modernist urban policies spatially segregated great parts of Oaxacan society from the formal city (this was a general trend in Latin America: see Davis, 2016b, p. 5).

Yet, in contrast to depictions of Oaxaca as 'traditional', 'unmodern' or 'isolated', Oaxaca city was and is powerfully shaped by the global scale of investment requirements, migration and tourism (Overmyer-Velázquez, 2007, p. 68). The global urban system integrated 'metropolitan and peripheral cities in the same scheme of uneven development' (see King 1990 cited in Laó-Montes & Dávila, 2012, p. 121). Through the turn-of-century Porfirian capitalist restructuring, Oaxaca's *vallistocracia* aimed to open Southern states up as a market and inject capitalist 'modernity' via infrastructure investments. The Mexican Southern Railway from 1892, connecting mining operations and later, passengers, to the international market, again links the local and global scales of Oaxaca's social relations and political economy. British firms invested, the Porfirian state planned, and Oaxacan upper middle classes embraced it as a symbol of modernity. New tobacco, coffee and rubber plantations, established after this infrastructural impulse, simultaneously pushed Oaxaca as a commercial hub and pressured peasants towards the city as workers (Romero Frizzi et al., 2016).

Both municipal and Oaxaca state institutional levels are located in the city. This convergence explains why local struggles continuously succeeded in expanding their scalar reach beyond local power relations and to institutional scales beyond the municipality. The involvement of Oaxaca state governments in urban disciplining acquired specific meaning in post-revolutionary Mexico: from the 1920s onwards, the state party PRI emerged as the institutional expression of a dynamic arrangement between forces prioritizing the internal market and broad social integration and forces geared towards global capital. In 1940, only 50,000 people inhabited the state capital Oaxaca, and its economy was still based on agriculture and mining. In a 'complex system of controlled integration, co-optation and repression' (Durazno Herrmann, 2011, p. 162; Morton, 2018), social organizations depended on ambiguous, informal arrangements with the PRI's regional expressions.

Growing discontent resulted in a limited guerrilla presence at the end of the 1970s, but federal and state institutions repressed these attempts at producing counter-spaces (Hesketh, 2017). Oaxaca was a node of this authoritarian scalar relationship (Bautista Martínez, 2010) through the twentieth century to the 1980s, when Mexico's debt crisis put the country at the vanguard of neoliberal restructuring. The crisis and subsequent restructuring finally shattered the PRI's promise of social mobility; social services became even more selective. Moreover, the closure of a number of federal state agencies strengthened the local state scale. The new Consejo Estatal del Café de Oaxaca, for example, rapidly became the one agency providing loans and market access to the region's primary export product: coffee. A new fiscal federalism allowed the expansion of Oaxacan state agencies external to the PRI's social base (Durazno Herrmann, 2011, p. 166f.). Oaxaca's own tax base, particularly property tax returns, remained low, so this structural phenomenon is not new (as it is for Peck, 2015). Despite general hints towards democratization, and Oaxaca state's formal recognition of *usos y costumbres* in 1995 – communal political mandates could now be selected according to customary practices rather than through parties – this appeared as strategically contentious measures seeking to prevent the Zapatista rebellion in neighbouring Chiapas from spilling over (Durazno Herrmann, 2011, p. 168).

In 2006, contradictions emerged between the hope for a more thorough democratic transformation and the achievements of local self-organization on the one hand, and neoliberal policies on the other hand, in the form of widespread social protests against the state's emerging efforts to privatize the Mexican educational system. The dissident local branch *sección 22* of the teachers' union, which historically enjoyed relative access to the PRI state, had opted for a more autonomous union stance in 1980. Their yearly demonstrations became a somewhat symbolic ritual surrounding wage renegotiations (Bautista Martínez, 2010; Durazno Herrmann, 2011, p. 171). In 2006, however, PRI governor Ulises Ruiz (whose government was already characterized by decidedly rigid, authoritarian mechanisms), exacerbated existing tensions by violently dispersing the march. Students and the APPO, an urban agglomeration of oppositional organizations and spontaneous participants, then converted the city centre into a 'space of resistance' between June and October; the government fled (Bautista Martínez, 2010, pp. 227–268; Hesketh, 2017; Magaña, 2016). Those fearing a radical change of government at the central Mexican state level shared interests with dominant Oaxacan fractions keen to maintain the social and political status quo (i.e. expressed in the governors association's press releases, Bautista Martínez, 2010, p. 250). This convergence of interests facilitated a highly authoritarian response which violently displaced the teachers' union and APPO from the city centre by the end of October 2006. Internal fragmentation, the *sección 22*'s own negotiations and the APPO's subsequent radicalization, all facilitated to reproduce 'spaces of capital' in former spaces of resistance (Hesketh, 2017).

The Federal Police crackdown on APPO had several effects for Oaxacan social relations. Most notably, authoritarian mechanisms emerged more clearly. Apart from federal transfers and a legitimizing decentralization discourse, Oaxaca's dominant fractions renewed their privileged position within the growing social polarization, by consolidating an authoritarian regime with a renovated extralegal dimension of counterinsurgency, intimidation and political violence (Bautista Martínez, 2010, p. 268). Special Federal Police forces trained by Guatemalan *kaibiles*, introduced the drug network ZETAs (which allegedly emerged from such Special Forces) and thus a transnational scale of illegal trade to the city (see IV07, IV02; Tello, 2016, p. 119). Consequently, instead of real alternatives, 'alternations of different neoliberal governments' now seemed to be 'the only choice … on offer' (Bruff, 2016, p. 113), in Oaxaca and in Mexico generally. After a period of right-wing PAN and Convergencia governments, the PRI won Oaxaca's municipal elections again. Demand for democratic change did not resonate in Oaxaca state's institutional ensemble until 2010, when a peculiar alliance between the right-wing PAN and the centre-left PRD took office. What these superficially differing governments had in common was that they continuously combined a range of authoritarian mechanisms such as direct coercion, the selective distribution of state funds, and personal ties within small dominant fractions that held economic and political power.

This section posited local contestation, and particularly the 2006 rebellion, as a point of departure for understanding today's urban AN in Oaxaca. The following sections explore the twin tendencies of rescaling and spatial restructuring that neoliberal policies have entailed, which have generated contradictions and also new possibilities for mobilization.

A competitive city? rebranding, rescaling, and fixing austerity

Oaxaca is one of four cities that the Mexican Economic Secretary included in its federal Competitive Cities programme in 2016 (Gobierno Federal de México, 2016). Various scales of policy-making recently converged in securing an entrepreneurial approach to urban governance in Oaxaca, under the same label of competitiveness. State agencies such as the Mexican Institute for Competitiveness (IMCO, 2016) ranked Oaxaca 53rd of 74 cities in their 'Competitive and Sustainable Cities Index 2016', demanding improvements in 'economic innovation', while the city achieved higher scores for a 'stable and functional political system' (Silva, 2015). The Secretary for Agricultural, Territorial and Urban Development (SEDATU, 2014) aims for 'compact, competitive cities' in its National Urban Development Programme. World Bank (Licciardi & Amirtahmasebi, 2012) and Interamerican Development Bank (Quartesan & Romis, 2010) documents argue Oaxaca should leverage its 1980s World Heritage City declaration to be more competitive.

The Competitive Cities programme aims to 'provide a better environment for business' by attacking 'specific problems that … hinder growth' in 'regulation, economic competition, facilitating commerce, and logistics' (Gobierno Federal de México, 2016). The discourse is one of 'privileged public private partnerships', and tries to appeal to academics by appointing universities as local coordinators (not municipal governments) (Gobierno Federal de México, 2016). This all comes in a context of debt, inequality and proclaimed austerity. Competitive Oaxaca can actually be seen as an *effect* of federal pressures on cities to attract foreign and/or private investment, to facilitate the central state's fiscal balance. The Oaxacan economy has been in recession, with a 5% negative growth rate in 2016 (México ¿cómo vamos?, 2017). In 2017, the *state* government declared a strict austerity plan that included the freezing of public officers' telecommunications costs (NVI, 2017b). To 'ensure fiscal sufficiency', the *municipality* stuck to 'maintaining current costs within control, austerity and discipline parameters' (Municipio de Oaxaca, 2016, pp. 58, 69), an agenda lauded by global ratings agencies (HR Ratings, 2016). Yet, the percentage of the population in Oaxaca (state) with a working wage below the established living minimum rose from 55.9% in 2005 to 64.2% in 2017 (CONEVAL, 2018, p. 35). Income inequality increased from 0.443 (2016) to 0.450 Gini points (2017); up to 70% of workers have neither formal contracts nor health or unemployment insurance through their workplace (México ¿cómo vamos?, 2017). Hence, the 'rollback' of the social state (Peck, 2015) is not the decisive factor in Oaxaca's case: austerity is often configured differently in the global North and South.

Oaxaca state reduced its public debt from a record 10.8 billion pesos in 2015 (half of which was accumulated from 2010 onwards) to 9.2 in 2017 (IMCO, 2017). Rescaling this effort to municipalities, the state development plan explicitly aimed to 'strengthen local finances' (Gobierno del Estado, 2011, p. 390). Cities increasingly bear the brunt of what, rather than temporary crisis management strategies, are permanent imbalances and socio-economic asymmetries. Federal investment in Oaxaca city, for example, is at 2.8 million pesos (INEGI, 2017, p. 1600), a fraction of the city's debt payments.[4] In a colonial variation of Peck's (2015) notions of 'deficit politics' and 'devolved risks' handed down to municipal authorities, the federal level increasingly presents poor budgets in historically poorer states and municipalities as caused by incomplete state-building processes and transitions to maturity. For instance, the National Mexican Institute for Competitiveness (IMCO, 2016) argues that 'it is more urgent than ever that municipalities transit from puberty to the adult phase to not depend as much anymore on the federation'. From 2016, the Law of Financial Discipline obliges municipalities to cut costs and eliminate public debt if they are unable to broaden their tax base – a complicated matter dependent on local power relations. This is the distinctly scalar element of neoliberal policies (on this general trend, Sevilla Buitrago, 2016, p. 39f.).

Recognizing its particular integration into the global economy (shaped by global requirements and structural constraints), and understanding neoliberal policies as responses to changes in accumulation regimes, tourism became Oaxaca's competitive 'advantage' – but one which exacerbates existing social contradictions. The number of hotels increased from 173 in 1999 to 240 in 2005 and again to 296 in 2016 (INEGI, 2017, p. 1385; Quartesan & Romis, 2010, p. 25). Wages in the tourism sector are generally about 70% of wages in other services sectors (Quartesan & Romis, 2010, p. 27). New employment created are, in almost half the cases, jobs below the minimum needed to acquire the basic basket of goods (NVI, 2017a).

The 'creative moment' of Oaxaca's tourism competitiveness (Peck, 2015) hinges on an entrepreneurial urbanity, which entails a specific set of accumulation strategies and is facilitated by an austere government (see also Di Giovanni, 2017 on Istanbul). Conflating the municipal and global scale, dominant local class fractions and an emerging community of US and European immigrants converge in promoting crafts and fashion under an 'ethnic' label, integrating indigenous 'authenticity' into the competitive package. These actors created an 'ethnic fashion' cluster and hold crafts and 'traditional cooking' fairs with the explicit aim to 'put Oaxaca on the global tourist map' (Municipio de Oaxaca, 2017). The municipal and state development plans likewise present indigenous crafts, culinary delights of 'traditional cooking', and modern design as Oaxaca's competitive advantages in an ever-renewed effort of city branding (Ayuntamiento Oaxaca, 2014; Municipio de Oaxaca, 2017), following up on the promotion of 'cultural tourism' (Quartesan & Romis, 2010). This folkloric usage of Oaxacan indigeneity points to the constitutive role racial hierarchies play in competitive urbanity (see also Swanson, 2007).

These combined measures of competitiveness and austerity have been promoted in a host of policy documents, impacting on the city's meagre social projects as well as possibilities for contestation. The AN literature calls this the 'constitutionalization of austerity' (Bruff, 2014, p. 117), as state agencies seek to fix austerity measures on various institutional levels and of variegated scale, partly dislodging the local as an arena of contestation (for a discussion of the relative strength of local struggles, see Hesketh, 2016). In Oaxaca, the 2006 conjuncture reconfigured political participation and prefigured the polarizing effects of the next decade. Relocating policies into an undebatable legal realm towards the national scale, 'scalar fixes' oscillate between downscaling of pressures and upscaling of control. Contesting these downward pressures is complicated by federal budget transfers which amount to around 90% of Oaxaca's budget (IMCO, 2017). The state government controls budget transfers and investments; it officially approves the municipalities' revenue planning (Ayuntamiento Oaxaca, 2017b).

The coloniality of power requires us to pay attention to: 1) racialized hierarchies in urban relations of forces – 'the multi-layered processes by which domination and hegemony (racial, class, patriarchal, cultural) are organized and contested across the institutions and throughout the social fabrics of urban space' (Laó-Montes & Dávila, 2012, p. 121); and 2) asymmetries between cities in the global economy, often based on (racialized) discourses of productivity, competitiveness, attractiveness, and the supposed lack of these qualities in the global South. The coloniality of power element in this rescaling is that Oaxaca's dominant forces secured their social position through urban redevelopment for the globally mobile, imbued with discourses of cleanliness and modernity versus local backward-, messi- and unproductiveness (NVI, 2017c; see also Swanson, 2007, p. 709). In fact, Oaxaca's 'low productivity' and high number of strikes lower its score on the Mexican state's Urban Competitiveness Index (IMCO, 2016).

The federal scale institutionalizes competition between subnational spaces in the context of economic globalization by controlling transfers, by imposing fiscal discipline, and by presenting competitiveness or Oaxaca's World Heritage Cities status as prime investment opportunities (IMCO, 2016, 2017; Municipio de Oaxaca, 2017) – in sum, via sets of new spatial strategies (Brenner, 2004) which resonate with local strategies of accumulation by emerging local real estate investors and neighbourhood renewal entrepreneurs. The local state invests in, regulates and opens these spaces – for example, it supports urban entrepreneurs by not enforcing the payment of property tax.

In the above section, I described the competitive cities rationale as an integral part of austerity in Oaxaca; various scales converge in its implementation and fixing. I now turn to the rescaling of security provision in particular, for the 'security' of the rebranded city is an integral part of the competitive rationale embedded in urban planning (see Cowen & Bunce, 2006, p. 430).

Securing austerity, rescaling discipline

Rather than simply making Oaxaca more secure for tourists as part of the competitive cities programme, security policies in times of austerity have been geared towards disciplining dissenters as well. Great efforts in the competitive city are geared towards the local protection of global property and investment, as more and more investors come from outside the city (NVI, 2017d; SILMéxico, 2017). For example, car theft has greatly diminished since 2012 (IMCO, 2016). A great number of prison inmates in Mexico are awaiting trial because of theft or robbery, often without a sentence (UNDP, 2013), so much that many authors position Mexico within a global tendency of punitive urbanism (Müller, 2016).[5] Austerity and policing discipline those that deviate from or dissent with urban renewal policies. Protestors against the privatization of education, for instance, who have regularly camped out in the *zócalo* (main square) since 2006, are perceived to hinder access to the historic centre (Quartesan & Romis, 2010, p. 20), and thus to the city's value-generating sections. Policing of protestors and informal vendors alike speaks of the anchorage of real estate investors, hotel owners and the tourist sector in general in the local state's institutional terrain.

Austerity has affected the pay, equipment and presence of the municipal police (IV02, IV07). Oaxaca *state's* public security budget has fluctuated greatly (NVI, 2017f). This is in dramatic contrast to overall considerable rises in the federal state budget for the military and Marines and thus their presence on the streets (Jenss, 2016). Even though Oaxaca's *municipal* budget for 'public security' grew considerably from 181 to 233.6 million pesos from fiscal year 2016 to 2017 alone (in line with the AN literature) (Municipio de Oaxaca, 2016), there is frequent discontent among the police about delays in payment, lack of equipment and low salaries, and the lack of adequate security subsidies from the federation (SUBSEMUN). Municipal *and* state police frequently go on strike (Diálogos Oaxaca, 2016; Pérez, 2015).

Austerity urbanism in Oaxaca has thus caused rivalries to emerge between local municipal police and federal police as part of a heterogeneous state ensemble. Disciplining dissenters seems more easily done through the Federal Police. The latter largely lack local connections and are sent to the city in moments of political crisis, i.e. in 2006, 2011, and 2015. They also appeared in 2017, when President Pena Nieto inaugurated the Convention Centre mentioned in the introduction, to counter protestors burning vehicles and launching handmade missiles against government helicopters. The state government invested 250 million pesos in 2017 alone in the Convention Centre, as part of the strategy to make Oaxaca 'globally competitive' (El Universal, 2017a; Matías, 2017).

Yet, the up- and downscaling of neoliberal policies also creates opportunities for contestation. Some spaces of contestation have (re)opened, underscoring the 'fragility of the "authoritarian fix"' (Bruff, 2016, p. 113). While the 2017 Law for Inner Security additionally facilitates the deployment of military forces to municipalities like Oaxaca and is an example of rescaled practices of coercion and their expression in the national legal realm, it has also served to reopen the urban debate on security, disciplining and protest, and their relation to the central state (IV06, IV07, IV03). For example, femicide has become more recognized as a problem in the city (IV07). Moreover, the fact that the competitive cities image in Oaxaca has been geared so much towards the folkloric integration of indigenous communities has created opportunities for contestation and the emergence of alternative communal development projects (for similar rural projects, see Hesketh, 2016). Some communities sell their own ecological products to tourists in the city, exposing and highlighting the contradictions between this folklore and the actual situation of poverty.

This section specifies the main argument: austerity programmes in Oaxaca have intertwined with the rescaling of security provision. These processes have had spatial effects, which are explored in the next section.

Spatial manifestations of austerity and discipline

Even if crime has been limited in Oaxaca compared to Northern Mexico, the increase in crime – homicides have risen by 33% since 2014 (NVI, 2017f) – in combination with a badly funded, low-salaried municipal police, makes Oaxaca a fragmented continuum of insecure spaces, which some people navigate more easily than others. One expression of this continuum are particular sites where the mostly middle-class owners of neighbouring shops and businesses have put up banners with lynch warnings against thieves ('against crime: *ratero*, if we catch you, we will lynch you. Tourist, if you feel in danger, shout out'). These *juntas vecinales* (neighbourhood associations) can be considered a particularly ambiguous form of the privatization of in/security, linked to austerity (NVI, 2017e; Zavala, 2017). They all refer to the lack of police action and the rise of robberies (IVs) (NVI, 2017f). How potential thieves are identified is unclear: this clearly stratifies security and potentially reinforces the spatial element of the coloniality of power. Competitiveness and austerity combined have resulted in some relatively safe areas where people move on foot undisturbed even at night (IV 01), while the relation with inhabitants from urban peripheries (perceived as indigenous) is uneasy.

Rebranding efforts to make Oaxaca a more competitive tourist destination have concentrated on the city's historic centre, in stark contrast to the so-called *colonias* on the city's fringes – a selectivity that underlines the coloniality of competitive austerity. The results of this are two-fold. In the urban periphery, state omission has facilitated the institutional communal condensation of 'indigenous' power relations, including rotation in non-remunerated public mandates (policing, particularly) (IV07). In other *barrios*, authoritarian forms of local political organizations, loosely connected to or ignored by the state, link to the fragmented continuum of in/security. While peripheries often appear in 'need to be made secure', in Oaxaca, these peripheral spaces often either lack police presence or are the scene of state-crime collusion. Various interviewees confirm the interpretation that some state agencies were involved in creating *grupos de choque* organized through former PRI corporatist organizations (CTM), that act against dissenters, e.g. at the Convention Centre's inauguration in 2017 (Interviews 02, 06, 07).

More generally, urban fiscal discipline is intertwined with spatialized processes of enclosure (cf. Sevilla Buitrago, 2015) that are facilitated by the state ensemble. The combined effect of austerity, the relegation of Oaxaca's social housing to the 'peripheries' (Davis, 2016a, p. 160), and the sharp rise in property prices strengthens the spatial element of the urban coloniality of power. Linked to and resulting from the competitive cities rationale, real estate prices are rising in Oaxaca's historic centre, as global capital is attracted towards this specific locale (including companies such as Airbnb). According to the World Bank and IADB, these prices doubled between 2000 and 2010 (from US$600 to US$1,200 per square metre unrenovated property) (Licciardi & Amirtahmasebi, 2012, p. 125), and rose 15% in 2016 alone and 65% between 2011 and 2017, making Oaxaca one of the most expensive places in Mexico, according to media and investors alike (NVI, 2017d; SIL-México, 2017). The disappearance of *vecindades* – buildings for several families with shared sanitary facilities, kitchens and a communal use *patio* – from the centre due to revalued property, has 'whitened' the city centre, assimilating it to colonial times. The 'peripheries', still less attractive in 2010 (even the well-off neighbourhood of La Reforma sold at US$430 per square metre) (Quartesan & Romis, 2010), are increasingly seen as a valuable commodity, i.e. by the current municipal development plan (aiming its planning at 'ordering' chaos in informal settlements). Rising prices in the formerly lower-class quarters around the new Convention Centre underline this (Ayuntamiento Oaxaca, 2014, IV01).

The site where this spatial disparity can be experienced most clearly is the *zócalo*, or main plaza. The *zócalo* now serves as a spatial boundary between the northern tourist centre of the city and a southern centre which has been described by interviewees as less organized, dirtier and poorer (IV 01, 05). The municipal police has been clearing spaces occupied by temporary vendors; it does not consider them part of the urban tourist sector. Their displacement towards the south of the centre has been crucial to Oaxaca's urban transformation. At the time of my research, frequent municipal police operations even within the southern part of the centre aimed to prevent informal vendors from resettling in streets they had recently been displaced from, forcing them towards the southern periphery of the city. In the northern centre, in 2014 snacks could be purchased from women vendors; by 2017, these had largely disappeared towards the southern part of centre. When informality is rigidly opposed to formality, the contradiction between informal labour and austerity seems logical, as urban informality does not add to the municipal budget via tax revenues. Yet, numerous authors (see, for example, Goldstein, 2016; Graaff & Ha, 2015) have exposed the regulated, coerced, if ambiguous relation between the local state and informality. While informal workers are often perceived as a problem (see Amar, 2013 on Cairo), simultaneously and continuously, the 'formal' city has depended on these elements of the urban via payable licenses. In Oaxaca, their payments are clearly regulated (Ayuntamiento Oaxaca, 2016) yet also dependent upon unequal power relations, e.g. their adherence to certain political groups apparently exempts some of them from inspections (NVI, 2017c).

Both the coloniality of power and the contestation of AN are visible in struggles over the *zócalo* itself. The state's specific making of space is shaped both by capitalism and coloniality, which produces hierarchies and homogeneity (see Morton, 2018). The site of power since colonialism, and the centre of month-long assemblies and protest particularly in 2006, the *zócalo* is central to an alternative continuum of 'spaces of resistance' (Hesketh, 2017; Magaña, 2016) to be navigated by dissenters. It is still an area of negotiation, political activism, and local trade. Municipal and state police displacing mostly indigenous vendors in joint operations (El Universal, 2017b) are reminiscent of regulation efforts to realize an ideal of white colonial/modern settlement (Goldstein, 2016) around the *zócalo*, in exchange for allowing urban growth and spatial disorder on the periphery. Following Goldstein (2016, p. 116ff; see also Morton, 2018), street vending 'disorder' around the *zócalo* in Oaxaca defies the urban forms of neoliberal, (post-)colonial order. Vendors and protestors alike tangibly defy displacements; they keep reappearing (El Universal, 2017b; NVI, 2017c). These tensions, above all, show that the *zócalo* has become a spatial arbiter of that which the state empowers, namely the competitive city (embodied by the beautifully painted houses and pedestrian walkways of the northern centre), and also what the state contains, namely social forces seeking to transcend the positions assigned to them (the southern centre, where vendors pushing their stands out into the streets, cars, motorcycles and pedestrians, struggle for every centimetre of the road) (cf. Lefebvre, 2003).

Conclusion: authoritarian neoliberalism in the urban global South

This article asked how rescaling processes implicit in neoliberal policies have been taking effect in spatially variegated ways in the intermediate city of Oaxaca in Southern Mexico. The core argument was that neoliberal policies, and more specifically, austerity programmes in Oaxaca and the rescaling of security provision are intertwined, rather than parallel, processes. I argued that the austerity programmes, which constitute a downscaling of fiscal discipline and institutionalize competition between subnational spaces, also rescaled security provision. To facilitate Oaxaca's entrepreneurial, competitive urbanity as a specific set of accumulation strategies, the upscaling of coercion relies on the Federal Police supporting municipal and state police affected by austerity. Oaxaca's austerity urbanism has caused rivalries to emerge between security agencies within the heterogeneous state ensemble; it has also created openings for contestation while simultaneously seeking to close them down – this see-saw effect sometimes taking place in the same space, such as the *zócalo*.

The article contributes in two ways to the AN literature. Firstly, it highlighted the multi-scalar character of state power in the urban 'rush towards balanced budgets' (Bruff, 2016, p. 112) and subsequent disciplining. I showed that Latin American urban fiscal discipline is intertwined with processes of spatial enclosure. Spatially, 'austerity urbanism' makes Oaxaca a fragmented continuum of insecure spaces. Revalued property, neighbourhood squads and displaced informal vendors may all constitute such spatial effects. Yet, the up- and downscaling of neoliberal policies also provide opportunities for contestation. Contestations of rescaled security have revived Oaxaca's urban debate on disciplining, protest, and its relation to the federal state.

The article secondly aimed to adapt AN to literatures on the postcolonial Latin American state. The notion of the coloniality of urban power relations differentiates our understanding of whose interests resonate with state policies. The selectivity of rebranding and competitiveness efforts concentrated on the city centre underlines the coloniality of competitive austerity. Municipal and state austerity, relegating Oaxaca's social housing to the 'peripheries', and rising property prices strengthen the spatial element of the urban coloniality of power. Both the coloniality of power and the contestation of authoritarian neoliberalism are visible in struggles over the main plaza, the *zócalo*. Both capitalism and coloniality shape the state's space-making practices, producing spatial hierarchies. The *zócalo*, simultaneously a site of power and contestation, has become a spatial arbiter of that which the state seeks to empower, namely the competitive city, and that which the state tries to contain, namely social groups attempting to transcend the social position assigned to them.

Notes

1. For an overview of the debate on austerity (definitions, effects and underlying power relations) mainly in Europe, see Sturm, Griebel, and Winkelmann (2017).
2. Made up of the Spanish words 'aristocratic' and (central Oaxaca) 'valley'.
3. As Porfirio Díaz's hometown, Oaxaca, more intimately than other Mexican cities, embodies the link between urban and state scales.
4. Oaxaca receives additional federal funds via the Mexican World Heritage Cities Programme (Ayuntamiento Oaxaca, 2017a, p. 95).
5. This tendency, however, appears less clear-cut now. The prison population has dropped to a rate below that of 2004, due to limits to pre-trial detention. Pre-trial detention dropped from a record 81 in 2010 to 64/100,000 inhabitants in 2017, and down to 38% of the prison population (World Prison Brief, 2017).

Acknowledgements

I would like to thank Ian Bruff and Cemal Burak Tansel for facilitating my participation in this special issue, as well as two anonymous reviewers for their helpful comments. I am also very grateful for comments Ian Bruff and Robert Gather provided on earlier versions of this paper.

Disclosure statement

No potential conflict of interest was reported by the author.

ORCID

Alke Jenss http://orcid.org/0000-0002-5751-7946

References

Amar, P. (2013). *Security archipelago: Human-security states, sexuality politics, and the end of neoliberalism*. London: Duke University Press.

Ayuntamiento Oaxaca. (2014). *Oaxaca plan municipal 2014–2018*. Oaxaca: Ayuntamiento.

Ayuntamiento Oaxaca. (2016). *Reglamento para el Control de Actividades Comerciales y de Servicios en Via Pública del Municipio de Oaxaca de Juárez*. Oaxaca: Ayuntamiento. Retrieved from http://www.ordenjuridico.gob.mx/Estatal/OAXACA/Municipios/Oaxaca/OAJReg32.pdf

Ayuntamiento Oaxaca. (2017a). *Informe municipal 2017*. Oaxaca: Ayuntamiento.

Ayuntamiento Oaxaca. (2017b). *Ley de Ingresos*. Oaxaca: Ayuntamiento. Retrieved from http://municipiodeoaxaca.gob.mx/uploads/archivos/reglamentos/LEY-DE-INGRESOS-OAXACA-2017.pdf

Bautista Martínez, E. (2010). *Los nudos del régimen autoritario. Ajustes y continuidades de la dominación en dos ciudades de Oaxaca*. Oaxaca: Pórrua.

Boudreau, J.-A. (2016). *Global urban politics: Informalization of the state*. Malden, MA: Polity.

Brenner, N. (2004). *New state spaces: Urban governance and the rescaling of statehood*. Oxford: Oxford University Press.

Bruff, I. (2014). The rise of authoritarian neoliberalism. *Rethinking Marxism*, *26*(1), 113–129.

Bruff, I. (2016). Neoliberalism and authoritarianism. In S. Springer, K. Birch, & J. MacLeavy (Eds.), *The handbook of neoliberalism* (pp. 107–117). New York: Routledge.

CONEVAL. (2018). *Índice de la Tendencia Laboral. Porcentaje de Población con ingreso laboral inferior al valor de la canasta alimentaria*. Oaxaca. Retrieved from https://www.coneval.org.mx/Medicion/Documents/ITLP-IS/2017/3t2017/ITLP_Nacional_y_estatal_noviembre_2017.pdf

Cowen, D., & Bunce, S. (2006). Competitive cities and secure nations: Conflict and convergence in urban waterfront agendas after 9/11. *International Journal of Urban and Regional Research*, *20*(2), 427–439.

Davis, D. (2016a). *Housing and habitus: Craft, politics and the production of housing in Oaxaca, México*. Harvard: Harvard Graduate School of Design.

Davis, D. (2016b). The production of space and violence in cities of the global South: Evidence from Latin America. *Nóesis. Revista de Ciencias Sociales y Humanidades*, *25*(1), 1–15.

Diálogos Oaxaca. (2016, September 29). Para labores policía municipal de Oaxaca de Juárez; exigen pago de bono. Retrieved from http://dialogosoaxaca.com/para-labores-policia-municipal-de-oaxaca-de-juarez-exigen-pago-de-bono/

Di Giovanni, A. (2017). Urban transformation under authoritarian neoliberalism. In C. B. Tansel (Ed.), *States of discipline: Authoritarian neoliberalism and the contested reproduction of capitalist order* (pp. 107–127). London: Rowman & Littlefield International.

Durazno Herrmann, J. (2011). Clientelismo y Democracia en Oaxaca. *Ulúa*, *17*, 159–180.

ECLAC. (2016). *Panorama Fiscal de América Latina y el Caribe 2016. Las finanzas públicas ante el desafío de conciliar austeridad con crecimiento e igualdad*. Santiago de Chile: Comisión Económica para América Latina y el Caribe (CEPAL).

El Universal. (2017a, September 6). Concluyen Centro de Convenciones de Oaxaca; lo inaugurará EPN. *El Universal*. Retrieved from http://oaxaca.eluniversal.com.mx/estatal/06-09-2017/concluyen-centro-de-convenciones-de-oaxaca-lo-inaugurara-epn

El Universal. (2017b, December 28). Invaden ambulantes, otra vez, el zócalo de Oaxaca. *El Universal*. Retrieved from http://oaxaca.eluniversal.com.mx/metropoli/28-12-2017/invaden-ambulantes-otra-vez-el-zocalo-de-oaxaca

Gobierno del Estado. (2011). *Plan Estatal de Desarrollo 2011–2016*. Oaxaca: Gobierno del Estado de Oaxaca.

Gobierno Federal de México. (2016). *Ciudades Competitivas*. México, DF: Gobierno Federal de México. Retrieved from http://www.gob.mx/se|mexicocompetitivo/acciones-y-programas/ciudades-competitivas?state=published

Goldstein, D. M. (2016). *Owners of the sidewalk: Security and survival in the informal city*. Durham: Duke University Press.

Graaff, K., & Ha, N. (2015). *Street vending in the neoliberal city: A global perspective on the practices and policies of a marginalized economy*. Oxford: Berghahn.

Graham, S. (2011). *Cities under siege*. London: Verso.

Guimarães, A. S. A. (2017). Racialisation and racial formation in urban spaces. *Social Identities*, 'Latest Articles' Section.

Harrison, G. (2018). Authoritarian neoliberalism and capitalist transformation in Africa: All pain, no gain. *Globalizations*. doi:10.1080/14747731.2018.1502491

Helmke, G., & Levitsky, S. (2006). *Informal institutions and democracy: Lessons from Latin America*. Baltimore: Johns Hopkins Univ Press.

Hesketh, C. (2016). The survival of non-capitalism. *Environment and Planning D: Society and Space*, *34*(5), 877–894.

Hesketh, C. (2017). *Spaces of capital/spaces of resistance: Mexico and the global political economy*. Athens: University of Georgia Press.

HR Ratings. (2016). *Rating Municipio de Oaxaca de Juárez*. New York: HR Credit Rating Agency. Retrieved from https://www.bmv.com.mx/docs-pub/eventoca/eventoca_704522_2.pdf

IMCO. (2016). *Índice de Competitividad Urbana 2016*. México, DF: Instituto Mexicano para la Competitividad (IMCO). Retrieved from http://imco.org.mx/indices/#!/reeleccion-municipal-y-rendicion-de-cuentas/resultados/entidad/031-oaxaca

IMCO. (2017). *Finanzas Públicas. Índice de Información Presupuestal Estatal 2017*. México, DF: Instituto Mexicano para la Competitividad (IMCO). Retrieved from http://imco.org.mx/finanzaspublicas/#!/indice-de-informacion-presupuestal-estatal/resultados/2017/20-oaxaca

INEGI. (2017). *Anuario Estadístico y Geográfico de Oaxaca 2017*. Méxcio, DF: INEGI. Retrieved from http://www.datatur.sectur.gob.mx/ITxEF_Docs/OAX_ANUARIO_PDF.pdf

Jenss, A. (2016). *Grauzonen staatlicher Gewalt: Staatlich produzierte Unsicherheit in Kolumbien und Mexiko*. Bielefeld: Transcript.

Kreitmeyr, N. (2018). Neoliberal co-optation and authoritarian renewal: Social entrepreneurship networks in Jordan and Morocco. *Globalizations*. doi:10.1080/14747731.2018.1502492

Laó-Montes, A., & Dávila, A. (2012). *Mambo montage: The latinization of New York city*. New York: Columbia University Press.

Lefebvre, H. (2003). *The urban revolution*. Minneapolis: University of Minnesota Press.

Licciardi, G., & Amirtahmasebi, R. (2012). *The economics of uniqueness: Investing in historic city cores and cultural heritage assets for sustainable development*. Washington, DC: World Bank. Retrieved from http://siteresources.worldbank.org/EXTSDNET/Resources/Economics_of_Uniqueness.pdf

Mabin, A. (2014). Grounding southern city theory in time and place. In S. Parnell & S. Oldfield (Eds.), *Routledge handbook on cities of the global South* (pp. 21–36). London: Routledge.

Magaña, M. R. (2016). Spaces of resistance, everyday activism, and belonging: Youth reimagining and reconfiguring the city in Oaxaca, Mexico. *The Journal of Latin American and Caribbean Anthropology*, *22*(2), 215–234.

Matías, P. (2017, September 7). Protestas contra Peña Nieto dejan 20 heridos, 20 detenidos, 10 vehículos destruidos y un helicóptero presidencial dañado. Retrieved from http://pagina3.mx/2017/09/protestas-contra-pena-nieto-dejan-20-heridos-20-detenidos-10-vehiculos-destruidos-y-un-helicoptero-presidencial-danado/

Mele, C. (2017). The strategic uses of race to legitimize 'social mix' urban redevelopment. *Social Identities*, 'Latest Articles' section.

México ¿cómo vamos? (2017). *Semáforo estatal: Oaxaca*. México, DF. Retrieved from http://mexicocomovamos.mx/

Moncada, E. (2009). Counting bodies: Crime mapping, policing and race in Colombia. *Ethnic and Racial Studies*, *33*(4), 696–716.

Monroe, K. V. (2016). *The insecure city: Space, power and mobility in Beirut*. New Brunswick: Rutgers University Press.

Morton, A. D. (2018). The architecture of 'passive revolution': Society, state and space in modern Mexico. *Journal of Latin American Studies*, *50*(1), 117–52.

Müller, M.-M. (2016). *The punitive city: Privatized policing and protection in neoliberal Mexico*. London: Zed Books.

Municipio de Oaxaca. (2016). *Presupuesto de Egresos 2017*. Oaxaca: Ayuntamiento Oaxaca de Juárez. Retrieved from https://www.municipiodeoaxaca.gob.mx/uploads/attachment/file/39/PRESUPUESTO_DE_EGRESOS_2017.pdf

Municipio de Oaxaca. (2017). *Impulsan la transformación de la capital desde la cultura, turismo y economía*. Oaxaca: Ayuntamiento Oaxaca de Juárez. Retrieved from http://municipiodeoaxaca.gob.mx/municipio-de-oaxaca/prensa/impulsan-la-transformacion-de-la-capital-desde-la-cultura-turismo-y-economia

NVI. (2017a). Se dispara la pobreza laboral en Oaxaca. NVI Noticias. Retrieved from http://www.nvinoticias.com/nota/82789/se-dispara-la-pobreza-laboral-en-oaxaca

NVI. (2017b, January 14). Oaxaca está quebrada; anuncia Murat plan de austeridad. *NVI Noticias*. Retrieved from http://www.nvinoticias.com/nota/48025/oaxaca-esta-quebrada-anuncia-murat-plan-de-austeridad

NVI. (2017c, January 25). Intocables, vendedores ambulantes en calles de Oaxaca. *NVI Noticias*. Retrieved from http://www.nvinoticias.com/nota/49190/intocables-vendedores-ambulantes-en-calles-de-oaxaca

NVI. (2017d, May 17). Oaxaca, con las casas más caras del país; incluso, más que frente al mar. *NVI Noticias*. Retrieved from http://www.nvinoticias.com/nota/59287/vivienda-mas-cara-en-oaxaca-que-en-paraiso-frente-al-mar

NVI. (2017e, October 17). Vecinos de Oaxaca. unidos contra la delincuencia. *NVI Noticias*. Retrieved from http://www.nvinoticias.com/nota/73543/vecinos-de-oaxaca-unidos-contra-la-delincuencia

NVI. (2017f, December 27). Prevención del delito en Oaxaca, 4 años perdidos. *NVI Noticias*. Retrieved from http://www.nvinoticias.com/nota/80232/prevencion-del-delito-en-oaxaca-4-anos-perdidos

Oberndorfer, L. (2015). From new constitutionalism to authoritarian constitutionalism: New economic governance and the state of European democracy. In J. Jäger & E. Springler (Eds.), *Asymmetric crisis in Europe and possible futures: Critical political economy and post-Keynesian perspectives* (pp. 186–207). Abingdon: Routledge.

Overmyer-Velázquez, M. (2007). Portraits of a lady: Visions of modernity in Porfirian Oaxaca City. *Mexican Studies/Estudios Mexicanos*, *23*(1), 63–100.

Parnell, S., & Oldfield, S. (2014). From the south. In S. Parnell & S. Oldfield (Eds.), *The Routledge handbook on cities of the global South* (pp. 1–5). London: Routledge.

Peck, J. (2015). *Austerity urbanism: The neoliberal crisis of American Cities* (City Series No. 1). Berlin: Rosa-Luxemburg Foundation.

Pérez, J. (2015, February 15). La Jornada: Fuerzas federales asumen vigilancia en Oaxaca por paro de 2 mil policías. *La Jornada*, p. 26.

Picker, G., Murji, K., & Boatcă, M. (2018). Racial urbanities: Towards a global cartography. *Social Identities*, 'Latest Articles' section.

Pimmer, S., & Schmidt, L. (2015). Dependenztheorien reloaded. *Journal für Entwicklungspolitik*, *31*(3), 4–10.

Poulantzas, N. (2002). *Staatstheorie. Politischer Überbau, Ideologie, Autoritärer Etatismus*. Hamburg: VSA-Verlag.

Quartesan, A., & Romis, M. (2010). *The sustainability of urban heritage preservation: The case of Oaxaca de Juarez*. Washington, DC: Interamerican Development Bank.

Quijano, A. (2000). Coloniality of power, Eurocentrism and Latin America. *Nepantla: Views from South*, *1*(3), 533–580.

Robinson, J. (2005). *Ordinary cities: Between modernity and development*. New York: Routledge.

Romero Frizzi, M., Sánchez Silva, C., Mendoza García, J., Bailón Corres, J., Ruiz Cervantes, F., Arrioja Díaz Viruell, L., & Celaya Nández, Y. (2016). *Historia breve*. Oaxaca: Fondo de Cultura Economica.

Rosales, M., Garay Reyna, Z., & Pedrazzani, C. (2016). *La espacialidad crítica en el pensamiento político-social Latinoamericano. Nuevas gramáticas de poder, territorialidades en tensión*. Buenos Aires: CLACSO.

SEDATU. (2014). *Programa Nacionald de Desarrollo Urbano, Diario Oficial 30.04.2014*. México, DF: Secretaria de Desarrollo Agrario, Territorial y Urbano. Retrieved from http://dof.gob.mx/nota_detalle.php?codigo=5342867&fecha=30/04/2014

Sevilla Buitrago, Á. (2015). Capitalist formations of enclosure: Space and the extinction of the commons. *Antipode*, *47*(4), 999–1020.

Sevilla Buitrago, Á. (2016). Crisis and the city: Neoliberalism, austerity planning and the production of space. In F. Eckardt & J. R. Sánchez (Eds.), *City of crisis: The multiple contestation of southern European cities* (pp. 31–49). Bielefeld: Transcript.

SILMéxico. (2017). *Now is the time to buy in Oaxaca: Real estate best value*. México, DF: SILMéxico Investment Properties.

Silva, P. (2015, October 26). Cojea Oaxaca en competitividad. *NVI Noticias*. Retrieved from http://old.nvinoticias.com/oaxaca/desifras/309600-cojea-oaxaca-competitividad

Sturm, R., Griebel, T., & Winkelmann, T. (2017). *Austerity: A journey to an unknown territory: Discourses, economics and politics*. Sonderband Zeitschrift für Politik. Baden-Baden: Nomos.

Swanson, K. (2007). Revanchist urbanism heads south: The regulation of indigenous beggars and street vendors in Ecuador. *Antipode*, *39*(4), 708–728.

Tansel, C. B. (2017). Authoritarian neoliberalism: Towards a new research agenda. In C. B. Tansel (Ed.), *States of discipline: Authoritarian neoliberalism and the contested reproduction of capitalist order* (pp. 1–28). London: Rowman & Littlefield International.

Tansel, B. (2018). Reproducing authoritarian neoliberalism in Turkey: Urban governance and state restructuring in the shadow of executive centralization. *Globalizations*. doi:10.1080/14747731.2018.1502494

Tello, N. (2016). De la violencia 'normal' a la 'guerra civil': La Central de Abastos después del 2006. In Laboratorio de Narrativas (Ed.), *Curándonos de Espanto. Oaxaca 2006–2016* (pp. 116–121). Oaxaca: Editorial Pez en el Arbol/SURCO A.C.

Tulumello, S. (2017). The multiscalar nature of urban security and public safety: Crime prevention from local policy to policing in Lisbon (Portugal) and Memphis (the United States). *Urban Affairs Review*, 'OnlineFirst' section.

UNDP. (2013). *Regional Human Development Report 2013–2014: Citizen security with a human face: Evidence and proposals for Latin America*. New York: United Nations Development Programme.

UN Habitat III. (2015). *Habitat III declaration intermediate cities (Cuenca)*. Cuenca: UN HABITAT. Retrieved from http://habitat3.cuenca.gob.ec/archivos/declaration/HIII-DeclarationCuencaES.pdf

Varley, A. (2013). Postcolonialising informality? *Environment and Planning D: Society and Space*, *31*(1), 4–22.

Vásquez Duplat, A. M. (2016). Feminismo y «extractivismo urbano»: notas exploratorias. *Nueva Sociedad*, *265*, 153–163.

World Prison Brief. (2017). *Mexico*. London: Institute for Criminal Policy Research.

Zavala, J. (2017, December 28). Llegan amenazas de linchamientos al Centro Histórico de Oaxaca. *El Universal*. Retrieved from http://oaxaca.eluniversal.com.mx/metropoli/28-12-2017/llegan-amenazas-de-linchamientos-al-centro-historico-de-oaxaca

7 Reproducing authoritarian neoliberalism in Turkey: urban governance and state restructuring in the shadow of executive centralization

Cemal Burak Tansel

ABSTRACT
The implosion of popular struggles against the erosion of economic and democratic rights in the Middle East has thrown into sharp relief the co-constitutive character of neoliberal reforms and authoritarian state practices. This article zooms in on this relationship, and traces the consolidation of a core component of authoritarian statisms by examining how the ruling AKP government in Turkey has facilitated executive centralization. This process refers to a form of state restructuring whereby key decision-making powers are increasingly concentrated in the hands of the central government while democratic avenues to contest government policies are curtailed through legal and administrative reforms, and the marginalization of dissident social forces. I unpack the mechanisms of executive centralization in Turkey by exploring the transformation of urban governance under AKP rule, which has promoted a spectacular degree of state-led commodification of land and housing while simultaneously recentralizing key decision-making powers. The investigation demonstrates that executive centralization in urban governance has paved the way for the swift implementation of contested urban transformation projects marked by a non-participatory approach to urban 'renewal', the reconfiguration of the state's redistributive function vis-à-vis low-income households, and a tendency to exacerbate existing patterns of inequalities in the housing market.

Introduction

Summer 2013 in Turkey was marked by an eruption of mass uprisings following an initial occupation aimed at the protection of green space in downtown Istanbul. The Gezi Park protests quickly spread throughout the whole country and mobilized an estimated 2.5 million participants in 79 provinces out of a total 81 (Amnesty International, 2013, p. 56). The rapidly developing wave of mobilization succeeded in bringing together a distinct coalition of social forces, which expanded the parameters of the protests to incorporate a set of broader issues related to the ruling Justice and Development Party (AKP) government's dubitable approach to democratic rights and accountability, economic development and public participation. This sustained and widespread mobilization, combined with the government's heavy-handed response to the protests, received considerable international attention and helped highlight what some considered the AKP's 'authoritarian turn' (Benhabib, 2013). While the AKP government's harsh response was, indeed, emblematic of a single-party rule that tolerated little opposition both in and outside the parliament, the violent spectacle of the state repression displayed at Gezi captures only a single facet of a broader governing logic of 'authoritarian neoliberalism' that had long defined the AKP era (Tansel, 2018). As such, it is necessary to contextualize Turkey's 'authoritarian turn' against the background of the systematic, yet perhaps less perceptible, transformations wrought in the fabric of the country's legal, administrative and bureaucratic mechanisms.

In order to contribute to recent discussions on the linkages between neoliberalism and authoritarian state practices across various socio-spatial contexts, here I argue that the AKP has relied on a high degree of political recentralization, which operates in conjunction with – not in spite of – its wholehearted adoption of a neoliberal macroeconomic programme (see also Cozzolino, 2018). This centralization not only privileged the executive as the sole arbiter of social and economic policy at various levels of governance, but also facilitated the party's increasingly recognized authoritarian drive by systematically blocking democratic and popular avenues for contesting its policies. I substantiate this argument by exploring the sweeping reorganization of the policy frameworks and institutions of urban governance with particular focus on the Housing Development Administration of Turkey (hereafter referred to as TOKİ, and the Administration). Analyzing the Administration's trajectory under the aegis of AKP rule provides us a productive avenue with which to disentangle the broader processes of executive centralization, whereby AKP-authored reform strategies have resulted in the domination of central decision-making bodies over residents, regulatory bodies and other stakeholders.

This argument is fleshed out through an analysis of the legislation produced or revised by AKP governments, which is then contrasted with a set of ethnographic insights on urban transformation projects compiled from the existing critical literature on urban governance. As the paper's primary aim is unpacking the legal and administrative facets of executive centralization, ethnographic material from urban transformation projects is harnessed as an auxiliary resource and the findings utilized from the literature are cross-referenced with multiple sources. Methodologically, while the paper is deeply rooted in the extant discussions on Turkish neoliberalism, it contributes to our understanding of the relationship between neoliberalism and authoritarianism in other contexts (see also numerous papers in this special issue, especially those by Jenss, 2018 and Kreitmeyr, 2018). The paper also highlights that a greater emphasis on unpacking this particular relationship is necessary to study similar cases of democratic debilitation that are commonly discussed under the aegis of democratic backsliding (see Tansel, 2018).

In the first section below, I provide an overview of the AKP-led neoliberalization and a preliminary conceptual map to highlight the linkages between executive centralization and neoliberalism, with particular reference to the transformation of urban governance. This is followed by an analysis of the sweeping legal and administrative reforms enacted by AKP governments in urban policy, which have greatly increased the competencies of TOKİ and restructured the Administration as the executive's arm in facilitating urban transformation projects. The final section offers a panoramic look at the ways in which the legal and administrative reforms have shaped urban transformation projects in the AKP era, and how these contested projects ended up commodifying land and housing while reproducing the extant lines of inequalities faced by the urban poor and low-income households that they were ostensibly designed to assist.

Executive centralization and neoliberalism in the urban frontier

Before detailing the transformation of urban governance in Turkey, it is important to briefly recount the parameters of the AKP-led neoliberalization, as it was against this background that the party instrumentalized urban transformation as an engine of economic growth and stability, and relied on a renewed TOKİ-driven agenda of public-private partnerships to commodify housing and land across the country.

The AKP assumed office in 2002 following the inability of a centrist coalition to resolve the twin crises of neoliberalization which fully broke out in the economic and political realms in 2000–2001. Instead of mounting a challenge to the principles of liberalization that underpinned the preceding decade of economic instability, the first AKP administration largely adopted a set of prescriptions provided by the IMF, and the successive governments have prioritized inflation targeting, fiscal austerity and a considerably broadened privatization programme (Yeldan & Ünüvar, 2015, pp. 15–16). These policy priorities have resulted in a macroeconomic balance sheet that boasts inflation reduction, high FDI inflows generated by speculative capital movements, an initial period of high GDP growth rates, and improvements in GDP per capita. The final two benchmarks mirror the coeval performance of many other 'emerging countries' rather than signal an exceptional feat (see Tansel, 2017a). Yet, despite the oft-overstated assessments of this performance, the AKP programme has failed to tackle unemployment and chart a route out of the country's trajectory of 'jobless growth' (Yeldan & Ercan, 2011). The aggressive labour market restructuring pursued by AKP governments has placed considerable constraints on the prospects of wage increases for most workers, while simultaneously buttressing the employers' ability to shrink employment rights (Bozkurt-Güngen, 2018). Coupled with the rapid expansion of the scope and availability of financial products, wage stagnation has precipitated a record level of household indebtedness whereby 'household debt reached 41% of disposable personal income in 2010, implying a 6-fold increase since the end of 2003' (Karaçimen, 2015, p. 752).

As many observers have noted, cities have not only played an instrumental role in the AKP's ability to undertake key pillars of its economic programme, but they have also become the concrete arenas for the party to demonstrate the apparent 'success' of its policy initiatives and its ability to 'serve' the people (Balaban, 2011). The urgently-needed capital inflows required by the rapid growth model propelled a search for new spaces to valorize and direct investment into, while the construction sector experienced a drastic expansion, thanks in no small part to the urban renewal and transformation projects devised and distributed by an increasingly ambitious TOKİ. TOKİ-initiated public-private partnerships effectively refashioned the Administration's operation as a 'catalyst for the private sector' (Atasoy, 2016, p. 671), a role explicitly championed by the Administration itself (TOKİ, 2011, p. 7).

TOKİ projects are responsible for 9.2% of Turkey's annual housing production. Between 2003 and September 2017, building permits for more than 2 billion m^2 were issued to facilitate the construction of approximately 1.7 million new buildings (TÜİK, n.d. a; Figure 1). Between 2003 and 2016, the Administration itself initiated the construction of 737,136 housing units with a stated aim to complete a total of 1.2 million units by 2023 (TOKİ, 2016, p. 10). This spectacular investment in built environment and state-supervised housing initiatives have propelled the construction industry to constitute an important share of the country's overall GDP – 8.9% in 2016 – and to grow by an average of 5.9% annually between 2003 and 2014 (Daily Sabah, 2017; Erol & Unal, 2015, p. 9). It is within this context that the role of the construction sector and the urbanization of capital have gained prominence as *explanans* of the AKP's hegemony, leading some scholars to establish a positive causal relationship between the AKP's housing policy and the party's electoral performance (see Marschall, Aydoğan, & Bulut, 2016). AKP cadres have also utilized the demonstrable transformation of cities with new spaces of consumption, housing and 'megaprojects' as direct evidence of the government's ability to modernize and transform the country, a strategy that aimed to appeal both to the Turkish electorate and the international capital that the government was keen to attract.

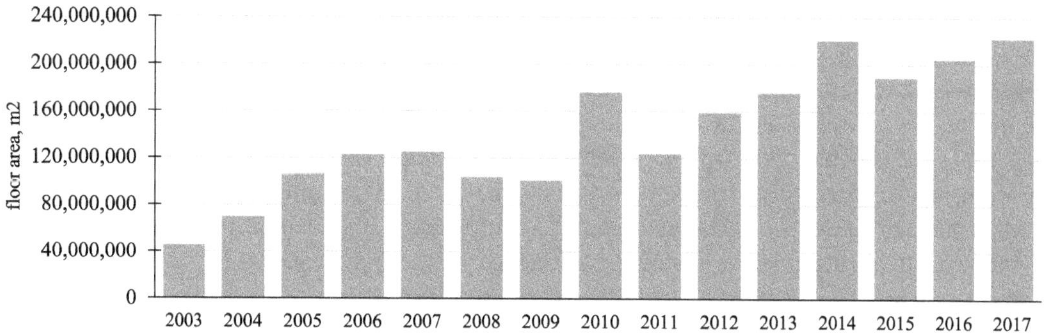

Figure 1. Total area of construction permits issued, 2003–2017; Source: Turkish Statistical Institute. Retrieved from http://www.turkstat.gov.tr/PrelstatistikTablo.do?istab_id=609.

While the AKP's agency in prioritizing this programme of economic development through urban transformation is undeniable, the socio-economic processes that facilitated this model should be linked both to earlier urbanization trends in Turkey as well as to the systemic pressures generated by the country's uneven liberalization. Rapid commodification of public land and the expansion of the real estate market under AKP rule were made possible by a proactive government policy that heavily relied on the state's expropriation and planning powers, and also by the antecedent, intensified urbanization of capital in the 1980s and 1990s. As Moreno (2014, p. 259) elucidates:

> urbanisation represented endless scope for capital to open up new channels of exploitation outside the closed field of the workplace. The city, comprising a fabric of social assets saturated with value, provided a space in which capitalism could re-fortify itself, through restructuring the ownership of the relations of production, consumption and collective consumption.

In Turkey, this process corresponded to a larger shift in economic management from import-substitution industrialization to neoliberalism, whereby the state's half-hearted attempts to regulate urbanization and the irregular housing stock began to clash with 'the emergence of entrepreneurial local government acting as a market facilitator, and the privatization of various municipal services such as transportation, housing, and provision of natural gas' (Bartu-Candan & Kolluoğlu, 2008, p. 12). Throughout the 1990s, the planned spaces of production and consumption increasingly infringed on public land in desired residential and commercial locations as well as on *gecekondu* neighbourhoods,[1] while the perceived *function* of urban land – from the perspective of both capital and the state – changed from being 'an instrument to accommodate the growing labouring classes' to becoming 'a new area of economic investment open to both national and international capital' (Saraçoğlu & Demirtaş-Milz, 2014, p. 192).

Yet the trend towards a greater concentration of capital in cities and a more permissive policy environment did not trigger the type of large-scale transformation and housing projects that now marks the AKP era. For example, between 1984 (the year the Mass Housing Fund was established) and 2002, the total area for which construction permits were granted was approximately 1.2 billion m^2 – roughly the same area for the construction permits issued *only* in Istanbul between 2003 and 2014 (Çavuşoğlu & Strutz, 2014, p. 142). Between 1984 and 2002, the average floor area for granted construction permits per annum roughly amounted to 64.6 million m^2, whereas it more than doubled to approximately 143 m^2 during the AKP's fourteen-year rule (2003–2017) (TÜİK, n.d. b; Figures 1 and 2).

This picture compels us to zoom in on the methods and mechanisms particular to the AKP-led state apparatuses and on the initiatives undertaken by the government since 2002. In addition to the availability of cheap credit, the AKP's key 'success' was its ability to deploy state apparatuses to facilitate and shelter capital flows. In effect, the policies have shepherded domestic and foreign capital flows into what Harvey (1985, pp. 6–7) termed 'the secondary circuit of capital', which consists of 'long-term assets, particularly those constituting the built environment'. Harvey suggested that the movement of capital from the 'first circuit' (comprising activities that produce surplus value) into the 'second' functions as a temporary displacement of the crisis tendencies of overaccumulation. Yet, this 'switching' between the circuits poses significant problems for individual capitalists, and Harvey indicated that it would be a feasible option only if a 'functioning capital market' and 'a state willing to finance and guarantee long-term, large-scale projects with respect to the creation of the built environment' existed (ibid., p. 7). My contention here is that AKP governments have effectively fulfilled this role by manoeuvring the Turkish state to become a facilitator of large-scale urban transformation and housing projects that both absorbed surplus capital – as Harvey's theory presumes it would – and heightened the scope and pace of the commodification of land through land and property transfer.

It is crucial to underscore that this process was made possible by a significant transformation of the state's administrative and legal branches in managing urban governance, as well as the deployment of its coercive apparatuses to secure the continuation of contested projects. The main mechanism I highlight here is executive centralization, which, in this particular context, refers to the degree to which the key decision-making powers in urban governance have been transferred to the central government through the empowerment of TOKİ – which operates under the Prime Ministry – and the legislative changes that have granted extraordinary expropriation powers to the state and invalidated the influence of relevant auditing and regulatory authorities, residents and civil society groups.

This trend towards 'centralization', rather than constituting an exception to an assumed neoliberal logic of 'marketization' or the privileging of private actors, *enables* further commodification while also signalling the importance of certain mechanisms that distinguish the Turkish case from some well-established examples of neoliberal urbanization. For example, Swyngedouw, Moulaert, and Rodriguez's (2002, p. 561) influential article on neoliberal urban policy in the European Union (EU) asserts that neoliberal urbanization is defined by a degree of institutional fragmentation, whereby the 'formal government structures' are 'subordinated to new institutions and agencies, often

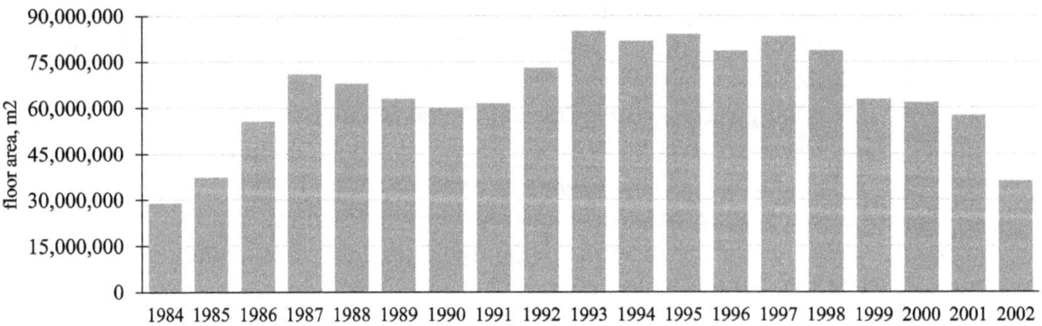

Figure 2. Total area of construction permits issued, 1984–2002; Source: Turkish Statistical Institute. Retrieved from http://www.turkstat.gov.tr/PreIstatistikTablo.do?istab_id=2010.

paralleled by a significant redistribution of policymaking powers, competencies, and responsibilities'. The case studies they cite suggest that neoliberal urbanization shifts the onus from public input to experts and a 'fusion of technical, economic, and political elites', and it reduces the 'role of the public in general and of traditional organized groups in particular, with a consequent loss of democratic accountability' (p. 579).

While the Turkish case mirrors many of these processes, it is important to highlight the following two qualifiers. First, the restructuring of urban governance during the AKP-led neoliberalization has not only excluded public participation in the design and implementation of large-scale projects, but it has also minimized the role of critical expertise. Centralization has consolidated and expanded the arms of the executive in shaping key decision-making processes, and has built a legal and administrative firewall around the urban transformation projects that many independent experts and professional associations have attempted to contest – all of which represent instances of 'preemptive discipline' (Bruff, 2014, p. 123; Tansel, 2017b, pp. 3–5). This does not contradict the overall thesis of Swyngedouw et al., as they also underline that the fragmented governance forged by neoliberal urbanization leads to 'the adoption of discretionary forms of management', and it helps create 'the conditions for the establishment of centralized and more autocratic' forms of decision-making (2002, p. 570). Nevertheless, the specificities of the Turkish case require some adjustment to the original argument.

Second, 'centralization' in the Turkish case does not necessarily refer to a complete reversal of the devolution of decision-making powers to local government. Many instances of administrative reform enacted by the AKP – particularly those that were propelled by EU accession negotiations in the first decade of AKP rule – explicitly aimed at furnishing greater powers to local authorities. Metropolitan Municipality Law No. 5216 and Municipality Law No. 5393 are clear examples of this orientation, as they both removed a number of central government controls over municipalities and encouraged the participation of civil society groups in local government initiatives (Bartu-Candan & Kolluoğlu, 2008, p. 13; Doğan & Stupar, 2017, p. 283; Lelandais, 2014, pp. 1792–1793). Yet the AKP's administrative restructuring has failed to produce a tangible decentralized structure of power at local and regional levels; or in other words, the reforms that were supposed to facilitate a transfer of authority, power and control to local governments rarely amounted to a genuine *institutional* restructuring. Despite broad-ranging changes in municipal laws, the central government and its affiliated bodies (e.g. TOKİ) have not relinquished their intervention powers; on the contrary, in most cases, they ended up extending their control over local authorities. Correspondingly, various local administration reforms have increasingly amounted to 'step towards strengthening the power of TOKİ while weakening that of local governments' (Kayasü & Yetişkul, 2014, p. 217; Bayırbağ, 2013).

Executive centralization has also reinforced the state's tendency to deploy coercion, and has resulted in the marginalization of public and non-governmental scrutiny of urban governance. As Di Giovanni (2017, p. 111) notes, coercion within the context of rapid urban transformation denotes a palpable increase in the scope and deployment of the state's repressive apparatuses, and 'a preemptive governance capable of legally restricting decision-making and auditing mechanisms. As polities must sustain the market of development investments and economic growth, policies are bound to restrict participation and accountability'. The expansion of the state's expropriation powers and TOKİ's exclusion from regulatory oversight have largely shielded urban transformation projects from legal contestation, while the heavy presence of the state's coercive apparatuses have aimed to minimize social mobilization against the projects.

Establishing the mechanisms of preemptive discipline in urban governance

This section examines how the AKP's legal and administrative reforms have repurposed TOKİ to function as an agent of land and property transfer, and how these changes have been instrumental in reinforcing the overall trend of executive centralization in public policy under AKP rule. TOKİ was established in 1984 with the stated aim of facilitating state-backed financing to housing projects. The Mass Housing Law of 1984,[2] which defined the parameters of the Administration's responsibilities, was envisioned as a potential panacea for the state's inability to expand housing provision for low-income families. Previous state-led efforts were largely defined by policies that prioritized offering subsidized credit, which often received criticism due to their tendency to contribute 'more to the development of middle-class and even luxurious residential construction than to the realization of social housing projects' (Buğra, 1998, p. 308).

TOKİ's second incarnation under AKP rule was facilitated by a series of sweeping legal and administrative changes that radically enhanced the Administration's planning and financial powers while also bringing its operation under the full control of the executive. These reforms have given TOKİ the ability to expand considerably the scope of its projects, while also situating the Administration in the housing market as a 'private enterprise' as well as the regulator and facilitator of public-private partnerships in large-scale urban transformation and housing projects (Kayasü & Yetişkul, 2014, p. 216; Kuyucu & Ünsal, 2010, p. 1485). Correspondingly, TOKİ's share of the housing market rose from 1.1% in 2003 to 18.6% within four years (Karaman, 2013, p. 3418), while the value of its housing investments at the municipal level reached $11 billion by 2014 (Marschall et al., 2016, p. 202).

The AKP's ambitious efforts to place urban transformation at the heart of its socio-economic programme began as early as 2003, with the passing of key legislation that considerably expanded TOKİ's competencies and attached the Administration more closely to the government. Law No. 4966 amended the Mass Housing Law of 1984 (Law No. 2985) and extended the responsibilities of the Administration to include the 'provision of individual and collective credit for housing… financing projects that aim to regenerate *gecekondu* areas, [and] to protect and restore historical and local architecture'.[3] TOKİ was also granted the option to request the ownership of treasury land designated to be used in its own projects without any compensation, subject to the approval of the Prime Minister. With Law No. 5018 on the management of public finances, TOKİ's accounts were reallocated to a 'special budget', thus removed from the Turkish Court of Accounts' auditing remit.[4] Shortly after this, the Administration itself was removed from the control of the Ministry of Public Works and Housing, and attached directly to the Prime Minister's office.[5]

2004–2008 represents a key juncture in urban governance in Turkey, as a series of laws passed in this period continued to expand TOKİ's powers. Law No. 5162 empowered the Administration to design and develop urban transformation projects, but also the authority to claim eminent domain, and thus the ability to expropriate any land or property owned by real or legal entities.[6] TOKİ gained the license to prepare and finance urban transformation projects in *gecekondu* neighbourhoods with a view to 'evacuating or reclaiming them through rejuvenation'. With Law No. 5162, the Administration was also authorized to establish partnerships with private companies, which would underpin its revenue-sharing partnership programme in the years to come.

Law No. 5273 strengthened the Administration's grip on public land by abolishing the Urban Land Office, 'which was formerly responsible for the development and allocation of urban land according to the needs of different institutions and local governments' (Türkün, 2011, p. 70), and transferring 64.5 million m^2 of public land to the TOKİ's own portfolio.[7] An amendment made to Law No. 775 in 2007 enabled TOKİ to take ownership of treasury lands without compensation.[8] Law No. 5366, ostensibly designed to protect and restore dilapidated buildings of historic importance, incorporated major conservation sites into the purview of urban transformation projects.[9] Directly empowering municipalities in implementing urban transformation projects in such areas, the law dismantled the regulations on 'historical and protection zones' and exposed these sites to the prospect of expropriation (Çavuşoğlu & Strutz, 2014, p. 143; Kayasü & Yetişkul, 2014, p. 217; Kuyucu, 2014, p. 616n.7).

The contingent empowerment of local authorities – in conjunction with the ongoing expansion of TOKİ – continued with Municipal Law of 2005 (No. 5393). Municipalities' competencies vis-à-vis urban transformation projects had already been enhanced with Law No. 5216 in 2004; but the 2005 law introduced a key new criterion for expanding the scope of urban transformation by entitling the municipalities with the authority to implement urban transformation projects to 'rebuild and restore decaying parts of the city'.[10] As Kuyucu (2014, p. 615) notes, the law 'specifies no concrete definitions or objective criteria of obsolescence, decay or dilapidation that should serve as the basis for designating areas as "transformation zones"', and this deliberate ambiguity 'opens up a dangerous degree of arbitrariness in decision making for municipal authorities' (see also Tepe, 2016, p. 77). These measures were designed to be implemented in partnership with TOKİ and did not amount to any systematic realignment towards institutional decentralization. Further pieces of legislation passed in this same four-year period demonstrate clearly that the AKP's approach to decentralization was highly contingent and did not aim to disassemble the central government's control over key decision-making mechanisms. For example, Law No. 5793, passed in July 2008, readjusted the scope of local government regulation in urban transformation projects and stipulated that TOKİ can authorize its own projects even if they are not approved by local authorities.[11]

Space does not permit a full exploration of all attempts to expand the scope of TOKİ's expropriatory powers and the public land available for urban transformation projects. However, two further key reforms should be briefly highlighted before unpacking how urban transformation projects are developed in practice. The first concerns the AKP's successful bid in 2012 to redefine the legal status of forests. Effectively revoking the pre-existing constitutional guarantees that protected forested areas from commercial use, Law No. 6292 legalized the sale of 'lands that have lost their "forest" status (due to burning and cutting of trees)' (Atasoy, 2016, p. 662).[12] By 2014, the state had completed cadastral work on the majority of lands that fell under this category, and sold 1.573 million m^2 lands out of a total 3.45 million m^2 (Atasoy, 2016, p. 662). Commodification of forest lands was accompanied by a twin act which was promulgated in the same year. Law No. 6306 was presented by the government as a state-led effort to increase cities' resilience to disasters and to strengthen building codes and regulations, yet it neatly fit into the existing trend towards executive centralization by empowering the Ministry of Environment and Urbanization and TOKİ in designating 'risk areas', which would then be earmarked for urban transformation projects under the guidance of the Administration.[13] The law enforced a highly ambiguous definition of 'risk areas', which includes specific buildings and zones under immediate 'disaster risk' and those in the proximity of such areas as well, thus allowing the Ministry and TOKİ to subject 'hypothetically all existing building stock' to the jurisdiction of the law (Eliçin, 2014, p. 151).

Broader reforms enacted by AKP governments have also had a significant impact on urban governance, as they have transformed the state's approach to informal housing. The new Criminal Code, passed in 2004, criminalized the construction of *gecekondu* housing for the first time and made it punishable by a five-year prison sentence.[14] Given the historical role *gecekondus* played in facilitating access to housing for the urban poor and the state's permissive approach to informal housing, criminalization was a major step in redefining the state's redistributive function vis-à-vis low-income households as well as its commitment to codifying, and further commodifying, land and housing (see also Jenss, 2018). The law has resulted in the escalation of disciplinary measures directed at *gecekondu* areas, which took the form of widespread demolitions of whole neighbourhoods and increased surveillance and policing (Lelandais, 2014, pp. 1793–1794).[15] The law also made the *gecekondu* neighbourhoods prime targets for TOKİ projects: the Administration was empowered to impose large-scale urban transformation projects in such areas and sought to transform them due to their high 'rent gap', i.e. 'the disparity between the potential ground rent level and the actual ground rent capitalized under the present land use' (Smith, 1996, p. 65; Karaman, 2014, p. 294; Saraçoğlu & Demirtaş-Milz, 2014, p. 179).

Reproducing authoritarian neoliberalism through urban governance

The above-discussed legal and administrative reforms in urban governance reveal the gradual assembly of an infrastructure that reinforced executive centralization under AKP rule, yet examining *how* these changes were reflected in urban transformation projects exposes an even more drastic realignment of the state's productive and regulatory role in cities, and its relationship with the urban poor and various fractions of capital. This section will unpack the ways in which the AKP's authoritarian neoliberal rule has manifested in urban governance by reviewing a series of snapshots taken from TOKİ's major urban transformation projects. The aim of this exercise is to establish how urban transformation projects have (I) limited popular participation by adopting a top-down approach; (II) intensified existing inequalities in the housing market; (III) displaced residents from their long-established spaces of social reproduction; (IV) exploited class and ethnicity-based divisions and deepened 'territorial stigmatization'; and (V) constituted a form of preemptive discipline by preventing (and, if necessary, violating) legal and social challenges mounted against the projects.

One of the most immediate effects of the way in which executive centralization has taken hold of urban governance is the degree to which key decision-making processes have been transferred to TOKİ and the Ministry of Environment and Urbanization at the expense of local authorities, residents, and civil society groups. As highlighted above, this trend emerged against the background of ostensible empowerment of municipalities to develop and implement urban transformation projects while their competencies were, in practice, regularly subjugated to the demands of TOKİ. Instead of producing an institutional structure capable of reflecting the needs of local authorities and populations, the reforms have placed the 'implementation of urban regeneration projects in the hands of central government from the beginning (land development and planning) to the end (property development and redistribution of property rights)' (Eraydın & Taşan-Kok, 2014, p. 119).

The ramifications of the AKP's top-down approach to urban governance can be traced in the way in which major transformation projects were conducted by the relevant local authorities and TOKİ, which are 'typically announced without any prior consultation with the locals and have resulted in the involuntary displacement of residents who have no right or means to participate in renewal schemes' (Erensü & Karaman, 2017, p. 26). The urban transformation project that aimed to 'regenerate' the neighbourhood of Sulukule in Istanbul embodies the contradictions of the AKP's contingent decentralization. Developed by TOKİ, the Istanbul Metropolitan Municipality and the local Fatih Municipality, the project began with an 'urgent expropriation decree' issued by the central government (Karaman, 2014, p. 296). While on paper the project aimed at the 'conservation of Sulukule' – a historic neighbourhood with a well-established majority Roma community – it was implemented without any substantial engagement with the residents, and widely criticized for the absence of participatory mechanisms that could integrate the needs and demands of the local population (Uysal, 2012, p. 16). A similar approach shaped the urban transformation project of the Fikirtepe neighbourhood in Istanbul, whose residents resisted the resettlement plans proposed by the TOKİ's private contractors. The project could only proceed after the central government invoked Law No. 6306 to declare Fikirtepe a 'risk area', thereby preempting and undermining the residents' efforts to mount legal and social challenges (Tepe, 2016, p. 88).

While TOKİ repeatedly underscores that the 'social housing projects' constitute the majority of its housing production (85.2%),[16] the development and implementation of these urban transformation projects serve to reproduce extant inequalities in access to housing. The projects' inability to offer substantial solutions to the existing lines of stratification in housing stems from both the highly financialized and non-participatory nature of the projects, and the specific history of the development of informal housing in Turkey. The *gecekondu* neighbourhoods that have been targeted by the TOKİ's 'renewal' projects proliferated within a context of uneven urbanization in, and migration to, the metropolitan areas in the second half of the twentieth century. Flows of migrant workers to the cities sustained the state's and the developing industries' labour needs, and successive governments' permissive approach to informal housing on public land – which gave birth to the *gecekondu* neighbourhoods – effectively helped keep labour costs down (Karaman, 2014, p. 296; Lelandais, 2014, p. 1792). With the passing of amnesty laws in 1984 and 1985, the occupiers of *gecekondu* properties started claiming legal ownership and use rights through the state's land titling initiatives. These legal reforms spawned what Erman (2001, p. 987) has called the 'apartmentalisation of *gecekondus*', whereby 'the once-owner-occupied/owner-built *gecekondus* were [replaced] by high-rise apartment buildings in which the owner of the *gecekondu* land owned several apartments'. Those *gecekondu* residents who were able to access title deeds and legalize their ownership status thus profited from either selling their piece of once-public land or further developing their properties into larger units – a process which 'created a lucrative and hierarchical market structure that disproportionately benefits the more economically resourceful and better politically connected inhabitants' (Kuyucu, 2014, pp. 618–619; Enlil, 2011, p. 20).

TOKİ's urban transformation projects exploited these legal ambiguities of informal housing tenure, and exacerbated the already stratified relationship between *gecekondu* tenants who lacked legal claims and protections and those who owned titles or use rights. In most transformation projects, 'legal' residents of the targeted neighbourhoods, i.e. those who can prove their ownership or use rights, retain the option to stay in the same area and move into a new-build TOKİ unit. The residents who opt for this scenario are required to pay a sum which is calculated as the difference between the value of their existing property and the value of the new TOKİ unit they would own. This arrangement thus offers 'the promise of acquiring a house with a significantly higher market value, and in the case of *gecekondu* settlers, the transition to formal ownership status' (Karaman, 2014, p. 297).

The translation of this arrangement into practice means that *gecekondu* tenants who lack established legal rights are not eligible for compensation, and often 'face direct eviction' (Karaman, 2014, p. 297). In the case of the Sulukule project, many tenants who could not afford the payment plan imposed by the project ended up abrogating their resettlement rights and selling their 'entitlement' to the new TOKİ properties to third parties (Karaman, 2014, p. 299; Uysal, 2012, p. 17). Meanwhile, residents who already possessed ownership rights had the opportunity to sell their properties at high profit margins (Uysal, 2012, p. 17). As such, the projects' promise of homeownership often applies to those who already enjoyed secure tenures via the possession of deeds or use rights, while tenants who lacked such legal claims are further pushed to a perpetual state of 'rental housing insecurity' (cf. Soederberg, 2018).

The exclusion of residents from participation in the planning and implementation of these projects, as well as the differential rights of resettlement possessed by owners and tenants, further serve to reproduce inequalities by displacing residents from their long-established communities and workplaces. The exclusionary effects often manifest in economic terms, as many resettled residents – particularly those who were tenants prior to resettlement – struggle to keep up with the mortgage payments and end up selling or leasing their new flats. Beyond this secondary cycle of displacement necessitated by economic hardship, the former residents of transformed neighbourhoods also face exclusion from their established spaces of reproduction. For example, Sulukule tenants were given the option to resettle in Taşoluk, a neighbourhood '40 km outside the city center' (Karaman, 2014, p. 299) and an unpopular alternative that was accepted by few residents. As Karaman (2014, p. 299) notes, 'almost all of the tenants had moved to smaller substandard houses in the immediate vicinity of Sulukule or were pushed further away from the city center'. Likewise, the resettlement plan implemented in Kadifekale envisioned that the residents would be moved to a peripheral suburb 'isolated from the economic and social opportunities on offer in the city' (Saraçoğlu & Demirtaş-Milz, 2014, pp. 181–182).

In addition to the difficulty of maintaining access to their workplaces after resettlement, residents have faced the prospect of being physically cut off from their established 'mutual assistance networks', which have been crucial in reinforcing the urban poor's ability to reproduce themselves outside the 'formal' framework of social reproduction via market mechanisms (Lelandais, 2014, p. 1798). As noted by ethnographic evidence, resettled residents have often lost access to informal practices that hitherto had increased their ability to purchase basic necessities (e.g. such as *veresiye*, a type of deferred payments commonly practiced in neighbourhood shops), and the stringently ordered TOKİ units built without the residents' input – and often administered by private companies – have resulted in the destruction of communal spaces where residents used to grow their own produce (Bartu-Candan & Kolluoğlu, 2008, p. 23). Simultaneously, there is growing evidence that resettled residents are attempting to 'reappropriate' these highly regulated and managed spaces to re-establish their everyday practices (Erman, 2016).

This consistent attempt to order informal spaces and submit them to the state's logic of formalizing property relations has also been reinforced by an explicit securitarian discourse which has exploited class and ethnicity-based differences to legitimize urban transformation. Public relations campaigns surrounding the urban transformation projects associated the targeted areas as zones of criminality and a general sense of urban decay, thus reinforcing an existing trend of 'territorial stigmatization' whereby 'discourses of vilification proliferate[d]' about neighbourhoods that had already been marked by a 'pervasive stigmata of poverty' (Wacquant, 1996, p. 125). This discourse manifested repeatedly in the statements and speeches of figures and authorities that played a key role in the projects. For example, in 2006, the then-Prime Minister Recep Tayyip Erdoğan described *gecekondu* neighbourhoods as a 'tumor that has surrounded our cities' and highlighted that 'removing this tumor' was the government's main priority (quoted in Kuyucu, 2014, pp. 613–614). The transformation of neighbourhoods with large Kurdish and Roma communities, such as Ayazma and Sulukule, has been justified by paternalistic narratives that emphasized the implicit otherness of such communities and an aggressive rhetoric that 'played upon the racist prejudice according to which Kurdishness is equated with political disloyalty, quasi-feudal primitivism, general anti-social attitudes and criminality' (Lovering & Türkmen, 2011, p. 84; Uysal, 2012, p. 15; Karaman, 2014, p. 293).

Finally, it is important to highlight that despite the preemptive disciplining of dissent against urban transformation projects, residents and civil society organizations succeeded in mounting important challenges. These mobilizations took the form of legal efforts aimed at chipping away at the judicial armour of the projects as well as grassroots movements that brought together residents and regional/national civil society organizations to contest the terms of the proposed transformation. Some of the legal challenges brought about by residents and NGOs have been successful in courts, resulting in temporary interruptions to constructions and the partial revision of transformation plans in neighbourhoods such as Başıbüyük and Tarlabaşı (Kuyucu & Ünsal, 2010, pp. 1488, 1495; Lovering & Türkmen, 2011, p. 91). The effectiveness of this strategy has been limited due to the previously-discussed legal reforms which have drastically increased the scope of TOKİ's competencies, and to the fact that many of those rulings in favour of the projects' cancellation were later annulled by appeal courts. Nevertheless, the legal firewall built around the AKP's urban transformation strategy as well as the state's deployment of its coercive arm to preserve the projects has created a mutually reinforcing cycle of grassroots activism. As Tepe (2016, p. 95) notes:

> The administratively nonnegotiable nature of URPs [urban renewal projects] introduces judicial venues as one of the most effective ways to contest them … Yet the local governments consistently disregard court decisions and reinforce the key role of central and local governments without judicial accountability. Paradoxically, the ineffectiveness of court decisions both increases political apathy and mistrust among residents as well as makes political activism the only viable option to challenge the URPs.

Therefore, while the extended judicial protection of the urban transformation projects, as well as TOKİ's ability to ignore contravening court decisions, constitute an important barrier to challenging these developments on legal grounds, the mechanisms of preemptive disciplining also heighten the possibility of coordinated grassroots action between residents, NGOs and other political actors by, in effect, channelling their opposition to the streets.

Conclusion

This article has analyzed the constitution of authoritarian neoliberalism through urban governance in Turkey, but the reader should not assume that the processes and practices that underpin the developments I have discussed are applicable only to questions of urban policy. It is vital to stress that the rapid centralization of decision-making processes and the accompanying legal and administrative measures taken in this specific policy area directly echo similar developments that AKP governments have put in motion in other key fields; hence the importance of recognizing them as individual nodes of a wider model of governance that I identify as authoritarian neoliberalism. The trajectory of administrative reform during the AKP era has followed the same pattern of recentralization in the guise of contingent decentralization. For example, the government's approach to privatization – the pace and value of which have increased dramatically since 2003 – reveals an identical tendency for 'streamlining' procedures with a view to removing institutional and regulatory barriers against privatization (Angın & Bedirhanoğlu, 2013; Tansel, 2017a). As Buğra and Savaşkan (2004, p. 82) have noted, since 2003 AKP governments have amended existing laws and passed new pieces of legislation which have 'simplified bureaucratic procedures, expanded and consolidated prime ministerial control over the Privatization Agency and eliminated the rules concerning partial public ownership of privatized enterprises'. This wave of regulatory liberalization vis-à-vis privatization initiatives went hand in hand with repeated efforts to utilize public procurement procedures to generate and further expand circuits of capital accumulation, particularly with a view to reinforcing the status and power of pro-government businesses. Loss of discretion and regulatory oversight in public procurement has resulted in ever-increasing market shares of pro-government conglomerates – many of them now possess monopolistic powers in key industries, such as in construction and media (Yeşil, 2016, p. 105). TOKİ itself has played a crucial role in this process, as its investment arm has distributed 60% of its procurements to the members of the pro-government Independent Industrialists' and Businessmen's Association (MÜSİAD) (Soyaltın, 2017, p. 147).

While the specificities of the Turkish case – the ways in which executive centralization has transformed the state's administrative, legal and coercive apparatuses – require a particular focus on the 'authoritarian' character of the AKP-led neoliberalization, it is important to note that 'centralization', in and of itself, has never been antithetical to the operation of actually existing neoliberalisms across the globe (see also Clua-Losada & Ribera-Almandoz, 2017; Cozzolino, 2018). A brief look at cases ranging from the restructuring of the British state's welfare provision during the New Labour years to the implementation of privatization programmes and bureaucratic reform in Mexico in the 1980s reveals that the adoption of neoliberal policies – often accompanied by an explicit discourse on the need to 'decentralize' decision-making – has repeatedly resulted in the 're-centralisation and formalisation of central state power' (May, Cloke, & Johnsen, 2005, p. 704; Aitken, 1996, p. 25).

The exclusionary and anti-democratic tendencies of these processes have been noted by many scholars, though in some cases, such propensities were attributed directly to local particularities. Castree (2010, p. 199), for example, has suggested that in neoliberal Britain, 'executive decisionmaking has become increasingly immune to public scrutiny or pressure' due to 'some peculiarities of British politics and society'. What the Turkish experience under AKP rule – and, indeed, many other cases explored in this special issue – attests is that we now have enough evidence of such executive centralizations to link them more systematically to a broader 'evacuation of capitalist democracy', namely, the increasing failure of the established political forms of capitalism to manage the 'tensions' between the necessity to safeguard capital accumulation while maintaining a healthy level of public legitimacy (Ayers & Saad-Filho, 2015, pp. 605–606). While the implementations of neoliberalism in different national contexts have had success in offering, albeit temporarily, a panacea for the crisis of profitability, the accompanying process of the transformation of governance has proven itself ill-equipped to resolve the inherent political contradictions of capitalism. The AKP-led attempts to expand the scope of commodification in the Turkish case underlines the magnitude of the structural power the state possesses to facilitate these projects, but also the vibrant potential of urban processes in broadening the space for collective action and in building concrete forms of solidarity from the bottom up to mount an effective resistance against neoliberalization.

Notes

1. *Gecekondu*, the literal translation of which is 'built overnight', denotes irregular and illegal housing often built on public land.
2. Law No. 2985, *Official Gazette*, 17 March 1984.
3. Law No. 4966, *Official Gazette*, 7 August 2003.
4. Law No. 5018, *Official Gazette*, 24 December 2003. See also Marschall et al. (2016, p. 205).
5. *Official Gazette*, 16 January 2004.
6. Law No. 5162, *Official Gazette*, 12 May 2004.
7. Law No. 5273, *Official Gazette*, 15 December 2004. The amount of public land controlled by TOKİ would increase to 110 million m^2 by 2011 (Atasoy, 2016, p. 671).
8. Law No. 5609, *Official Gazette*, 28 March 2007.
9. Law No. 5366, *Official Gazette*, 5 July 2005.

10. Law No. 5216, *Official Gazette*, 23 July 2004; Law No. 5393, *Official Gazette*, 13 July 2005.
11. Law No. 5793, *Official Gazette*, 6 August 2008.
12. Law No. 6292, *Official Gazette*, 26 April 2012.
13. Law No. 6306, *Official Gazette*, 31 May 2012.
14. Law No. 5237, *Official Gazette*, 12 October 2004.
15. 'Between 2004 and 2008, 11,543 [*gecekondu*] units in Istanbul were demolished, a record high for any period' (Kuyucu & Ünsal, 2010, p. 1484).
16. The figure includes housing projects constructed for the urban poor, low- and middle-income groups, disaster housing as well as urban renewal projects (i.e. *gecekondu* transformation projects) and agricultural villages (TOKİ, 2016, p. 16).

Acknowledgements

I would like to thank Ian Bruff, Roberto Roccu and the two reviewers for comments on an earlier draft.

Disclosure statement

No potential conflict of interest was reported by the author.

ORCID

Cemal Burak Tansel http://orcid.org/0000-0001-7586-459X

References

Aitken, R. (1996). Neoliberalism and identity: Redefining state and society in Mexico. In R. Aitken, N. Craske, G. A. Jones, & D. E. Stansfield (Eds.), *Dismantling the Mexican state?* (pp. 24–38). London: Palgrave Macmillan.

Amnesty International. (2013). *Gezi Park protests: Brutal denial of the right to peaceful assembly in Turkey*. Retrieved from https://www.amnesty.org/download/Documents/12000/eur440222013en.pdf

Angın, M., & Bedirhanoğlu, P. (2013). AKP döneminde Türkiye'de büyük ölçekli özelleştirmeler ve devletin dönüşümü. *Praksis*, *30/31*, 75–95.

Atasoy, Y. (2016). Repossession, re-informalization and dispossession: The 'muddy terrain' of land commodification in Turkey. *Journal of Agrarian Change*, *17*(4), 657–679.

Ayers, A. J., & Saad-Filho, A. (2015). Democracy against neoliberalism: Paradoxes, limitations, transcendence. *Critical Sociology*, *41*(4/5), 597–618.

Balaban, O. (2011). İnşaat sektörü neyin lokomotifi? *Birikim*, *270*, 19–26.

Bartu-Candan, A. B., & Kolluoğlu, B. (2008). Emerging spaces of neoliberalism: A gated town and a public housing project in İstanbul. *New Perspectives on Turkey*, *39*, 5–46.

Bayırbağ, M. K. (2013). Continuity and change in public policy: Redistribution, exclusion and state rescaling in Turkey. *International Journal of Urban and Regional Research*, *37*(4), 1123–1146.

Benhabib, S. (2013). Turkey's authoritarian turn. *The New York Times*. Retrieved from http://www.nytimes.com/2013/06/04/opinion/turkeys-authoritarian-turn.html

Bozkurt-Güngen, S. (2018). Labour and authoritarian neoliberalism: Changes and continuities under the AKP governments in Turkey. *South European Society and Politics*, *23*(2), 219–238.

Bruff, I. (2014). The rise of authoritarian neoliberalism. *Rethinking Marxism*, *26*(1), 113–129.

Buğra, A. (1998). The immoral economy of housing in Turkey. *International Journal of Urban and Regional Research*, *22*(2), 303–317.

Buğra, A., & Savaşkan, O. (2014). *New capitalism in Turkey: The relationship between politics, religion and business*. Cheltenham: Edward Elgar.

Castree, N. (2010). Crisis, continuity and change: Neoliberalism, the left and the future of capitalism. *Antipode*, *41*(S1), 185–213.

Çavuşoğlu, E., & Strutz, J. (2014). Producing force and consent: Urban transformation and corporatism in Turkey. *City*, *18*(2), 134–148.

Clua-Losada, M., & Ribera-Almandoz, O. (2017). Authoritarian neoliberalism and the disciplining of labour. In C. B. Tansel (Ed.), *States of discipline: Authoritarian neoliberalism and the contested reproduction of capitalist order* (pp. 29–45). London: Rowman & Littlefield International.

Cozzolino, A. (2018). Reconfiguring the state: Executive powers, emergency legislation, and neoliberalization in Italy. *Globalizations*. doi:10.1080/14747731.2018.1502495

Daily Sabah. (2017). Turkey's public housing body TOKI eyes building 425,000 houses in 7 years. Retrieved from https://www.dailysabah.com/real-estate/2017/03/26/turkeys-public-housing-body-toki-eyes-building-425000-houses-in-7-years

Di Giovanni, A. (2017). Urban transformation under authoritarian neoliberalism. In C. B. Tansel (Ed.), *States of discipline: Authoritarian neoliberalism and the contested reproduction of capitalist order* (pp. 107–127). London: Rowman & Littlefield International.

Doğan, E., & Stupar, A. (2017). The limits of growth: A case study of three mega-projects in Istanbul. *Cities*, *60* (A), 281–288.

Eliçin, Y. (2014). Neoliberal transformation of the Turkish city through the urban transformation act. *Habitat International*, *41*(C), 150–155.

Enlil, Z. M. (2011). The neoliberal agenda and the changing urban form of Istanbul. *International Planning Studies*, *16*(1), 5–25.

Eraydın, A., & Taşan-Kok, T. (2014). State response to contemporary urban movements in Turkey: A critical overview of state entrepreneurialism and authoritarian interventions. *Antipode*, *46*(1), 110–129.

Erensü, S., & Karaman, O. (2017). The work of a few trees: Gezi, politics and space. *International Journal of Urban and Regional Research*, *41*(1), 19–36.

Erman, T. (2001). The politics of squatter (*Gecekondu*) studies in Turkey: The changing representations of rural migrants in the academic discourse. *Urban Studies*, *38*(7), 983–1002.

Erman, T. (2016). Formalization by the state, re-informalization by the people: A *gecekondu* transformation housing estate as site of multiple discrepancies. *International Journal of Urban and Regional Research*, *40* (2), 425–440.

Erol, I., & Unal, U. (2015). *Role of construction sector in economic growth: New evidence from Turkey* (MPRA Paper No. 68263). Retrieved from https://mpra.ub.uni-muenchen.de/68263/

Harvey, D. (1985). *The urbanization of capital*. Oxford: Basil Blackwell.

Jenss, A. (2018). Authoritarian neoliberal rescaling in Latin America: Urban in/security and austerity in Oaxaca. *Globalizations*. doi:10.1080/14747731.2018.1502493

Karaçimen, E. (2015). Interlinkages between credit, debt and the labour market: Evidence from Turkey. *Cambridge Journal of Economics*, *39*(3), 751–767.

Karaman, O. (2013). Urban neoliberalism with Islamic characteristics. *Urban Studies*, *50*(16), 3412–3427.

Karaman, O. (2014). Resisting urban renewal in Istanbul. *Urban Geography*, *35*(2), 290–310.

Kayasü, S., & Yetişkul, E. (2014). Evolving legal and institutional frameworks of neoliberal urban policies in Turkey. *METU Journal of the Faculty of Architecture*, *31*(2), 209–222.

Kreitmeyr, N. (2018). Neoliberal co-optation and authoritarian renewal: Social entrepreneurship networks in Jordan and Morocco. *Globalizations*. doi:10.1080/14747731.2018.1502492

Kuyucu, T. (2014). Law, property and ambiguity: The uses and abuses of legal ambiguity in remaking Istanbul's informal settlements. *International Journal of Urban and Regional Research*, *38*(2), 609–627.

Kuyucu, T., & Ünsal, Ö. (2010). 'Urban transformation' as state-led property transfer: An analysis of two cases of urban renewal in Istanbul. *Urban Studies*, *47*(7), 1479–1499.

Lelandais, G. E. (2014). Space and identity in resistance against neoliberal urban planning in Turkey. *International Journal of Urban and Regional Research*, *38*(5), 1785–1806.

Lovering, J., & Türkmen, H. (2011). Bulldozer neo-liberalism in Istanbul: The state-led construction of property markets and the displacement of the urban poor. *International Planning Studies*, *16*(1), 73–96.

Marschall, M., Aydoğan, A., & Bulut, A. (2016). Does housing create votes? Explaining the electoral success of the AKP in Turkey. *Electoral Studies*, *42*, 201–212.

May, J., Cloke, P., & Johnsen, S. (2005). Re-phasing neoliberalism: New Labour and Britain's crisis of street homelessness. *Antipode*, *37*(4), 703–730.

Moreno, L. (2014). The urban process under financialised capitalism. *City*, *18*(3), 244–268.

Saraçoğlu, C., & Demirtaş-Milz, N. (2014). Disasters as an ideological strategy for governing neoliberal urban transformation in Turkey: Insights from Izmir/Kadifekale. *Disasters*, *38*(1), 178–201.

Smith, N. (1996). *The new urban frontier: Gentrification and the revanchist city*. London: Routledge.

Soederberg, S. (2018). The rental housing question: Exploitation, eviction and erasures. *Geoforum*, *89*, 114–123.

Soyaltın, D. (2017) *Europeanisation, good governance and corruption in the public sector: The case of Turkey*. Abingdon: Routledge.

Swyngedouw, E., Moulaert, F., & Rodriguez, A. (2002). Neoliberal urbanization in Europe: Large-scale urban development projects and the new urban policy. *Antipode*, *34*(3), 542–577.

Tansel, C. B. (2017a). *The shape of 'rising powers' to come? The antinomies of growth and neoliberal development in Turkey* (Working paper).

Tansel, C. B. (2017b). Authoritarian neoliberalism: Towards a new research agenda. In C. B. Tansel (Ed.), *States of discipline: Authoritarian neoliberalism and the contested reproduction of capitalist order* (pp. 1–28). London: Rowman & Littlefield International.

Tansel, C. B. (2018). Authoritarian neoliberalism and democratic backsliding in Turkey: Beyond the narratives of progress. *South European Society and Politics*, *23*(2), 197–217.

Tepe, S. (2016). Urban renewal projects and democratic capacities of citizens. *Mediterranean Quarterly*, *27*(1), 71–96.

TOKİ. (2011). Building Turkey of the future. Corporate profile 2010/2011. Retrieved from http://www.toki.gov.tr/content/images/main-page-slider/30102016224921-pdf.pdf

TOKİ. (2016). Corporate profile 2016. Retrieved from http://www.toki.gov.tr/content/images/main-page-slider/16012017212815-pdf.pdf

TÜİK. (n.d. a). New buildings and additions by use of building, since 2002. Retrieved from http://www.turkstat.gov.tr/PreIstatistikTablo.do?istab_id=609

TÜİK. (n.d. b). New buildings and additions by use of building, (1954–2003). Retrieved from http://www.turkstat.gov.tr/PreIstatistikTablo.do?istab_id=2010

Türkün, A. (2011). Urban regeneration and hegemonic power relationships. *International Planning Studies*, *16* (1), 61–72.

Uysal, ÜE. (2012). An urban social movement challenging urban regeneration: The case of Sulukule, Istanbul. *Cities*, *29*(1), 12–22.

Wacquant, L. (1996). The rise of advanced marginality: Notes on its nature and implications. *Acta Sociologica*, *39*(2), 121–139.

Yeldan, A. E., & Ünüvar, B. (2015). An assessment of the Turkish economy in the AKP era. *Research and Policy on Turkey*, *1*(1), 11–28.

Yeldan, E., & Ercan, H. (2011). *Growth, employment policies and economic linkages: Turkey* (ILO Employment Working Paper, No. 84). Geneva: ILO.

Yeşil, B. (2016). *New media in Turkey: The origins of an authoritarian neoliberal state*. Urbana-Champaign, IL: University of Illinois Press.

8 Reconfiguring the state: executive powers, emergency legislation, and neoliberalization in Italy

Adriano Cozzolino

ABSTRACT

The article examines the evolution of legal and institutional mechanisms over four decades in Italy (1976–2015). Through an original data analysis of legislation on macroeconomic and financial measures, the paper investigates the reconfiguration of state institutions during the rise, consolidation and crisis of neoliberalism. I argue that the strengthening of the policy-making role of the executive, in particular through emergency legislation, proved to be key in the insulation and imposition of neoliberal and austerity policies. Furthermore, in the post-2008 period further coercive dynamics, such as the abuse of confidence question, the abuse of decree laws to impose austerity measures, and the constitutionalization of the balanced budget principle gained momentum. The data presented in this article also shows that the rise of executive power is paralleled by a gradual but steady marginalization of the policy-making role of the parliament, now often relegated to a mere ratifying institution of decisions taken elsewhere. Moreover, the growing tendency to resort to emergency and delegated legislation can be found in centre-left, centre-right and technocratic governments. Accordingly, the paper calls attention not only to the increasingly coercive legal and institutional dynamics that enshrine neoliberal policy-making, but also to an intrinsic and structural tension between the liberal democratic form of the state and increasingly authoritarian forms of neoliberalization.

Introduction

In November 2011, during the height of the sovereign debt crisis in Europe, Mario Monti,[1] under the aegis of the former president of the Republic Giorgio Napolitano, formed the third technocratic government in Italian history (the first two being in 1992–3 and 1994–5). Mario Monti had the cabinet conferred by Napolitano without 'officially declaring the government crisis [i.e. the crisis of the confidence between the executive and parliament], the early end [of the legislature], or calling for regular elections to attain the formation of a new government' (Calvano, 2014, p. 7; author's translation). Napolitano bypassed the electoral process by nominating Mario Monti as first life-senator and then Prime Minister – two acts that effectively amounted to a significant contortion of formal constitutional procedures.[2] At the same time, the previous right-wing government led by Silvio Berlusconi did not receive a formal no-confidence vote by the parliament (Article 94 of the Constitution) (Tebaldi, 2014). Monti (2012, p. 21; author's translation) himself admitted the extraordinary character of this process by noting that '[n]ot a single Italian … has chosen me except for the President of the Republic. I feel the importance of this task as we have to impose, without the citizens asking for it, unpopular measures'. The main task of his government was to win back the country's lost international 'credibility' in order to calm the financial markets and implement an extensive package of structural reforms. In the months after its formation, the Monti government managed to pass reforms concerning the pension system, the liberalization of services, labour market, public administration, fiscal adjustment, and, above all, the constitutionalization of the balanced budget principle (Article 81 of the Constitution). In this framework, the regular operations of liberal democratic procedures *appeared* to be suspended in favour of the necessity to fast-track the decision-making processes and launch, in the shortest time possible, large-scale macroeconomic reform programmes to avoid a sovereign debt default.

The question at stake is the extent to which this type of government can really be conceived as exceptional – in terms of policy content and decision-making procedures – within the trajectory of the reconfiguration of the state in the neoliberal phase of capitalism (see also Bruff & Tansel, 2018; Tansel, 2018; Wigger, 2018). Put differently, to what extent – drawing on Giorgio Agamben (2003) – is the permanent state of exception structurally inscribed in the neoliberal order and its legal and institutional practices? Scholarship on authoritarian neoliberalism has aptly stressed that the post-2007-8 and post-sovereign debt crisis phase did exacerbate – and with further innovations – the institutional and legal tendencies that had already emerged in the previous decades of neoliberal governance (Bruff, 2014; Tansel, 2017), furthering also the crisis of political authority and legitimation (Fraser, 2015). In particular, increasingly coercive neoliberalization dynamics can be detected in the 'loss or weakening of forums where social compromises can be established, maintained and strengthened' (Bruff, 2014, p. 115). The case of the marginalization of the policy-making function of the Italian Parliament is a relevant example and demonstrates important parallels with other cases, where the systematic use of emergency legal mechanisms by the executive to fast-track economic reforms and fiscal adjustment programmes have been documented (see Clua-Losada & Ribera-Almandoz, 2017; Sotiris, 2017). Such interrelated tendencies constitute, at the same time, the 'reconfiguration of state institutions and institutional power in an attempt to insulate certain policies and institutional practices from social and political dissent' in the name of market-based forms of political rule (Bruff, 2014, p. 115).

In order to assess, on empirical grounds, the long-term relation between the reconfiguration of the state and processes of neoliberalization, this article takes into account how fiscal and macroeconomic[3] policies were legislatively implemented in Italy from 1976 to 2015. A specific focus, moreover, is devoted to the post-2008 phase, when previous legal and institutional patterns went through further centralization and thus embodied increasingly coercive impositions of austerity (see also Obendorfer, 2016; Sandbeck & Schneider, 2014; Sotiris, 2017). The legislative production is linked to specific institutional sources of policy-making. In other words, the analysis of the patterns of law-making allows us to detect how the policy-making role of domestic institutions changes over time. The types of law analyzed in this article are the main legislative instruments provided for by the Italian Constitution, respectively: (I) ordinary law, namely the parliamentary legal act; (II) decree law, i.e. a legal tool at the disposal of the executive branch to be used in cases of extraordinary necessity and urgency[4] in line with Article 77 of the Constitution; and (III) the legislative decree, a further government-sponsored legal tool, issued by the executive after a formal delegation of the Parliament.[5] By tracing the distributional frequency of such laws, it is possible to assess the extent to which fiscal and macroeconomic policy can be explained in terms of the enhanced law-making activity of the executive. This, in turn, is conceived as a process of centralization and insulation of the decision-making process, which has dramatically reduced the political and institutional space for alternatives, dissent and compromises (see also Tansel, 2018).

The paper is organized as follows. The first section advances a critical political economy conceptualization of the relation between the strengthening of the executive branch and neoliberalization. This is followed by an analysis of the historical roots of the rise of executive power in Italy. In contrast to some of the well-established positions in the literature which locate the emergence of the stronger executive in the early 1990s, I argue that the growing influence of executive power emerged as a political-institutional response to the crisis of the Keynesian welfare state. The executive's enhanced agency, thus, needs to be linked back to the late 1970s and early 1980s, even though the critical juncture of the early 1990s provided a key window of opportunity to consolidate the intertwined dynamic of executive strengthening and neoliberalization. The final section sheds light on several legal and institutional innovations introduced in the post-2007-8 phase, which is understood as a period where the previously established trends towards the enhanced activism of the executive gained a further boost. The study is therefore based on a periodization of Italy's neoliberalization in three historical phases: (I) the early neoliberal phase, from the mid-1970s to the late 1980s, in which the institutional and macroeconomic foundations of neoliberalism were laid (Saad-Filho, 2010); (II) the consolidation of neoliberalism, from the early 1990s to the global financial crisis of 2007–8, which marks the beginning of the crisis of neoliberalism (Duménil & Lévy, 2011); (III) the 'late neoliberalism' phase (cf. Della Porta et al., 2017), which can be conceived as a stage of permanent socio-economic and political crisis, in which the past authoritarian tendencies came much more to the fore. The concluding remarks discuss the question of the reconfiguration of the state in the neoliberal era.

A critical political economy conceptualization of the strengthening of executive power

The strengthening of the executive branch, especially from the early 1990s onwards, has increasingly featured as a recurring theme in political science scholarship (Foleys, 1993; Poguntke & Webb, 2005). The Italian case was flagged as one of the key examples of this trend (Calise, 2005). The Italian executives, and in particular the chief executives, enhanced their policy-making leverage through several reforms passed in late 1980s and throughout the 1990s,[6] in conjunction with the consolidation of neoliberalism (Criscitiello, 2004). In large part, such institutional transformations are generally related to the crisis of the early 1990s, which opened a window of opportunity for state officials to strengthen the government vis-à-vis the Parliament in the wake of the European integration process (Della Sala, 1997). In this orientation, emphasis is placed on the role of the executive in European integration negotiations due to their complexity and to the necessity of presenting a unitary stance in Europe – which also empowered national technocrats in supranational fora (Dyson & Featherstone, 1996). A strand of this literature has stressed that the Europeanization process, by placing further constraints on national institutions, 'increased domestic policy-making capabilities both in terms of efficiency and fairness' (Radaelli & Franchino, 2004, p. 945). According to this scholarship, thanks to their participation in the European integration, domestic institutions were dragged out of the long-standing post-war institutional inertia – prevalent especially during the 1970s and 1980s – and from the ideological and political conflicts raging from the early 1960s to the late 1970s. Italy was, in other words, *rescued by Europe* (the title of Ferrera & Gualmini, 2004).

I now reconsider such explanations by adopting a critical political economy perspective on the reconfiguration of the state and the empowerment of the executive (see also Tansel, 2018;

Wigger, 2018). The first theoretical problem in 'mainstream' scholarship is that 'the economic' and 'the political-institutional' spheres are conceptualized as structurally *exterior* to each other; that is, they are considered as autonomous layers of social reality. As a result, the state is understood as a neutral site externally related to 'the economy'; the economy, in turn, emerges as a static domain in which the social relations of production and the dynamics of capitalism disappear from the outset (see, for compelling critiques, Bruff, 2011; Bruff & Hartmann, 2014). As such, the institutional transformation of the state and the transformation of capitalism are rarely regarded as structurally interlinked processes; hence, the implications of capitalist crisis for state institutions are dramatically overlooked. As maintained by Bruff and Horn (2012, p. 163), 'capitalism is a historically specific system of production and … institutions are part of this system, not in some ill-defined external relationship with it'. On the contrary, for mainstream scholarship, the sources of systemic stability or instability are exclusively located *within* the institutional system, which – with the 'right reforms' – is positioned as tendentially attaining political-institutional stability, with crises seen as anomalous or epiphenomenal. In turn, this political-institutional stability is considered essential for the stabilization of markets, especially finance. This stance has implied, first and foremost, a dramatic neglect of the increasing social inequalities that have characterized neoliberalism from the outset (see Alvaredo & Pisano, 2010, for the Italian case), and an inability to recognize neoliberalism as the primary trigger of the current political crisis of authority and legitimation in Europe – hence, a source of instability spanning over the whole social *and* institutional spectrum.

In historical terms, the institutionalist-oriented literature emphasizes that executive strengthening has largely taken place in Italy from the early 1990s onwards. This study, on the contrary, aims to provide a different periodization of the phenomenon in order to better identify the changes in executive agency in conjunction with the crisis of the broader Keynesian paradigm. In Italy, the fiscal crisis of the state and the slowdown of capital accumulation in the mid-1970s were amplified by widespread political and social conflicts triggered by one of the best-organized working classes in Europe (Bellofiore, 2001). Between 1959–67 and 1968–73, Italy experienced the most intense wave of strikes in its postwar history, as well as a mutually reinforcing improvement in unions' capacity and political participation which lasted until the late 1970s (Accornero, 1992; Franzosi, 1989). The response of state officials to the stalemate of the late 1970s emerged within a double movement of state reconfiguration and empowerment of financial markets through austerity and monetarist-oriented policy. As the following sections will demonstrate, the use of emergency legislation to enact supply-side and fiscal adjustment policies started in the late 1970s and early 1980s, rose sharply during the 1990s, and increased further in the post-2007-8 phase.

In other words, more than ten years before the beginning of the Maastricht Treaty negotiations, the legal activism of the Italian executive was already on the rise (see Figure 1). Along with other segments of the state apparatus – most prominently, the Bank of Italy and the Treasury[7] – the government started to outline and implement reform projects concerning the liberalization of financial markets, wage devaluation (especially the agreements of 1983–4), fiscal adjustment, and a monetarist policy focused on low inflation rather than economic growth (Crescenzi, 2007). Such reforms were later implemented in larger scale during the 1990s, when the power of the executive and the marginalization of Parliament were further consolidated. Moreover, in 1993 the electoral law was reformed, following a similar majoritarian logic. The objective of the reform was to ensure the stability (*governabilità*) of the politico-institutional system, fiscal consolidation and the implementation of structural reforms. In fact, the majoritarian system reduced the full representation of different societal interests to promote the formation of large coalitions of the centre-left and centre-right, which converged on supporting the same neoliberal macroeconomic programme.

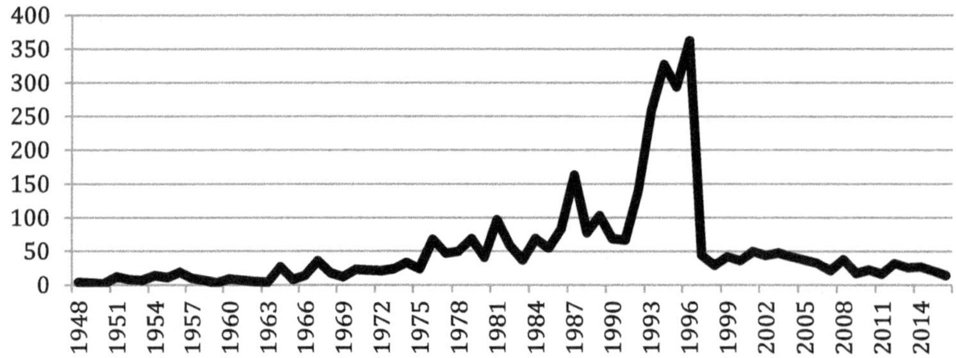

Figure 1. Decree laws passed in Italy, 1945–2016. Source: Data collected from Normattiva. Available at: http://www.normattiva.it

The final part of the puzzle revolves around the role of the European Union (EU). Generally, the EU proved to be *strategically* essential in terms of the establishment of a common continental strategy to consolidate – especially in the 1990s – large-scale processes of macroeconomic restructuring. The EU, for all intents and purposes, was the 'supranational anchor for the domestic pursuit of market freedom' (Bonefeld, 2010, p. 3). This stands in stark contrast to other perceptions of the Union as an enlightened and benevolent model (cf. Hine, 2000), capable of improving from above policy-making capabilities at the domestic level through an institutional process of adaptation to EU constraints. Nevertheless, the importance of the EU in fostering economic reform should not be overstated or simply accepted without reference to domestic institutional and macroeconomic dynamics. What is at stake here is the recognition that parallel processes of institutional reconfiguration at the domestic level and institutional building at the EU level (especially after the Maastricht Treaty) both aimed at launching and consolidating programmes of financial and macroeconomic restructuring.

This critical political economy perspective on executive strengthening has reframed the theoretical and historical dynamics of the phenomenon. The article now turns to reviewing the evidence on the relation between the enhanced law-making capacity of the executive and the consolidation of neoliberal rule.

The historical roots of the executive's law-making activism in Italy

As noted already, the 1990s in Italy are seen as the juncture in which state managers in the executive were able to exploit the window of opportunity created by the crises to consolidate the executive's leverage on domestic policy-making. The domestic scandal of *Tangentopoli*,[8] the introduction of the majoritarian system in 1993, the enactment of the Maastricht Treaty and the fiscal crisis of 1992 emerge as familiar motifs in this narrative. In light of the below data on the executive's legal activism, this claim holds true: there is a clear tendency to resort to emergency legislation in the early 1990s which contradicts the constitutional prescription to use such legislation *only* in extraordinary cases (Figure 1). Moreover, it is worth noting that throughout the 1990s several governments were led by experts/technocrats,[9] who regularly turned to emergency legislation to carry out their *ordinary* policy-making functions (Musella, 2014).

Despite this explicit trend in the first half of the 1990s, the rise of emergency legislation needs to be contextualized further. The evidence demonstrates that the use of decree laws started to increase in connection with the fiscal and social crises which erupted in mid-1970s, and the number of decree laws passed rapidly increased from 18 measures in 1975 to 51 in the next year, and steadily grew during the 1980s (Figure 1). The data concerning emergency legal mechanisms reveal that the improved law-making capacity of the executive pre-dates the advanced phase of the European integration process in the 1990s by at least one decade, notwithstanding the fact that in the 1990s the abuse of decrees achieved a historical peak with 139 decrees issued in 1992, 259 in 1993, 327 in 1994, 294 in 1995 and 362 in 1996. In 1996, a ruling of the constitutional court (No. 360/1996) censored this practice due to its plain violation of the Constitution.

The 1980s should also be considered as a period in which the Parliament maintained a substantial role in policy-making and legislative production. As shown in Figure 2,[10] in the 1980s the ordinary law still accounted for the majority of the legislative output. In other words, this period witnessed the growth of executive power on the one hand, but this was still marked by a strong parliament and party-system on the other. The marginalization of the ordinary law and of parliamentary policy-making activity gained pace from 1992 onwards, whereby the executive-parliament relations were transformed (Figure 2). In this juncture, the aforementioned window of opportunity led to the consolidation of the earlier patterns of executive strengthening, and fostered the vertical centralization of legislative and policy-making power.[11]

The analysis, so far, reveals three main trends: (I) a significant increase in the executive's law-making capacity from the late 1970s via emergency legislation and, from mid-1990s, also via legislative decrees; (II) the steady and ultimately substantial marginalization of parliamentary law from the early 1990s onwards; (III) the reduction, over the four decades considered in this study, of the volume of legislative production, which achieved its peak during the 1990s in terms of both overall law-making activity and politico-economic legislation more specifically (see Figure 6), and decreased from the early 2000s and even further from 2008 onwards. The next section will demonstrate that, in the last decade of crisis, the overall output of the legislation concerning all policy sectors shrunk, while the legislation relative just to macroeconomic and fiscal policy increased. In other words, we witness a selective mobilization of state power, via the executive's emergency legislation, aimed at enforcing neoliberal reforms.

State reconfiguration by neoliberal means: more state in the name of more market

This section analyzes the correlation between legislative patterns and the neoliberalization of Italian capitalism. To unpack this relationship, I have collated all of the legal acts issued in Italy from 1976 to

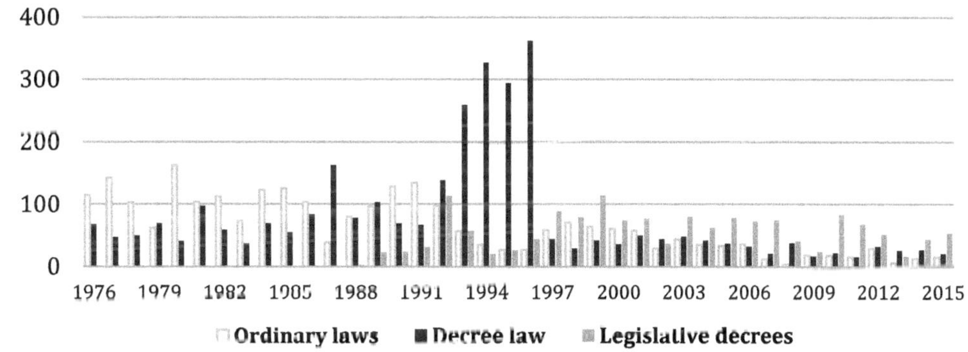

Figure 2. Ordinary laws, Decree laws, and Legislative decrees, 1976–2015. Source: Data collected from Normattiva. Available at: http://www.normattiva.it

2015 concerning macroeconomic policy, local and regional finance, and fiscal policy. The aim is to assess the frequency of the distribution of the legislation types employed in these key policy sectors, and to shed light on the evolving agency of state institutions over time.

Macroeconomic policy

Supply-side oriented macroeconomic reforms started to be implemented from the early 1980s (Graziani, 1998), when the regime change in monetary policy (July 1981) and the liberalization of financial markets were accompanied by a series of legislative interventions aimed at favouring entrepreneurship and enhancing 'the market'. The data concern a wide range of supply-side oriented interventions, such as the initiatives aimed at the reduction of labour cost, tax breaks for enterprises, enhancement and protection of competition and markets, competitiveness, subsidies for entrepreneurship, and the wider (re)regulation of market and productive activity (cf. note 3).

The distributional frequency of these legislation types shows the crucial role of executive-sponsored laws. From the early 1980s and throughout the whole period under scrutiny, there is a clear prevalence of the law of conversion of decree law (except for the five-year period between 1996 and 2000). Specifically, ordinary law accounts for 19% of the total legislation, legislative decree for 12%, and the law of conversion of decree law for 70%.

With respect to the historical trends in legislative production, the law-making activity reveals a growing tendency in two periods: from 1981 to 1995, and from 2001 to 2015. In the second period, the legislative output is higher when compared to the first phase of significant increase between 1981 and 1995. After the eruption of global economic crisis in 2007–8 and the sovereign debt crisis of 2010–11, the legislative output increased further and reached its historical peak. While 14 measures were passed through the law of conversion during the height of the crisis (2007–10), the post-crisis period of 2010–15 witnessed the consolidation of the trend with the enactment of a further 22 measures (Figure 3).

Local and regional finance

As the fiscal crisis of the Keynesian state emerged in the early 1970s, and heightened in the second half of the 1970s (see O'Connor, 1973), the first phase of austerity in Italy (1977) was punctuated by a series of measures enacted by the executive, which was concerned with the adjustment of regional

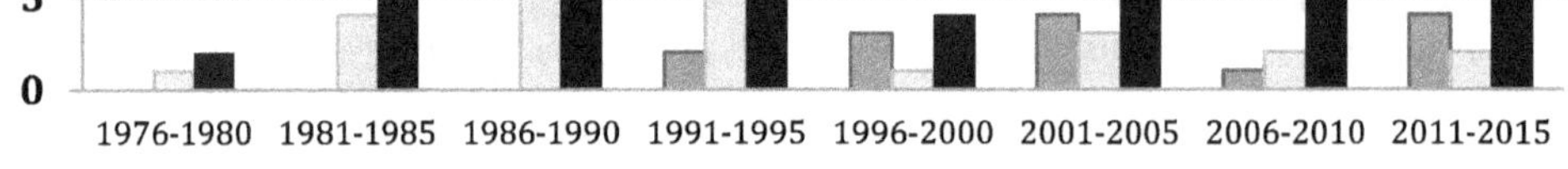

Figure 3. Legislation of macroeconomic policy, 1976–2015. Source: Data collected from Normattiva, Available at: http://www.normattiva.it

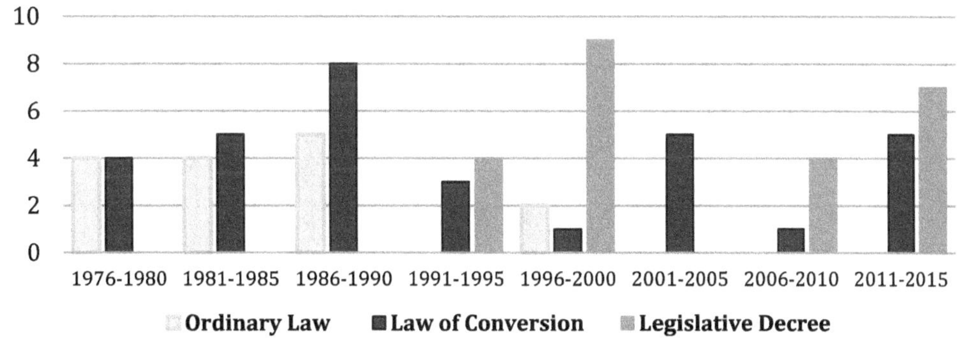

Figure 4. Legislation of local and regional finance, 1976–2015.
Source: Data collected from Normattiva. Available at: http://www.normattiva.it

and local government expenditures. Such uses of the decree law continued in the following decade, when they were employed to pass a series of extraordinary measures on local spending. In relation to the role of the Parliament, from the late 1970s and during the 1980s the ordinary law was mainly used to issue general dispositions concerning the coordination between the budget of the state and that of the regions (Figure 4).

Following the first phase of fiscal adjustment, from the early 1990s new legislative tendencies arose: the parliamentary law became marginal and the frequency of decree laws decreased. The legislative decree, on the other hand, became the main instrument of law-making activity. Throughout the 1990s, the Italian executives, influenced by the rising hegemony of the New Public Management (Capano, 2003), employed legislative decrees to pass several major reforms on public administration, taxation, education, and the pension and health systems. Local spending was part of this 'permanent cycle of reform' (Capano, 2003, p. 787), which aimed to implement the fiscal federalism project and, thus, to ration the financial transfers to local government. The reform cycle also aimed at strengthening the fiscal autonomy of local government within the framework of the Stability and Growth Pact (1997) and of business-oriented management.

After a decline in the overall volume of legislative activity from the early to mid-2000s, legislation on local and regional finance grew again in the last decade, especially in the 2011–15 period. In this recent historical juncture, the content of the policy was likewise mainly devoted to enhancing fiscal federalism (in this case, also at municipal level) and reforming local government budgets. In terms of legal mechanisms, from the early 1990s to 2015 the decree law and legislative decrees were the only types of law utilized. They accounted for, respectively, 45% and 34% of total legislation, while ordinary law only accounted for 21%. Thus, the role of the Parliament with regards to local and regional finance policy-making shrank considerably from the 2000s.

Fiscal policy

Fiscal policy includes dispositions concerning general spending mechanisms, fiscal adjustment, interventions to guarantee financial stability, and budgetary reform.[13] The fiscal measures in the first five-year period (1976–1980) were rare. In the following five years – in the beginning of the first phase of fiscal consolidation – the overall measures quadrupled due to the rise of decree laws. Importantly, the executives started to pass decree laws on fiscal adjustment measures, especially with respect to public expenditures related to the health system and welfare. From the second half of

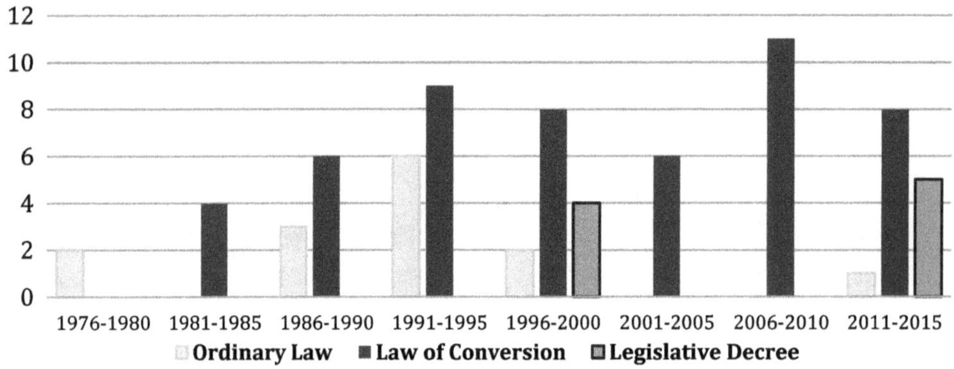

Figure 5. Legislation of fiscal policy, 1976–2015. Source: Data collected from Normattiva. Available at: http://www.normattiva.it

the 1980s, the use of decree law for the purposes of fiscal adjustment has grown consistently. The single ordinary law passed in this period is the Law No. 362 in 1988, which reformed the budget procedure and tightened the control of the executive vis-à-vis the Parliament. In conjunction with the consolidation of neoliberalism and austerity in the 1990s, the use of decrees for fiscal policy grew further (Figure 5). Fundamental measures on fiscal consolidation and reduction-cum-restructuring of public spending passed mainly through emergency legislation – even when the ordinary law was still present.

At the beginning of the twenty-first century, and as with local and regional policy, ordinary law disappeared as a legislative tool of fiscal policy. Fiscal policy, therefore, became fully associated with the law-making activity of the executive, with the Parliament acting merely as a ratifying or delegating institution. Use of the legislative decree in this sector is relatively marginal; nevertheless, this use can be linked to important general reforms of state budget and spending mechanisms, especially in the periods 1996–2000 and 2011–15. The law of conversion stands out as the legal instrument recurring with the highest frequency – 68.5% of the overall legislation – followed by ordinary law (17%) and legislative decree (14%) (Figure 5).

In the last decade, the legislative production continued to increase. This trend materialized just before the global crisis, when in 2006–7 several decrees enacted measures of fiscal consolidation (e.g. 248/2006; 286/2006). After the breakout of global economic crisis in 2007–8 and the sovereign debt crisis in 2010–11, policy-makers systematically resorted to emergency legislation and legislative decrees to pass austerity measures.

Reconfiguring the state, strengthening 'the market'

From the above empirical analysis, we can reach two main conclusions:

(I) There is a clear domination of emergency legislation, which accounts for 63% of total law-making activity from 1976 to 2015. Combined with the executive's other legal tool, the legislative decree (18%), the role of the executive proves to have been key to the long-term enforcement of market-oriented political rule and fiscal adjustment.

(II) If parliamentary legislative output in the late 1970s and throughout the 1980s was generally higher than the executive's, in macroeconomic and fiscal policy there was a steady increase

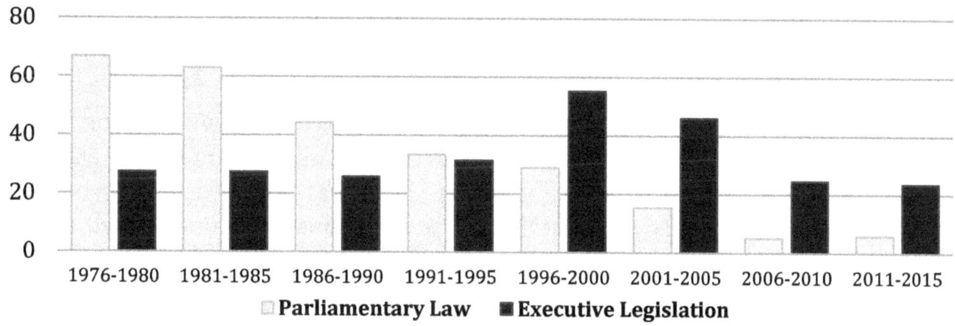

Figure 6. Parliamentary and executive political economy legislation (yearly average), 1976–2015. Source: Data collected from Normattiva. Available at: http://www.normattiva.it

in the prevalence of executive legislation. And yet, throughout the 1980s and in the first years of the 1990s, the Parliament still had a say in policy-making. It is in the consolidation phase of neoliberalism in the 1990s, and certainly from the early 2000s onwards, that the policy-making role of the Parliament was marginalized.

With respect to the patterns of overall law-making activity, the levels from the 2000s onwards are persistently lower than in the previous decades (see Figure 2). Moreover, the quantitative legislative trend in the *aggregate* political economy sector shows a declining output from the early 2000s to 2015 in terms of both the Parliament's and executive's law making activity[13] (Figure 6). Thus, while the general legislative output declined in the last fifteen years with respect to the political economy as a whole, law-making activity in the highlighted three sectors grew steadily (Cozzolino, 2018). Given this trend, the 'late neoliberalism' phase is therefore increasingly characterized by a *selective mobilization* of state powers, via and through the executive's agency, to enforce austerity policies. This now represents the predominant component of legislative output. This last evolution is analyzed in the following section.

Legal and constitutional dynamics in the post-2007-8 period of crisis: advancing the coercive practices

During and since the global economic crisis, the legal and institutional mechanisms of austerity evolved further, sharpening neoliberalism's intrinsically coercive and post-democratic tendencies. This trend emerged at both supranational and domestic levels. At the supranational level, for instance, Lukas Obendorfer (2016; see also Bruff, 2016, Sandbeck & Schneider, 2014) has aptly noted that the innovations concerning the EU legal structures introduced during the crisis phase – Fiscal Compact, Six-Pack, Two-Pack, and the overall framework of the European Semester – can be conceived as a *formal* break with representative democracy and, at the same time, as a tool of further empowerment of the European executive – the Commission in particular (cf. Bauer & Becker, 2014).

This final section reviews several institutional and legal mechanisms employed to impose austerity policies in the wake of the global economic crisis. The aim is to emphasize how the post-2007-8 innovations follow the long-term direction of neoliberalizing governance while also strengthening its coercive core. In particular, the analysis takes into account several legal and constitutional changes that emerged in the post-2007-8 period, namely: (I) increased domination of decree laws; (II) abuse of the question of confidence; (III) constitutionalization of the principle of the balanced budget – the successful attempt, but not the only one, to change the Constitution.[14]

The data presented in the previous sections already showed the long-standing relationship between neoliberalism and emergency legislation. Nevertheless, from the mid-2000s and systematically from the 2007–8 crisis onwards, the use of this type of law has gone through a further evolution. Up until the mid-2000s, decree laws on fiscal and macroeconomic policy were used to introduce quite specific measures. In the last decade, however, single decree laws became increasingly utilized as 'maxi-containers' to pass measures in different areas of policy, in some cases even anticipating the fiscal measures usually enacted by the budget and financial law of the Parliament. This novel practice consolidated from 2008 onwards, as the laws of conversion accounted for 80% of the 'multi-sectoral' bills in Italy (Di Cosimo, 2013, p. 5; the data relate to the XVI legislature; see also Delledonne, 2011). From 2007 to 2008, emergency legislation started to be *systematically* used in such a way (Francaviglia, Laze, Maccabiani, Tira, & Parmigiani, 2012; Zaccaria, 2011), representing the outstanding part of the politico-economic legislation – to the extent that the parliament's *Report on Legislation 2012* defined this practice as a 'genetic mutation' of the decree law, particularly in relation to economic and fiscal policy (quoted in Di Cosimo, 2013, p. 4). Single 'maxi-decrees', as they are labelled in legal scholarship, passed measures concerning fiscal consolidation and cuts to public expenditures, budget reform, reform of public administration and bureaucracy, privatizations, liberalizations, reduction of labour cost, labour reform, higher education reform, competitiveness and entrepreneurship, public works and infrastructures, reform of tax administration and tax reliefs for enterprises.[15] This legal mechanism also explains why, along with the dramatic reduction in the prevalence of parliamentary law (Figure 2), there has also been a quantitative reduction of the general legislative output concerning the political economy more broadly (Figure 6) – with the already-mentioned notable exception of sectors like fiscal policy and macroeconomic issues.

This plainly anti-constitutional use of decrees has been interlinked with another recent practice which was introduced in the aftermath of the 2007–8 crisis: the abuse of the confidence question. The confidence question, introduced in 1988 (Law No. 400) to strengthen executive power vis-à-vis the Parliament, can be brought by the cabinet to the Parliament with respect to key bills, so as to reduce the risk of a parliamentary rejection. In this case, the executive advises its parliamentary majority to call for new elections in case of a negative vote on the bill covered by the confidence question. At the same time, this legal mechanism serves to fast-track the approval of the specific bill, reducing the time allocated for discussion and thus for the amending power of parliamentary forces to potentially be exercised (Criscitiello, 2004). The confidence question can also be imposed on the law regarding conversion of decree laws, which has occurred regularly in the post-crisis period.

Use of the question of confidence rose in the 2008–2011 period under the Berlusconi government,[16] but the real increase occurred under Monti's technocratic government, when it skyrocketed from 15 to 45% of bills (Calvano, 2014; OpenPolis, 2015), with an average of three confidence questions per month on financial measures (Savini, 2012). From the Monti cabinet onwards, the executives have been requesting the confidence question, especially with respect to the law regarding conversion of decree laws, on economic policies. According to a dossier of the research centre OpenPolis (2015), the Monti government imposed eight confidence votes on labour reforms, five on the Stability Law of 2013, four on *Decreto Sviluppo* (a maxi-decree covering many economic issues), and another four on fiscal reform. The 'crisis executives' also systematically imposed the confidence vote on their macroeconomic policies, such as *Decreto del Fare* and *Destinazione Italia* (Letta government), the Jobs Act – i.e. more labour reform – and the Competitiveness Decree (Renzi government).[17]

The last major change introduced during the years of crisis was the constitutionalization of the balanced budget principle (Article 81) under the Monti government, which was approved by a large centre-left and centre-right coalition (Olivito, 2014; Rivosecchi, 2012). This reform, presented as the application of the EU's Fiscal Compact, occurred after two decades of fiscal consolidation, and Italian policy-makers' 'achievement' of a long-term series of primary budgetary surpluses from the early 1990s and structural cuts in primary expenditures (Balassone, Francese, & Pace, 2011).[18] This constitutional reform, thus, rather than introducing a wholesale new orientation concerning fiscal policy and the state budget, had a strong symbolic impact – it codified and embodied a real paradigm change (Mone, 2014; see also Ciervo, 2015). The Italian post-WWII Constitution posited the primacy of human beings and a socially oriented economy. Article 3, for instance, states that 'the Republic removes any economic and social barrier that, precluding freedom and social justice, would obstruct the full development of a person and the effective participation of the *workers* in the political, economic and social organization of the Country' (author's translation and emphasis). This reform – which directly contravenes the Constitution – imposed a paradigm based on market imperatives, price stability, and the 'sustainability' of debt, and reassured the EU institutions and international financial investors that the ordoliberal 'stability culture' has been finally established in Italy by constitutional means and therefore with the intention of permanent means (Rivosecchi, 2012).

Conclusion

Many scholars have demonstrated that neoliberalism has been associated with the restoration of class power and capital accumulation after the crisis of the Keynesian paradigm (Duménil & Lévy, 2011; Harvey, 2005). Others, stressing the authoritarian dimensions of neoliberalism, have laid emphasis on the impact of neoliberal governance on the institutional structures of liberal democracies (Bruff, 2014; Obendorfer, 2016) – in and beyond Europe (Tansel, 2017). This article, acknowledging the analytical pre-eminence of such social and institutional dynamics, focused on the relation between institutional change and neoliberalism in Italy. The aim of the paper was to demonstrate empirically that the historical emergence of neoliberalism is structurally linked to the reconfiguration of the state, in particular by empowering the principal decision-making institution: the executive. In Italy, the empowerment of the executive appeared mainly via the use of the legislative instrument granted to it by the Constitution: the decree law. The Constitution envisaged the power to resort to the decree only in extraordinary cases of necessity and urgency. However, as this study has revealed, executives have turned to emergency legislation on a regular basis, dramatically reducing the space for socio-economic compromises and alternatives to be considered.

The empirical analysis of the executive's legislative activism has produced several important findings. The empowered executive emerged from the late 1970s and early 1980s onwards, within the materiality of social conflicts raging during the dying days of the preceding Keynesian paradigm. Therefore, to interpret the executive's strengthening merely as a learning process of improved governing capacity facilitated by the Europeanization process entails, at best, a failure to understand the nature and historical temporality of this phenomenon. On the contrary, the data demonstrate the strong connection between macroeconomic and financial policy – core aspects of the political economy – and the executive's enhanced legal activism from the late 1970s and early 1980s onwards.

The reconfiguration of the state in the neoliberal era should be seen as an incremental process, punctuated intermittently by capitalist crises. With respect to the Italian case, the 1992–93 and

2008–11 junctures proved to be key windows of opportunity to enhance a 'market'-like rule and government's overall power. Both these junctures presented similar dynamics marked by fiscal crisis and emergency, as well as political uncertainty. The sense of emergency was invoked to legitimize further institutional restrictions on the possibilities for political accountability and for the pursuit of goals linked to alternative social and political programmes. Moreover, the data demonstrate that the use of emergency legislation to enact neoliberal reforms was equally supported by the centre-right and the centre-left, thus dramatically restricting the possibility for Italian voters to opt for a *real* alternative. This, for instance, explains the collapse of the Democratic Party – broadly associated with wealthy elites in the country – in the general elections of March 2018 and the rise of populist and eurosceptic forces such as the Five Star Movement and the Northern League. These two parties subsequently formed a government, but not before the President, Sergio Mattarella, vetoed the original choice of Paolo Savona as finance minister due to Savona's hostility to the euro and to Eurozone governance structures. The ensuing controversy should be viewed in light of the argument found in this article. Mattarella's decision was rather unexceptional given the prior, steady enhancement of executive powers, and his actions were thus analogous to those of Napolitano in 2011 – not least because Mattarella invoked the possibility that Savona would alarm financial markets and discourage foreign investment into Italy.

Such dynamics are therefore inscribed into the long-term trajectory of the anti-democratic restructuring of democratic procedures. The institutional changes which occurred after the crisis of 2007–8 and the sovereign debt crisis of 2010–11 can be regarded as the mature phase of neoliberal governance, the foundations of which had been laid and consolidated in the previous decades. What is at stake in this overall trajectory of neoliberalization is the need to recognize the structural tension between the liberal-democratic state form and 'market' – especially finance – rule. While the crisis of neoliberalism unfolds, the crisis of parliamentary democracy continues to intensify: the obsessive quest for stability via empowering 'markets' through decision-making centralization has left us with systemic instabilities and a structural crisis of political legitimation.

Notes

1. Mario Monti was Professor of Political Economy and Dean of the Italian private business school Luigi Bocconi; head and/or member of several Italian reform commissions for the liberalization of financial markets during the 1980s; adviser to the global investment bank Goldman Sachs; president of the Italian group of the Trilateral Commission; and former European Commissioner of the Internal Market DG (1995–1998) and Competition DG (1999–2004).
2. Cf. Articles 92, 93, and 94 of the Italian Constitution. More importantly, this period was characterized by the unprecedented stretching of the political power of the Presidency of the Republic under the aegis of Giorgio Napolitano.
3. 'Macroeconomic issues' in the areas of political economy policy-making include measures on competitiveness, productivity, supply-side oriented reforms, tax breaks for enterprises, general market regulations and multiple economic dispositions.
4. According to the Italian Constitution (Article 77.2), the executive has the power to enact a decree law *only* in cases of extraordinary necessity and urgency. The decree law comes automatically into force; nonetheless, the Parliament has to ratify the decree within sixty days through a specific bill called law of conversion. If the Parliament does not issue the law of conversion of the decree law after 60 days, the *status quo ante* of the decree law is restored. Importantly, the decree law, due to the strict deadline, is a way to impose the policy priorities of the executive over those of parliamentary forces.
5. The delegating law is a law formally approved by the Parliament that contains one or more provisions through which it delegates the executive to enact legislative decrees. In the delegating act, the Parliament

states the general criteria and the timeline of the legislative activity, while the specific content of the law is left to the executive (Article 76).

6. The first major reform occurred in 1988, when Law no. 400 reorganized and strengthened the overall structure of the presidency of the council. The presidency of the council was reformed again by two-centre left governments in 1997 (Law no. 59) and 1999 (Law no. 303).
7. In July 1981, the Treasury and the Bank of Italy split (the so-called 'divorce'). Central bank independence was thus fundamental to the imposition of monetarist policy.
8. A system of illegal financing to political parties that in a few months wiped out, directly or indirectly, a large portion of the political establishment of the time. The scandal erupted in 1992.
9. The first government was led by Giuliano Amato, a law professor (June 1992 to April 1993); the second was a technocratic government, and was led by the governor of the Bank of Italy, Carlo Azeglio Ciampi (April 1993 to May 1994); the third, similarly a fully technocratic cabinet, was led by Lamberto Dini, general director of the Bank of Italy (January 1995 to October 1998).
10. Ordinary laws of ratification of international treaties, budget law and *finanziaria* were not included in Figure 2, for they would have biased the result.
11. See, for example, the rising frequency of the other type of government-sponsored law: the legislative decree. The legislative decrees, which were marginal until the early 1990s, substituted the decree law after the censorship ruling of the constitutional court in 1996 (Figure 2).
12. The data excluded budget laws (Article 81 of the Constitution) and financial bills (meaningfully introduced in 1978) in order to place emphasis on the specific interventions implemented 'outside' these laws.
13. The data concerning macroeconomic policy, local and regional finance, and fiscal policy are part of a broader dataset constructed for my PhD project and based on the collection and classification of all the laws passed in the Italian Parliament between 1976 and 2015 regarding the political economy in general (Cozzolino, 2018).
14. Attempts to reform the Constitution materialized in 2006 and in 2016, respectively under the centre-right Berlusconi government and the centre-left Renzi government. Such attempts, both rejected by a popular referendum, aimed at changing the architecture of government in order to speed up the legislative process and enhance further the centralization of decision-making. Their rejection indicated the growing structural crisis of political legitimation in Italy, as further exemplified in the March 2018 elections.
15. The use of decrees to implement measures was systematic in the crisis years. See, among others, Salva Italia Decree (214/2011), Cresci Italia Decree (27/2012), Decreto Sviluppo (134/2012) (Monti government); Decreto del fare (98/2013), Decreto Imu (124/2013), Destinazione Italia (9/2014) (Letta government), decree no. 80/2014, 89/2014, Decreto Competitività (116/2014) (Renzi government).
16. Among others, see the reform packages 'Anti-crisis Decree' (no. 2/2009), 'Anti-crisis Measures' (no. 102/2009), 'Urgent measures to reduce public spending of local public authorities and regions' (no. 42/2010), 'European semester – first urgent economic dispositions' (no. 106/2011), 'Urgent measures for financial stabilization' (no. 111/2011).
17. According to my own calculations based on the database Normattiva.it and the statistics produced in the Senate database, out of 24 bills (mainly decree laws) regarding the political economy from 2008 to 2016, the confidence question was imposed on 21 bills (in several cases, also more than once).
18. See the note of the parliamentary activity *Il Pareggio di Bilancio in Costituzione*, available at http://leg16.camera.it/465?area=1&tema=496&Il±pareggio±di±bilancio±in±Costituzione.

Acknowledgements

Many thanks to Angela Wigger for comments on the first draft of the paper. Thanks also to the two anonymous reviewers and to the editors of this special issue, who carefully read and commented on the paper.

Disclosure statement

No potential conflict of interest was reported by the author.

References

Accornero, A. (1992). *La parola del sindacato. Ascesa e declino di una cultura*. Bologna: Il Mulino.

Agamben, G. (2003). *Lo Stato di Eccezione*. Torino: Bollati Boringheri.

Alvaredo, F., & Pisano, E. (2010). Top incomes in Italy 1974–2004. In A. B. Atkinson & T. Piketty (Eds.), *Top incomes: A global perspective* (pp. 625–658). Oxford: Oxford University Press.

Balassone, F., Francese, M., & Pace, A. (2011, October 12–15). *Public debt and economic growth in Italy*. Paper presented at the Conference 'Italy and the World Economy, 1861–2011' Rome, Banca d'Italia.

Bauer, M., & Becker, S. (2014). The unexpected winner of the crisis: The European Commission's strengthened role in economic governance. *Journal of European Integration*, *36*(3), 213–229.

Bellofiore, R. (2001). I lunghi anni Settanta. Crisi sociale e integrazione economica internazionale. In L. Baldissara (Ed.), *Le radici della crisi* (pp. 57–102). Rome: Carocci.

Bonefeld, W. (2010). Free economy and the strong state: Some notes on the state. *Capital & Class*, *34*(1), 15–24.

Bruff, I. (2011). Overcoming the state/market dichotomy. In S. Shields, I. Bruff, & H. Macartney (Eds.), *Critical international political economy: Dialogue, debate and dissensus* (pp. 80–98). Basingstoke: Palgrave Macmillan.

Bruff, I. (2014). The rise of authoritarian neoliberalism. *Rethinking Marxism*, *26*(1), 113–129.

Bruff, I. (2016). Neoliberalism and authoritarianism. In S. Springer, K. Birch, & J. MacLeavy (Eds.), *The handbook of neoliberalism* (pp. 107–117). New York, NY: Routledge.

Bruff, I., & Hartmann, E. (2014). Neo-pluralist political science, economic sociology and the conceptual foundations of the comparative capitalisms literatures. *Capital & Class*, *38*(1), 73–85.

Bruff, I., & Horn, L. (2012). Varieties of capitalism in crisis? *Competition & Change*, *16*(3), 161–168.

Bruff, I., & Tansel, C. B. (2018). Authoritarian neoliberalism: Trajectories of knowledge production and praxis. *Globalizations*. doi:10.1080/14747731.2018.1502497

Calise, M. (2005). Presidentialization: Italian style. In T. Poguntke & D. Webb (Eds.), *The presidentialization of politics: A comparative study of modern democracies* (pp. 88–106). Oxford: Oxford University Press.

Calvano, R. (2014). La Decretazione d'urgenza nella stagione delle larghe intese. *Associazione Italiana dei Costituzionalisti*, *2*, 1–23.

Capano, G. (2003). Administrative traditions and policy change: When policy paradigms matter. The case of Italian administrative reform during the 1990s. *Public Administration*, *81*(4), 781–801.

Ciervo, A. (2015). Con la scusa della crisi. Il neo-liberismo e le trasformazioni dello stato costituzionale. Riflessioni a partire da due recenti volumi di Pierre Dardot e Christian Laval. *Costituzionalismo.it*, *3*, 29–68.

Clua-Losada, M., & Ribera-Almandoz, O. (2017). Authoritarian neoliberalism and the disciplining of labour. In C. B. Tansel (Ed.), *States of discipline: Authoritarian neoliberalism and the contested reproduction of capitalist order* (pp. 29–45). London: Rowman & Littlefield International.

Cozzolino, A. (2018). *The political economy of state transformation from the crisis of the Keynesian welfare state to the crisis of the neoliberal paradigm* (unpublished doctoral dissertation). University L'Orientale, Naples, Italy.

Crescenzi, A. (2007). *I documenti di programmazione: una lettura della politica economica in Italia dal Piano Marshall al DPEF 2008–2011*. Rome: LUISS University Press.

Criscitiello, A. (2004). *Il cuore dei governi. Le politiche di riforma degli esecutivi in prospettiva comparata*. Napoli: Edizioni Scientifiche Italiane.

Della Porta, D., Andretta, M., Fernandes, T., O'Connor, F., Romanos, E., & Vogiatzoglu, M. (Eds.). (2017). *Late neoliberalism and its discontents in the economic crisis: Comparing social movements in the European periphery*. London: Palgrave Macmillan.

Della Sala, V. (1997). Hollowing out and hardening the state: European integration and the Italian economy. *West European Politics*, *20*(1), 14–33.

Delledonne, G. (2011). Decretazione d'urgenza, indirizzo politico e programma di governo. In R. Zaccaria (Ed.), *Fuga dalla legge? Seminari sulla qualità della legislazione* (pp. 74–77). Brescia: Grafo.

Di Cosimo, G. (2013). Il Governo pigliatutto: la legislazione d'urgenza nella XVI legislatura. *Osservatorio sulle fonte*, *1*, 1–9.

Duménil, G., & Lévy, D. (2011). *The crisis of neoliberalism*. Cambridge: Harvard University Press.

Dyson, K., & Featherstone, K. (1996). Italy and EMU as a 'Vincolo Esterno': Empowering the technocrats, transforming the state. *South European Society and Politics*, *1*(2), 272–299.

Ferrera, M., & Gualmini, E. (2004). *Rescued by Europe? Social and labour market reforms in Italy from Maastricht to Berlusconi*. Amsterdam: Amsterdam University Press.

Foleys, M. (1993). *The rise of the British presidency*. Manchester: Manchester University Press.

Francaviglia, M., Laze, M., Maccabiani, N., Tira, E., & Parmigiani, F. (2012). L'attività normativa del governo Monti. *Associazione Italiana dei Costituzionalisti*, *4*, 1–40.

Franzosi, R. (1989). Strike data in search of a theory: The Italian case in the postwar period. *Politics & Society*, *17*(4), 453–480.

Fraser, N. (2015). Legitimation crisis? On the political contradictions of financialized capitalism. *Critical Historical Studies*, *2*(2), 157–189.

Graziani, A. (1998). *Lo Sviluppo dell'Economia Italiana. Dalla Ricostruzione alla Moneta Europea*. Torino: Bollati Boringheri.

Harvey, D. (2005). *A brief history of neoliberalism*. Oxford: Oxford University Press.

Hine, D. (2000). European policy-making and the machinery of Italian government. *South European Society and Politics*, *5*(2), 25–46.

Mone, D. (2014). La costituzionalizzazione del pareggio di bilancio ed il potenziale vulnus alla teoria dei controlimiti. *Associazione Italiana dei Costituzionalisti*, *3*, 2–29.

Monti, M. (2012). *Le parole e i fatti*. F. Fubini (Ed.). Milan: Rizzoli.

Musella, F. (2014). A premier without parliament: The legislative process in the Italian second republic. *Journal of Comparative Politics*, *7*(1), 4–17.

Obendorfer, L. (2016). A new economic governance through secondary legislation? Analysis and constitutional assessment: From new constitutionalism, via authoritarian constitutionalism, to progressive constitutionalism. In N. Bruun, K. Lorcher, & I. Schomann (Eds.), *The economic and financial crisis and collective labour law in Europe* (pp. 25–54). London: Bloomsbury.

O'Connor, J. (1973). *The fiscal crisis of the state*. New York, NY: Saint Martin's Press.

Olivito, E. (2014). Crisi economico-finanziaria ed equilibri costituzionali. Qualche spunto a partire dalla lettere della BCE al governo italiano. *Associazione Italiana dei Costituzionalisti*, *1*, 1–18.

Open Polis. (2015). Premierato all'Italiana. Retrieved from https://www.openpolis.it/dossier/premierato-allitaliana

Poguntke, T., & Webb, D. (Eds.). (2005). *The presidentialization of politics: A comparative study of modern democracies*. Oxford: Oxford University Press.

Radaelli, C., & Franchino, F. (2004). Analysing political change in Italy. *Journal of European Public Policy*, *11* (6), 941–953.

Rivosecchi, G. (2012). Il c.d. pareggio di bilancio tra Corte e legislatore, anche nei suoi riflessi sulle regioni: quando la paura prevale sulla ragione. *Associazione Italiana Dei Costituzionalisti*, *3*, 1–28.

Saad-Filho, A. (2010). Monetary policy in the neo-liberal transition: A political economy critique of Keynesianism, monetarism and inflation targeting. In B. Jessop, R. Albritton, & R. Westra (Eds.), *Political economy and global capitalism* (pp. 89–119). London: Anthem Press.

Sandbeck, S., & Schneider, E. (2014). From the sovereign debt crisis to authoritarian statism: Contradictions of the European state project. *New Political Economy*, *19*(6), 847–871.

Savini, C. (2012). Note brevissime sull'uso della questione di fiducia nell'esperienza del Governo Monti. *Osservatorio sulle Fonti*, *3*, 2–8.

Sotiris, P. (2017). The authoritarian and disciplinary mechanism of reduced sovereignty in the EU: The case of Greece. In C. B. Tansel (Ed.), *States of discipline: Authoritarian neoliberalism and the contested reproduction of capitalist order* (pp. 171–187). London: Rowman & Littlefield International.

Tansel, C. B. (Ed.). (2017). *States of discipline: Authoritarian neoliberalism and the contested reproduction of capitalist order*. London: Rowman & Littlefield International.

Tansel, C. B. (2018). Reproducing authoritarian neoliberalism in Turkey: Urban governance and state restructuring in the shadow of executive centralization. *Globalizations*. doi:10.1080/14747731.2018.1502494

Tebaldi, M. (2014). From notary to ruler: The role of the president of the republic during the Italian crisis (2010–14). *South European Society and Politics*, *19*(4), 561–581.

Wigger, A. (2018). The new EU industrial policy: Authoritarian neoliberal structural adjustment and the case for alternatives. *Globalizations*. doi:10.1080/14747731.2018.1502496

Zaccaria, R. (Ed.). (2011). *Fuga dalla legge? Seminari sulla qualità della legislazione*. Brescia: Grafo.

OPEN ACCESS

9 The new EU industrial policy: authoritarian neoliberal structural adjustment and the case for alternatives

Angela Wigger

ABSTRACT

In 2017, European Commission President Jean-Claude Juncker declared the re-industrialization of the European Union (EU) a top priority. The new EU industrial policy seeks to boost industrial competitiveness and leverage investments into manufacturing, thereby increasing industry's share of EU Gross Domestic Product (GDP) to 20% by 2020. What may appear to be a Keynesian industrial policy and thus a move away from the EU's previous neoliberal agenda, however, seeks to calibrate a further neoliberal structural adjustment in a highly authoritarian fashion. Internal devaluation through devaluing labour, intensifying competition and reducing corporate taxes takes centre-stage. As an auxiliary to the European Semester, national productivity boards have been established to monitor wage developments alongside labour productivity and to suggest policy adjustments when cost competitiveness lags behind the Eurozone average and that of the main trading partners. Not only have formal democratic institutions and organized labour been circumvented in the decision-making process regarding such boards, they will have little voice in the future, and this an area that hitherto fell largely within the scope of member states: wage bargaining. Hence, the new EU industrial policy needs to be discredited, de-legitimized and thus, politicized. A political counter-project, rooted in an alternative industrial policy geared towards fostering horizontal and democratic solidarity economy initiatives which have proliferated since 2008, is discussed in the article's closing pages.

Introduction

With the ascendancy of neoliberalism at the European Union (EU) level since the 1980s, industrial policy came to be denounced as old-fashioned and inefficient, rescuing only temporarily 'sunset industries' or 'lame duck' companies from their inevitable downturn. Today, ten years after the 2008 crisis hit, industrial policy seems to be rising like a phoenix from its ashes. Aware that EU austerity politics in response to the crisis has been anything but successful, and alarmed by the rapid deindustrialization of EU economies, the European Commission (2014) heralded the 'European Industrial Renaissance' as the next step in EU crisis management. In theory, the new EU industrial policy will trigger a back-shoring of manufacturing capacity in knowledge-intensive sectors from China and other emerging markets to Europe. The Commission prophesied an increase of the manufacturing share of EU GDP from currently 15% to 20% by 2020, provided that competitiveness reforms would be adopted. The view is that the EU's future prosperity depends on export-led growth, which in turn relies on the ability to attract investments into the real production economy, most notably Foreign Direct Investment to compensate for low domestic investment.

Scholars and politicians have considered the new EU industrial policy a turn away from previous neoliberal austerity politics (see Pochet, 2016). Indeed, the Council of the European Union (2017)[1] affirmed that a holistic industrial policy will be central, and Dijsselbloem (2017), social democrat and former head of the Eurogroup,[2] announced a change in the policy mix of the EU crisis management: 'moving away from austerity and putting more emphasis on deep reforms.' Similarly, when his successor Mário Centeno, incumbent since January 2018, echoed Dijsselbloem, Gianni Pittella (in CNBC, 2017), the leader of the Socialists and Democrats grouping in the European Parliament, triumphed: 'We are finally overcoming the era of blind and stupid austerity that has left behind even more poor and divided societies across Europe.' Against the backdrop of widespread popular fatigue with fiscal austerity and persistently high unemployment since 2009, reforms that counter the decline of the EU's industrial base appear much-needed. However, what may seem at first glance to be a Keynesian industrial policy instead promises to intensify the neoliberal structural adjustment that we have seen hitherto.

What is not immediately visible is that the new EU industrial policy, in addition to various funds leveraging private investments, has a strong internal devaluation component. Internal devaluation is a strategy that seeks to substitute for currency devaluations as a way to reduce (export) prices and increase industrial competitiveness relative to other economies.[3] It can entail a mix of structural changes, such as labour and product market reforms that increase wage and price flexibility (Armingeon & Baccaro, 2012, p. 256), or a reduction of trade costs and corporate taxes (Petroulakis, 2017). The European Commission (2016) declared improving the global 'price' and 'cost' competitiveness of EU manufacturers a central goal, and envisaged a three-tier internal devaluation strategy: first, depreciating real wages and inducing further labour market reforms; second, intensifying inter-company competition to lower prices; and third, lowering the overall level of corporate taxation.

Adopting a historical materialist perspective, the article argues that the suggested internal devaluation strategy will devalue labour in turbospeed, putting the burden of adjustment once more on labour rather than capital. While wage repression, labour market reforms, and intense price competition directly and indirectly deflate the cost of labour, the reduction of corporate taxes also expedites a further redistribution of wealth from labour to capital. Consequently, the share of 'working poor' and precarious workers is likely to increase further, with particularly severe impacts on the youth, women, and migrants, and low-skilled workers. Moreover, structural asymmetries within the EU will only worsen, and with it the propensity to invest. In addition to constituting a major assault on labour, the article shows that the chosen institutional architecture for internal devaluation reveals highly authoritarian traits, epitomizing what Bruff (2014) termed authoritarian neoliberalism (see also Oberndorfer, 2014; Sandbeck & Schneider, 2014; Tansel, 2017; Cozzolino, 2018).

Particularly, the recently established national productivity boards, which will function as an auxiliary to the reforms conducted under the European Semester,[4] form the touchstone for the governance framework for internal devaluation. In sharp contrast to studies that consider the new EU industrial policy as 'horizontal in nature' and national productivity boards as politically 'neutral' (Berglof, 2016; Pochet, 2016; Schout & Schwieter, 2018), the article demonstrates that not only have national parliaments and the European Parliament been circumvented in the decision-making process regarding such boards, but formal democratic institutions will also remain structurally disempowered in the future. Set up as 'politically independent' institutions, national productivity boards have been entrusted with the task of ensuring that member states raise productivity while containing unit labour costs, and suggesting policies when cost competitiveness lags behind the euro area average and the main trading partners (Council of the European Union, 2016; European Council, 2016). The democratically unelected and unaccountable European Commission will supervise these boards, formulate common standards for measuring productivity, and make use of ensuing annual reports in the European Semester. Thereby, EU executive and bureaucratic powers will be strengthened in the wage-setting process, an area that hitherto has fallen outside of EU competences, while the role of organized labour is likely to be marginalized, if not completely ruled out.

The article primarily discusses internal devaluation with reference to the labour market and intensified capitalist competition.[5] The next section locates the internal devaluation programme within the new EU industrial policy and outlines why it will only increase structural asymmetries in the EU. Section two reveals the authoritarian neoliberal character of national productivity boards. As there is a need to not just explain and critique the ongoing neoliberal reconfigurations of the EU state apparatus, but also to consider how the contradictions immanent to such reconfigurations provide opportunities for groups struggling for a post-neoliberal and a post-capitalist world, section three discusses what an alternative EU industrial policy could look like, and suggests policies that support solidarity economy initiatives. The conclusions summarize the article's main contributions.

The new EU industrial policy: internal devaluation through the backdoor

In its Communication 'For a European Industrial Renaissance', the European Commission (2014) set the target to make 'the EU a more attractive location for the production of goods and services', and to reverse the ongoing deindustrialization in Europe reflected in the transfer of manufacturing capacity to China and other emerging markets. The Commission acknowledged that the pace of economic recovery since 2008 has been slow, and ascribed this to the absence of investment into European industries. Indeed, both private and public investment in production has undergone a downward trend since the 1970s, which has been due to saturated markets, lingering industrial overcapacity alongside slowly growing aggregate demand, as well as a vast outsourcing and offshoring of labour-intensive production to low-wage countries. Moreover, the tertialization of European economies required far less investment, while the ever-expanding financial sector absorbed vast shares of surplus capital not invested in industrial production (Wigger, 2017). The decline of investment has accelerated further since the turn of the century, and particularly since the imposition of austerity: in the absence of public investment, private investments have also been withheld (Barbiero & Darvas, 2014). Measured in terms of gross fixed capital formation, investment in the EU decreased from 22.1% of GDP in 2000 to 19.2% in 2013, with only a marginal increase to 19.8% in 2016 (Eurostat, 2017). This compares poorly to China and India, with roughly 45% and 30% respectively (World Bank, 2018). While the investment downturn also affected services, manufacturing saw most of the reductions, albeit in an uneven fashion, hitting particularly hard the EU's South, with shortfalls ranging here from 25% to 60% (European Commission, 2017a).

The new EU industrial strategy consists of multiple funds and policy measures that seek to leverage private investments into manufacturing. The European Fund for Strategic Investments (EFSI), established in 2015, is probably the most prominent measure. Also referred to as the Juncker Funds, named after Commission President Jean-Claude Juncker, the EFSI seeks to co-finance private financing for risky 'infrastructure and innovation projects' that would not otherwise be funded. Similarly, the Programme for the Competitiveness of Enterprises and Small and Medium-sized Enterprises (COSME), established in 2014, seeks to improve SMEs' access to credit on the basis of EU guarantees and counter-guarantees, as well as through using the securitization of debt-finance portfolios as leverage: every euro invested in a loan guarantee is expected to release up to 30 euros of private investment (European Commission, 2018a). In a similar vein, the European Steel Action Plan, Horizon2020 and even the European Defence Action have been subsumed under the new EU industrial policy, and the Commission (2017b) announced future specific action plans for almost every imaginable industrial sector. Additionally, flanking programmes such as 'Better Regulation', 'Regulatory Fitness and Performance Programme' (REFIT) or 'Competitiveness Proofing' have been employed for the sake of simplifying or removing existing legislation considered costly for business, as well as for screening new legislation regarding its impact on the global competitiveness of EU industries.

While the above-mentioned funds and programmes seek to unlock private investments in one way or another, the Commission also seeks to boost the 'cost' and 'price' competitiveness of EU manufacturing industries as a way of attracting investments, ultimately serving the goal of catalyzing export-led economic growth. According to the Commission (2013), manufacturing, which currently accounts for 40% of all EU exports, will be the main driver for future innovation, jobs, growth and wealth. Hence, improving 'cost' and 'price' competitiveness is considered a prerequisite for allowing EU manufacturing industries to compete successfully on global markets.

Improving 'cost' competitiveness through deflating the cost of labour

A central yardstick for assessing and comparing the evolution of 'cost' competitiveness is unit labour costs, a ratio between productivity and total labour compensation indicating whether labour costs rise in line with productivity gains. The components can vary and range from direct and indirect labour cost structures (which include wages and employers' contributions as well as social security and pension schemes), vis-a-vis units of produced output or hours worked (measured either at company, industry, regional or national level). The general idea is that reducing unit labour costs will have positive signalling effects to investors, eventually leading to a re-industrialization process across Europe, higher net exports and economic growth, with a positive trickle-down effect on employment. Unit labour costs can be reduced by increasing productivity or by reducing elements of the total labour costs structure. However, as productivity in the EU has slowed considerably alongside vast deindustrialization since the 1970s, and as productivity gains in the tertiary sector are difficult to achieve, supply-side strategies, such as labour market adjustments, including wage suppression or labour market flexibilization, generally receive all of the emphasis.

Internal devaluation through deflating labour has been on the EU agenda for quite some time. The rigid disciplinary rules and institutions of the Economic and Monetary Union (EMU) already prefigured internal devaluation: exchange rate adjustments to cheapen export prices in a context of low inflation and a single currency were no longer an option, while budgetary straitjackets ruled out national deficit spending and thereby also interventionist industrial policies. Under this yoke, labour market adjustments therefore became a prominent strategic goal. When the crisis hit in 2008 and trade balances worsened, the Commission (2011b, p. 22) advocated internal devaluation as a way to 'mimic the expenditure-switching effects of "external" exchange rate devaluation'. Scoreboards of unit labour costs were subsequently used as headline indicators in the so-called Memoranda of Understanding between member states and the Troika or the IMF/EU, the 2011 European Semester, the 2011 Euro Plus Pact or the Six Pack (European Commission, 2018b; see also Erne, 2015).[6] Losses in cost competitiveness and overall low investment levels in so-called deficit countries were linked to sustained increases of unit labour costs and/or the persistence of restrictive employment protection legislation, both of which were, it was argued, detrimental to Europe's economic prospects (European Commission, 2014, 2017c). The argument generally was that countries such as Greece, Ireland, Spain and Portugal had real wage increases far beyond what could be justified on the basis of their productivity performances. Indeed, since 2000 unit labour costs in the Southern periphery increased 25–30% faster than those of Germany (Stockhammer & Onaran, 2012, p. 198).

Germany's comparatively low unit labour costs served as a benchmark for a reason: Chancellor Schröder's Agenda 2010 reforms of 2003–5 entailed a far-reaching internal devaluation programme, consisting of reducing job protection, tightening job acceptance regulations for the unemployed (including so-called 1 euro jobs outside regular labour markets), deregulating temporary work agencies, dismantling social welfare and reducing social contributions for long-term unemployed, decentralizing collective bargaining, and cutting corporate taxes (see also Bruff, 2015). As part of the EU's crisis management strategy, 'Modell Deutschland' seems to have been elevated as the EU standard (see also Beck & Germann 2018, on Modell Deutschland). In fact, German Chancellor Merkel (2013) repeatedly emphasized that it was vital to keep driving down labour costs in order to create a regulatory environment in Europe that is attractive to investors. Merkel articulated what organized (transnational) industrial interests, such as in the configuration of the so-called Captains of Industry, assembled in the European Round Table of Industrialists (ERT), have been pushing for over the last few decades. It is not a coincidence that Merkel invited the ERT to Berlin in 2013, together with the-then French President Hollande and Commission President Barroso, where it was jointly agreed that industrial competitiveness should be at the centre of EU policy-making (ERT, 2013). More concretely, it was agreed that business-friendly regulations, such as tax reductions, less labour protection and thus more labour market flexibilization, and lower wages and severance payments were needed, in addition to further privatizations as well as the facilitation of mergers and acquisitions – or what the ERT called 'market-driven consolidation' (ERT, 2013). To put industrial competitiveness 'at the core of each and every European policy' has moreover been iterated in joint declarations by nationally organized industrial capital groups, such as the German BDI, the Italian Confindustria and the French MEDEF (BDI, 2014a, 2014b), as well as a joint declaration handsigned by 125 CEOs in the European manufacturing industry (see Joint Declaration of Industry Representatives, 2017). And when the ERT in 2014 issued the 'EU Industrial Renaissance: Agenda for Action 2014–2019', consisting of policy priorities and a set of instructions for the then newly appointed Commission (see ERT, 2014, p. 1), the Commission (2014) soon after followed with its eponymic 'For a European Industrial Renaissance' Communication.

The industrial competitiveness agenda has also been pushed by organized labour. In 2016, the European Trade Union Confederation (ETUC), the umbrella organization of national trade unions, joined forces with BusinessEurope, calling 'on EU institutions to bring competitive and sustainable industry back to the core of the EU policy agenda' (ETUC & BusinessEurope, 2016). Surely, ETUC does not subscribe to an industrial policy based on devaluing labour, but construals that link the crisis' root causes to a lack of industrial competitiveness, and that seek solutions in attracting industrial investments, seem to have an enthralling effect. Against the backdrop of 'America First', or the 'Make in India' or 'Made in China 2025' strategies (which seek to transform India into the next manufacturing destination and China into the leading manufacturing power), both organized labour and the statist centre-left seem preoccupied with winning the global competitiveness race and thus can be supportive of schemes that come with the air of a Keynesian industrial strategy, despite their concrete implications.

Scoreboards of unit labour costs, alongside other competitiveness performance indexes and benchmarks of best practices, are disciplinary policy tools that constitute the apex of the neoliberal organization of capitalism. As Marx observed in the *Grundrisse* (1973 [1939], p. 164), under capitalism, individuals are ruled by abstractions and the character of these abstractions is 'a product of historic relations'. Unit labour costs are such an abstraction. They are what Marx called a crude reductionist travesty that dehumanizes and objectifies commodified labour. As a calculus for competitive comparisons, EU member states will have to undercut each other's unit labour costs in a 'beggar-thy-neighbour' fashion. This is likely to exacerbate existing structural asymmetries in the EU (see also ETUI, 2016). To begin with, internal devaluation in Germany has been anything but a success story. While three-quarters of the German GDP has indeed been driven by net exports since 2000, job growth was mostly due to the expansion of precarious and part-time employment (Sandbu, 2016, pp. 27–28). Rather than investing in Germany, manufacturers relocated production to cheap labour areas in Central and Eastern Europe from where they imported components and processed material more cheaply.

As EU economies mainly trade with each other, albeit in a highly uneven manner, Germany's export competitiveness led to a contraction of manufacturing industry in other EU member states. German surplus capital, or what has not been paid out in wages, moreover has been valorized through credit extension to the EU's periphery, where it spurred the growth of fiscal deficits and/or household debt, while debt-fuelled consumption further augmented the trade surplus of the EU's North vis-a-vis the South. Therefore, as long as the bulk of trade is intra-EU and extra-EU exports account for a relatively small share of EU GDP (ranging between 12–15%; see Eurostat, 2017), EU economies cannot *all* expand their industries and pursue an export-led growth pattern with large trade surpluses. In the absence of strong global demand, internal devaluation will have only a moderate effect on the EU's net-export position (Stockhammer & Onaran, 2012, pp. 195–196). Thus, reducing unit labour costs in one member state will weaken unit labour costs in others, and wage repression, combined with austerity, will undermine domestic and also intra-EU consumption, as well as trigger deflation – all factors that render the success of the proclaimed investment-cum-export-led growth strategy highly unrealistic.

Improving 'price' competitiveness through intensified competition

In addition to boosting the 'cost' competitiveness of European industries by targeting unit labour costs and reducing so-called 'rigidities of the labour market', the Commission has been determined to improve 'price' competitiveness by reducing 'rigidities in product markets' (European Commission, 2015a, p. 57). A strict enforcement of EU competition policy has been advocated as the main lever to reduce the costs of capital, energy, electricity, raw materials and other variable production inputs. According to the Commission (2017a), 'competition policy is an important driver for firms to innovate and invest', and to ensure 'that firms can source their inputs at optimum conditions and benefit from competitive outlets for their products'. Intense price competition is moreover believed to lead to higher productivity (European Commission, 2017a). Flanking 'pro-competition' reforms have already been adopted, such as the above-mentioned REFIT or 'Competitiveness Proofing', in addition to reforms targeting barriers that inhibit cross-border corporate expansion and investments in product and service markets (European Commission, 2017a).

Competition policy has functioned as an industrial policy at the outset. Although the Treaty of Rome of 1957 did not mention industrial policy by the word, the preambles declared 'a high degree of competitiveness' a Community goal (see Article 2). In the postwar decades of European integration, the enforcement of supranational competition rules had a strong neo-mercantilist and protectionist outlook (Wigger & Buch-Hansen, 2014). Distortions to (supranational) competition rules were commonplace, and the Commission generously permitted direct or indirect state aid such as friendly loans, financial support for investments or R&D projects, as well as tax reductions or guaranteed procurement. Over time, the Commission became more activist, and sought to create European champions rather than allow national governments to pick their winners. It facilitated all sorts of cross-border industry collaboration and economic consolidation through mergers and acquisitions (Wigger & Buch-Hansen, 2014, p. 67). Primacy was given to bolstering European industries that were lagging behind the much larger and technologically more advanced American counterparts in high-value added sectors, such as computing and aerospace, and to protecting industrial sectors considered 'too important to fail', such as steel, coal, electricity, railways, textiles, shipbuilding, infrastructure or defence industries (Wigger & Buch-Hansen, 2014, p. 69). During the stagflation crisis of the 1970s, the Commission even tolerated crisis cartels setting prices and limiting outputs (Wigger & Buch-Hansen, 2014, p. 69).

Although with the neoliberal turn in the 1980s industrial policy was denounced as part of what Giersch (1985) diagnosed as 'Eurosclerosis', the rhetoric of competitiveness stayed. Rather than curbing competition to improve the competitiveness of European industries, intense competition was propagated to enhance competitiveness. The neoliberal logic entailed that if a plethora of discrete companies strive to become more efficient, increase their productivity and stay ahead of rivals through lower prices, higher levels of competitiveness of entire economies can be expected. In this vein, state aid was curtailed, cartels stringently prosecuted and public utility sectors privatized. Moreover, the notion 'fair competition' was replaced with 'free competition' in the consolidation of the treaty texts through the 1991 Maastricht Treaty. The logic of competition leading to competitiveness was also entrenched in the Lisbon Agenda of 2000 and its successor strategy Europe 2020. It is therefore not surprising that former Competition Commissioner Almunia (2014) announced that the new EU industrial policy would differ markedly from that of the 1970s. According to Almunia, strict enforcement of EU competition rules was 'the cheapest and most effective structural reform', 'at no extra cost for the taxpayer' (Almunia, 2012a, 2012b). By intensifying competition as a way to lower price levels, EU economies, so the idea goes, can compete themselves out of the crisis.

Lower prices may appear much-needed in times of economic recession, and a strict enforcement of competition rules may seem less painful than fiscal austerity, onslaughts on social rights and the repression of wages. However, competition facilitated by strict rules enforcement can intensify to an extent that prices of competitors can only be undercut by a further exploitation of labour (Wigger, 2017). While it makes sense from an individual capitalist perspective to maximize the freedom to exploit labour, this is not the case on an aggregate level. If less surplus from the production sphere is redistributed to wage earners, and by extension to society at large, the macro-effect will be reduced aggregate demand. The competitive lowering of prices moreover tempers future profit expectations, and thereby the propensity to invest in new production capacities. The coercive nature of capitalist competition can therefore precipitate what Harvey (2010, p. 29) called a peculiar combination of low profits, low wages, and low investments. Hence, by increasing privatized control over surplus capital, the new EU industrial policy is unlikely to channel investments to the real production sphere but rather to free even more liquid capital for speculative activities in the financial sphere.

The authoritarian neoliberal traits of internal devaluation

The governance framework for the internal devaluation component within the new EU industrial policy is yet another domain where neoliberal solutions are imposed in a highly authoritarian fashion. In 2009, the Commission appointed a 'high level group of experts' to develop a long-term common industrial strategy, and thus from the outset sought to avoid a broad-based debate with various societal stakeholders. The resulting policy suggestions informed the Commission's Communication 'Industrial Policy Reinforcing Competitiveness' of 2011, calling for deep structural reforms and coherent and coordinated policies, including policies that target unit labour costs (European Commission, 2011a). In 2012, the Four Presidents' Report[7] took up the competitiveness agenda, suggesting that EU governments should conclude annual contractual arrangements with the Commission, targeting areas where competitiveness was weak. In 2013, at the World Economic Forum in Davos, Switzerland, Chancellor Merkel advocated 'Competitiveness Pacts', which similar to the Fiscal Compact should create the prerequisite to get access to financial aid under what euphemistically had been termed the 'solidarity mechanism'.

Only one month later, the Commission (2013) launched a proposal for a 'Convergence and Competitiveness Instrument', which suggested a procedure according to which the Commission would make recommendations to individual member governments on how to regain competitiveness. Almost simultaneously, the European Council (2013, pp. 17–20) committed itself to negotiate 'Partnerships for Growth, Employment and Competitiveness', which entailed that individual governments and the Commission would conclude bilateral reform contracts that were subject to approval by the Council, notably in the configuration of its Competitiveness Council. In contrast to the reform requirements spelled out in the Memoranda of Understanding, the bilateral competitiveness treaties would not only demand reform efforts from the most crisis-hit but from *all* Eurozone members. Moreover, in contrast to the Country-Specific Recommendations issued *ex ante* by the Commission under the European Semester, the competitiveness treaties would be legally binding, and thus be enforceable through *ex post* litigation before EU Courts. The view was that the 2011 Euro Plus Pact and the European Semester failed to deliver the expected results – not because of the substance of the policies but due to their non-binding nature.

In a political climate of growing Euroscepticism and outright anti-EU sentiments, the subsequent Five Presidents' Report[8] in 2015 no longer mentioned the involvement of the courts but proposed establishing national competitiveness authorities, entrusted with the supervision of policies and the analysis of performances in the field of competitiveness. These authorities were to be functionally autonomous and politically independent from ministries and public authorities, and enjoy a statutory basis in national law, while their decisions should have the authority of law (Five Presidents' Report, 2015). Establishing national competitiveness authorities, rather than competitiveness pacts, had to create a strong sense of 'national ownership' of the 'necessary policies and reforms', while leaving sufficient room for national disparities and legal traditions.

According to the Five President's Report, 'Member States have a responsibility and self-interest to maintain sound policies and to embark on reforms that make their economies more flexible and competitive' (Five Presidents' Report, 2015, p. 4). What may appear to be a decentralized approach actually involved a high degree of centralization: the Commission would supervise the national competitiveness authorities, formulate common templates and standards, and then use the reported progress as a basis for the 'country-specific recommendations' in the European Semester (Five Presidents' Report, 2015, pp. 7–8). Common standards had to span the field of 'labour markets, competitiveness, business environment and public administrations, as well as certain aspects of tax policy (e.g. corporate tax base)' (Five Presidents' Report, 2015, p. 9). Importantly, national competitiveness authorities had to 'assess whether wages are evolving in line with productivity' and in comparison with other Eurozone members and 'the main comparable trading partners' (Five Presidents' Report, 2015, p. 7). EU economies thus had to undercut each other's cost and price competitiveness plus those of their main non-EU trading partners. Furthermore, national competitiveness authorities had to promote the 'flexicurity' concept, the contradictory combination of 'flexible labour contracts' coupled with 'lifelong learning strategies' and 'modern social security systems' (Five Presidents' Report, 2015, p. 9).

When these proposals still caused reservations to be expressed, the Commission subsequently changed the name, and national competitiveness 'authorities' were downgraded to national competitiveness 'boards'. In October 2015, it issued a 'Recommendation for a Council Recommendation on the Establishment of National Competitiveness Boards' (European Commission, 2015b). The Ecofin Council[9] revised the Commission's Recommendation in June 2016, and shortly after, in September, the European Council endorsed these changes and issued a recommendation, calling upon Eurozone members to establish national productivity boards within 18 months (European Council, 2016). In addition to dropping the word competitiveness and replacing it with productivity, there were minor revisions, such as degrading the Commission's supervisory role from a 'coordinator' to a 'facilitator' of the exchange of views and best practices among national productivity boards. The overall substance of the mandate entrusted upon national productivity boards, however, remained unchanged: the 'boards should analyse productivity and competitiveness developments' not only among Eurozone members but also 'relative to global competitors', and 'address cost and non-cost factors that can affect prices' (Council of the European Union, 2016; European Council, 2016).

National productivity boards should moreover be 'in charge of the design and implementation of policies in the field of productivity and competitiveness in the Member State or at European level' (Council of the European Union, 2016), and be able to react to national developments and initiatives proposed by national authorities, reinforce the policy dialogue at the national level and have an impact on national debates. National productivity boards may sound more trivial than the initially suggested competitiveness pacts or national competitiveness authorities. However, reporting on unit labour costs developments, and suggesting policy reforms that seek to raise productivity while containing unit labour costs and making adjustments when cost competitiveness lags behind the Eurozone average or the main trading partners, remain core activities. In addition, the annual reports will inform the Commission's country-specific recommendations in the European Semester and the Macroeconomic Imbalance Procedure processes (Council of the European Union, 2016; European Commission, 2016). This has also been emphasized in the Communication 'A renewed EU Industrial Policy Strategy', where the Commission (2017a) announced that it intended 'to work with member states in the European Semester to deliver on the main needs for industrial competitiveness'.

The strengthening of the European Semester through national productivity boards surveilling and attempting to enforce internal devaluation is yet another instance of authoritarian neoliberalism at the EU level, which seeks to insulate certain policies and institutional practices from social and political dissent (cf. Bruff, 2014, p. 115). To begin with, the European Commission deliberately sidestepped the ordinary legislative procedure and thereby the involvement of the European Parliament when *recommending* that the Council should *recommend* such boards at national level, ruling out any parliamentary oversight and debate over the role and function of national productivity boards (European Parliament, 2015). Furthermore, the neoliberal adjustment agenda will in the future, at least by intention, be hermetically sealed from institutionalized channels for contestation and democratic accountability (see also Cozzolino, 2018; Tansel, 2018). Indeed, one can be easily deceived when reading that these boards should be 'unbiased' and their expert analyses 'formulated in the general interest' instead of containing 'only or mainly views of specific groups of stakeholders' (Council of the European Union, 2016). However, by enjoying 'functional autonomy' and political independence vis-à-vis any public authority, these boards are designed as a one-way street when informing 'the national debate in the field of productivity and competitiveness'. As Dijsselbloem (2016) tweeted, these boards 'should primarily objectify the national debate'.

Not only formal democratic bodies like the European Parliament and national parliaments but also organized labour has been, and will also in the future be, sidestepped. Although in response to criticism, the 2016 Council Recommendation included a notion that productivity boards should 'respect the national practice and institutions for wage formation', the Commission had already advocated that 'social partners' should use the annual reports as guidance during wage-setting negotiations, and ought to take into account productivity developments in order to avoid 'misalignments between wages, productivity and skills', or what is also referred to as wage formation rigidities (European Commission, 2017c). Whereas the Commission already had a foot in the door regarding the wage formation process and labour cost adjustments on the basis of the European Semester, the Euro Plus Pact or the Six Pack (see Erne, 2015), the competitiveness governance framework now seeks to put an end to tripartite social dialogue at the national level. Arguably, none of the EU austerity or the hasty bailout packages has been implemented in cooperation with organized labour, but the Commission, by proxy of national productivity boards, can now fully intrude on a policy domain that used to be a national preserve. Ironically, national trade unions and the ETUC have long pushed for wage coordination at EU level; however, certainly not in the way it is materializing now. As a representative of ETUC (2015) remarked: 'we are only a hair's breath away from setting maximum wage standards for collective bargaining that are legally binding, or from questioning the validity of strike action'.

The fact that there have been only minor changes since the first proposal is indicative of yet another feature of authoritarian neoliberalism, namely that fewer attempts are being made to achieve consent from contesting groups through policy and/or material concessions. Against the backdrop of growing dissent, protest and resistance to neoliberal EU integration from (radical) left movements and organizations, and the recent landslide electoral victories of neo-populist Eurosceptic, radical right and even neo-fascist parties, the neoliberal agenda can only be pursued through a pre-emptive administrative, legal and coercive apparatus sealed off from popular contestation (cf. Bruff, 2014, p. 116). Thus, despite heightened contestation EU institutions continue to follow a neoliberal course, thereby relying on various complex, multi-layered and cross-cutting EU economic governance packages, and newly erected bodies with seemingly harmless names, such as the national productivity boards. The sheer complexity of this authoritarian surge is paired with an active marginalization and increasingly also the criminalization of oppositional forces (Tansel, 2017, p. 2).

Nevertheless, it is important to stress that this is all indicative of the deep political crisis in which the EU finds itself. As Poulantzas (1978, p. 241) aptly put it: '[a]uthoritarian statism does not correspond to a univocal strengthening of the State: it rather involves the dual aspect of strengthening-weakening'. He observed that weakening with regard to, for instance, shortfalls in legitimacy and ongoing states of crisis offers 'fresh possibilities to the Left' and creates 'new forms of popular struggle' (Poulantzas, 1978, pp. 245–246). Democratizing the EU and its institutions to remedy the vast legitimacy shortfall may seem out of reach, if not entirely impossible; yet, there are also indicators of a political counter-project that directly or indirectly discredits, delegitimizes and politicizes the authoritarian reconfiguration of EU institutions and the imposition of neoliberal race-to-the-bottom structural adjustment policies and procedures. The new forms of popular struggles that Poulantzas (1978, p. 246) observed in the late 1970s exhibited 'a characteristic anti-statism and express themselves in the mushrooming of self-management centres and networks of direct intervention by the masses in the decisions which affect them'.

As will be discussed below, these struggles have indeed surfaced again in the last decade, against the backdrop of protracted and multiple crises.

Discussion: an alternative EU industrial policy fostering solidarity economy initiatives

A range of scholars and organizations have suggested an alternative, employment-friendly, ecologically sustainable, transparent and democratically accountable EU industrial policy that ensures social participation and tackles the vast structural asymmetries across the EU (see Rosa Luxemburg Stiftung, 2017). Putting labour at the core is certainly the way to go; however, most of these suggestions remain implicitly or explicitly within the capitalist social relations of (re)production. Arguably, fixed blueprints for a post-neoliberal and post-capitalist society are neither possible nor desirable, if democratic processes are to be taken seriously, but we should not refrain from discussing at least the contours of such alternatives. From a historical materialist vantage point, changing the social relations of (re)production should constitute the bedrock for a systemic change, while competition on prices and wages need to be ruled out (Wigger, 2018). There is nothing wrong with producing higher quality and more innovative products in a competitive spirit; yet production should be reoriented towards what Marx (1965 [1887]) called 'use value', rather than 'exchange-value' relying on labour as a comparative advantage. Competition originates from the Latin word *competere*, which refers to striving and running together and learning from each other. Giving significance to the original sense of the word could be a step in the right direction. Ideally, democratic or consensual decision-making should take centre-stage. However, as there is and cannot be a 'one size fits all' solution, free experimentation of different formats, evolving from bottom-up grassroots initiatives, should prevail, leading to a coexistence of multiple laboratories for the production, distribution and consumption of goods and services, as well as the reproduction of the wider 'social factory' beyond the workplace (see Cleaver, 2000 in Bieler & Jordan, 2017).

Real existing 'solidarity economy' initiatives in many ways prefigure more equitable, horizontally- and democratically-managed social relations of (re)production. Over the last decade, workers' collectives, cooperatives, mutuals, associations or foundations have proliferated, particularly in the most crisis-hit EU member states (Wigger, 2018). Estimates suggest that there are currently more than 250,000 grassroots cooperatives in the EU, which are owned by 163 million citizens (equivalent of one-third of the EU population), and which employ 5.4 million people (Cooperatives Europe, 2018). Although solidarity economy initiatives can be more or less radical in resisting prevailing capitalist logics, overall they can be seen as a coagulation of structures of resistance against authoritarian neoliberalism in contemporary capitalism (Wigger, 2018). Solidarity economy initiatives frequently include communal ownership and horizontal direct-democratic decision-making structures, with fewer supervisory and management layers and a higher degree of social inclusion in terms of gender, age and (dis)ability, as well as migrants (Wigger, 2018). They tend to give primacy to equity, reciprocity, cooperation, mutual aid, solidarity and environmental sustainability – all antidotes to cut-throat capitalist competition and the maximization of profits (Kokkinidis, 2015a, 2015b).

Importantly, solidarity economy initiatives come with a high transformative potential. Rather than operating in isolation, they often form part of dense network structures that cluster complementary products and services, and create new synergies among local, regional, national and also international peer-to-peer producer and consumer networks. As a result, they often rely on shorter supply chains, rendering the production and consumption of goods and services less alienated, while also reducing energy-wasteful transportation (Wigger, 2018). The transformative potential also lies in the fact that solidarity economy initiatives offer an infrastructure of dissent, making new political imaginaries possible (Vogiatzoglou, 2015). Solidarity, after all, is a relation forged through political struggle, which reshapes 'the terrain of what is politically possible and what counts and what is recognized as political' (Featherstone, 2012, p. 7).

The recent surge of solidarity economy initiatives is closely linked to the disruptive mass protests against the neoliberal EU crisis management, where hundreds of thousands took to the streets, occupied central squares, held popular assemblies or engaged in strikes or acts of civil disobedience, leading to the emergence of new social movements, like the 15-M in Spain or the Syntagma Square movement in Greece, as well as a myriad of new political parties or party-like platforms (Wigger, 2018). In particular, the square occupations and neighbourhood assemblies that started after the mass demonstrations in Spain provided an arena for solidarity economy networks to engage with a more heterogeneous audience, bringing together different activist groups and previously non-politicized individuals (Wigger, 2018, p. 44). These initiatives have offered a more concrete, praxis-oriented form of resistance compared to the often short-lived and fragmented protest actions in the streets, and have attracted the political support from a disparate set of progressive social forces.

One of the most radical examples, which emerged as an activist response to the crisis and the unbridled power of the financial sector in contemporary capitalism, is the Cooperativa Integral Catalana (CIC), the Integrated Cooperative. The CIC seeks to synthesize all activities of social life under an umbrella framework of mutual help that transcends capitalist forms of organization and production (see CIC, 2018). Established in 2010 in Catalonia with the aim of promoting degrowth ideas, self-management, direct democracy and the empowerment of local nodes by cutting out intermediaries between production and consumption, the CIC has grown into a network involving several thousand people and has progressively moved into new activities, subsuming a network of ever more cooperatives (Dafermos, 2017). The CIC model has been copied, with sister networks emerging all over Europe (CIC, 2018). For example, similar initiatives can be found in Greece, such as Syn.al-l.ois, a Cooperative for Alternative and Solidarity Trade that was established in 2011 (see Kokkinidis, 2015a, 2015b).

While the CIC seeks to establish autonomous alternatives and deliberately operates beyond the remit of the state and the capitalist market, other solidarity economy initiatives are fighting for legal recognition at national and EU levels, demanding for example more lenient tax treatment and exemptions from national and EU competition rules (CIRIEC International, 2016; Cooperatives Europe, 2018). While the European Court of Justice (ECJ) ruled in 2011 that a specific tax treatment can indeed be justified based on their different nature compared to for-profit-enterprises, the ECJ also interpreted associations or federations among solidarity economy initiatives as illicit and anti-competitive agreements (CIRIEC International, 2016, p. 39). Similarly, the European Commission has hitherto paid no attention to the specific needs of the solidarity economy, and holds on to its neoliberal mantra that capitalist competition should receive primacy at all times. In a Communication on cooperative societies, the Commission (2004, p. 13) argued that despite their distinctive features, cooperatives 'do not need preferential treatment', have 'to compete effectively in their markets and on equal terms with other forms of enterprise' and 'are therefore subject to competition rules'. Concretely, this means that there are no exemptions regarding state aid or cooperative agreements between different solidarity initiatives. This illustrates that the Commission employs EU competition rules as a fictitious equalizer, which standardizes corporations irrespective of their size, purpose and economic power into something they are not, namely equal market players. Cooperation and mutual aid, the antitheses of capitalist competition, are thereby marginalized or ruled out entirely as organizing principles. This is to the detriment of solidarity economy initiatives, which can only thrive and exploit their transformative potential with the capacity to cooperate and form associations and federations.

Ironically, the Commission's (2017d, p. 6) recent 'White Paper on the Future of Europe' starts with a reference to the *Manifesto di Ventotene* ('For a Free and United Europe'), written by Altiero Spinelli and Ernesto Rossi, who were imprisoned by the fascist regime on the isle of Venetone during the Second World War and whose federalist ideas formed part of the very impetus for kickstarting European integration. Not only was Spinelli a communist, and Rossi the founder of a cooperative, but in the Manifesto they also suggested an 'industrial reform which will extend workers' ownership in non-nationalized sectors, through co-operative adventures, employee profit-sharing, and so on' (quoted in Mayo, 2018). The current EU economic policies, including industrial and competition policy, are a far cry from the 'free and united Europe' as envisaged by the Italian anti-fascists. Against the backdrop of increasingly authoritarian traits in which the neoliberal course is solidified in so-called independent and democratically non-accountable bodies, the Commission's (2017d, p. 6) invocation for Europe's future that the hard-earned human dignity, freedom and democracy in Europe can never be relinquished seems merely a platitude.

Conclusion

Ten years after the global economic crisis, various EU institutions and politicians have come to realize that low inflation, low public debt-GDP ratios and tight budget deficits have not led to the promised economic convergence, let alone to a sustained and balanced economic recovery. It has also been acknowledged that reforms are needed to tackle the vast structural asymmetries that have opened up a North–South and West–East divide. Likewise, it has been recognized that financial markets have grown out of proportion vis-à-vis the production economy, and that measures are needed to channel financial excess capital into European industries. In this vein, the new EU industrial policy is meant to serve as one big lever to attract private investments.

This article has revealed that the new EU industrial policy, in addition to various funds and regulatory packages, endorses the very same neoliberal internal devaluation measures that have underpinned the EMU since Maastricht, and that were also included into the Macroeconomic Imbalance Procedure of the European Semester in 2010. The chosen way forward is as follows: to compensate for the loss of exchange rate flexibility within the Eurozone as a way of cheapening EU exports, all emphasis is given to improving the cost and price competitiveness of European industries — mostly through wage adjustments and further labour market flexibilization — as well as lower prices following from unbridled competition, alongside a lowering of corporate tax rates. As has been shown in this article, in addition to directly and indirectly depreciating the costs of labour, internal devaluation also comes with an authoritarian reconfiguration of the EU state apparatus. With the establishment of allegedly 'independent' national productivity boards, keeping track of wage vis-à-vis productivity developments, and suggesting national reforms in sectors and areas deemed to lack competitiveness, the unelected and unaccountable European Commission finds itself once more in a fortified position when 'commanding' structural adjustments through the European Semester. Against the backdrop of growing popular contestation of the European integration project, it remains to be seen whether and how national productivity boards, as vassals of the European Commission's new industrial policy, will indeed manage to foster internal devaluation.

The solidarity economy initiatives, as discussed in the last section, may appear marginalized and disparate struggles, but they are also indicative of concrete utopias that already exist and thus provide the foundations for an alternative EU industrial policy. They are a crucial part of ongoing attempts to discredit, de-legitimize and politicize authoritarian neoliberal crisis management strategies at national and EU levels and capitalism in Europe more generally.

Notes

1. The Council of the European Union, or the Council of Ministers, is an EU body where national ministers meet in policy-specific areas to adopt legislative acts and coordinate policies, mostly together with the European Parliament through the so-called ordinary legislative procedure or what used to be termed codecision. The Council should not be mistaken for the European Council, consisting of the heads of state of the member state governments, the European Council President, and the President of the European Commission, which defines the general course and priorities of European integration.
2. The Eurogroup is an informal and democratically unaccountable body without a statutory basis in the Treaties, consisting of the finance ministers of the Eurozone members, the Commissioner for economic and financial affairs, and the president of the European Central Bank. The Eurogroup enjoys vast discretionary powers and coordinates economic policies among Eurozone members.
3. As unilateral currency devaluations by individual member states have become impossible with the establishment of the Economic and Monetary Union (EMU) and euro as the common currency, internal devaluation strategies offer an 'alternative' option to cheapen exports.
4. The European Semester was introduced in 2010 and forms part of the annual supranational economic policy coordination process, which allows the European Commission to surveil economic and fiscal policies, including budget plans, as well as macroeconomic and structural reforms, and issue country-specific recommendations for the next 12 to 18 months.
5. At the time of writing (March 2018), the broader EU package of corporate tax reforms is in the process of being launched and thus falls outside the scope of the article. Nevertheless, its direction of travel is clearly towards the overall goals mentioned already, i.e. lower levels of taxation.
6. Memoranda of Understanding (MoU) are bilateral contracts specifying the reform conditions for member states that requested financial assistance. The Europlus Pact, signed in 2011, seeks to strengthen economic policy coordination among Eurozone and other member states with the aim to improve 'economic competitiveness'. The Six Pack, also adopted in 2011, consists of five regulations and one directive that seek to strengthen the Commission's budgetary and macroeconomic surveillance powers under the new macroeconomic imbalance procedure – a procedure installed to detect risky economic developments.
7. The Four Presidents' Report is a joint report by the presidents of respectively the European Council, the European Commission, the Eurogroup and the European Central Bank.
8. In comparison to the Four Presidents' Report of 2012, the Five Presidents' Report of 2015 also included the President of the European Parliament.
9. ECOFIN is short for the Economic and Financial Affairs Council.

Acknowledgements

I would like to thank the anonymous reviewers and the editors for their very helpful and constructive comments and suggestions, plus the participants of the 2017 'Neoliberalism's Complexities' workshop at the University of Newcastle in Sydney, Australia, and the participants of the Critical Political Economy Research Network (CPERN) panels at the 2017 European Sociological Association conference in Athens, Greece, for very fruitful discussions of an earlier version of this paper.

Disclosure statement

No potential conflict of interest was reported by the author.

References

Almunia, J. (2012a). *The role of competition policy in times of crisis.* Speech/12/917, Brussels.
Almunia, J. (2012b). *Competition policy for innovation and growth: Keeping markets open and efficient.* Speech 12/172, Copenhagen.
Almunia, J. (2014). *Competition policy enforcement as a driver for growth.* Speech 14/178, Brussels.
Armingeon, K., & Baccaro, L. (2012). Political economy of the sovereign debt crisis: The limits of internal devaluation. *Industrial Law Journal, 41*(3), 254–275.
Barbiero, F., & Darvas, Z. (2014). In sickness and health: Protecting and supporting public investment in Europe. *Bruegel Policy Contribution, 2014*(2), 1–18.
BDI. (2014a). A call from BDI and Confindustria to the German and Italian government ahead of the Spring European Council. *Joint declaration with Confindustria.* Retrieved from http://www.bdi.eu/bdi_english/download_content/BDI_Confindustria_Joint_Declaration_EN.pdf
BDI. (2014b). Strengthening competitiveness and creating more jobs in Europe our priorities for the future. A call from BDI and MEDEF to the European Council. Retrieved from http://www.medef.com/fileadmin/www.medef.fr/documents/BDI-MEDEF/20140205/BDI-MEDEF-Declaration-EN-201402005.pdf
Beck, M., & Germann, J. (2018). Managerial power in the German model: The case of Bertelsmann and the antecedents of neoliberalism. *Globalizations.* doi: 10.1080/14747731.2018.1502490
Berglof, E. (2016). European industrial policy. Tapping the full growth potential of the EU. *Intereconomics, 51* (6), 335–340.
Bieler, A., & Jordan, J. (2017). Commodification and 'the commons': The politics of privatizing public water in Greece and Portugal during the Eurozone crisis. *European Journal of International Relations.*
Bruff, I. (2014). The rise of authoritarian neoliberalism. *Rethinking Marxism, 26*(1), 113–129.
Bruff, I. (2015). Germany and the crisis: Steady as she goes? In R. Westra, D. Badeen, & R. Albritton (Eds.), *The future of capitalism after the financial crisis: The varieties of capitalism debate in the age of austerity* (pp. 114–131). London: Routledge.
CIC. (2018). *Cooperativa Integral Catalana.* Retrieved from https://cooperativa.cat/en
CIRIEC International. (2016). *Recent evolutions of the Social Economy in the European Union.* Retrieved from http://base.socioeco.org/docs/qe-04-17-875-en-n.pdf
Cleaver, H. (2000). *Reading capital politically.* Oakland: AK Press.
CNBC. (2017). *In shift away from austerity, euro countries pick new leader.* Retrieved from https://www.cnbc.com/2017/12/05/in-shift-away-from-austerity-euro-countries-pick-new-leader.html
Cooperatives Europe. (2018). *What is a cooperative?* Retrieved from https://coopseurope.coop/sites/default/files/Flyer%20Cooperatives%20Europe_0.pdf
Council of the European Union. (2016). *Recommendation for a Council recommendation on the establishment of national productivity boards,* ECOFIN 590, UEM 248, Brussels.
Council of the European Union. (2017). *Conclusions on a future EU industrial policy strategy.* Press Release 283/17, Brussels.
Cozzolino, A. (2018). Reconfiguring the state: Executive powers, emergency legislation, and neoliberalization in Italy. *Globalizations.* doi:10.1080/14747731.2018.1502495
Dafermos, G. (2017). *The Catalan Integral Cooperative. An organizational study of a post- capitalist cooperative.* P2P Foundation and Robin Hood Coop. Retrieved from https://p2pfoundation.net/wp-content/uploads/2017/10/The-Catalan-Integral-Cooperative.pdf
Dijsselbloem, J. (2016, February 17). Tweet by Jeroen Dijsselbloem@J_Dijsselbloem.

Dijsselbloem, J. (2017). *Remarks following the Eurogroup meeting of 20 February 2017*. Press Release 77/17, Brussels.

Erne, R. (2015). A supranational regime that nationalises social conflict: Explaining European trade unions' difficulties in politicizing European economic governance. *Labor History*, *56*(3), 345–368.

ERT. (2013). *ERT meets with Merkel, Hollande and Barroso on Europe's competitiveness*. Press Release, 18 March, Brussels.

ERT. (2014). *EU industrial renaissance*. ERT agenda for action 2014–2019. Brussels.

ETUC. (2015). *ETUC's position on national competitiveness boards*. Retrieved from https://www.etuc.org/en/document/etuc-position-national-competitiveness-boards

ETUC & BusinessEurope. (2016). BusinessEurope and ETUC call on EU institutions to bring competitive and sustainable industry back to the core of the EU policy agenda. Brussels.

ETUI (Ed.). (2016). *Unemployment, internal devaluation and labour market deregulation in Europe*. Brussels: European Trade Union Institute.

European Commission. (2004). *On the promotion of co-operative societies in Europe*. COM(2004) 18 final, Brussels.

European Commission. (2011a). *Industrial policy: Reinforcing competitiveness*. Brussels: Communication.

European Commission. (2011b). Quarterly report on the Euro Area, *10*(3), Brussels.

European Commission. (2013). *Towards a deep and genuine Economic and Monetary Union. The introduction of a convergence and competitiveness instrument*. COM(2013) 165 final, Brussels.

European Commission. (2014). *For a European industrial renaissance*. Communication COM/2014/014 final Brussels.

European Commission. (2015a). *EU structural change 2015*. Luxembourg: Publications Office of the European Union.

European Commission. (2015b). *Recommendation for a Council recommendation on the establishment of national competitiveness boards within the Euro Area*. COM(2015) 601 final: Brussels.

European Commission. (2016). *Recommendation for a Council recommendation on the economic policy of the euro area*. Brussels.

European Commission. (2017a). *Investing in a smart, innovative and sustainable industry: A renewed EU industrial policy strategy*. Brussels: Communication.

European Commission. (2017b). *EU industrial policy*. Retrieved from https://ec.europa.eu/growth/industry/policy/eu_en

European Commission. (2017c). *Investment in the EU member states: An analysis of drivers and barriers*. Retrieved from https://ec.europa.eu/info/sites/info/files/ip062_en.pdf

European Commission. (2017d). *White paper on the future of Europe*. Retrieved from https://ec.europa.eu/commission/sites/beta-political/files/white_paper_on_the_future_of_europe_en.pdf

European Commission. (2018a). *COSME financial instruments*. Retrieved from https://ec.europa.eu/growth/access-to-finance/cosme-financial-instruments_nl

European Commission. (2018b). *Macroeconomic imbalance procedure scoreboard*. Retrieved from https://ec.europa.eu/info/business-economy-euro/economic-and-fiscal-policy-coordination/eu-economic-governance-monitoring-prevention-correction/macroeconomic-imbalance-procedure/scoreboard_en

European Council. (2013). *Conclusions*. EUCO 217/13: Brussels.

European Council. (2016). *Council recommendation on the establishment of National Productivity Boards*. 2016/C 349/01: Brussels.

European Parliament. (2015). European Parliament resolution of 17 December 2015 on completing Europe's Economic and Monetary Union 2015/2936(RSP): Brussels.

Eurostat. (2017). *International trade*. Retrieved from http://ec.europa.eu/eurostat/

Featherstone, D. (2012). *Solidarity: Hidden histories and geographies of internationalism*. London: Zed Books.

Five Presidents' Report. (2015). *Completing Europe's Economic and Monetary Union*. Brussels. Retrieved from https://ec.europa.eu/commission/sites/beta-political/files/5-presidents-report_en.pdf

Four Presidents' Report. (2012). *Towards a genuine Economic and Monetary Union*. Retrieved from http://www.consilium.europa.eu/uedocs/cms_Data/docs/pressdata/en/ec/134069.pdf

Giersch, H. (1985, January 2). Eurosclerosis: The malaise that threatens prosperity. *The Financial Times*, p. 9.

Harvey, D. (2010). *The enigma of capital and the crises of capitalism*. London: Profile Books.

Joint Declaration of Industry Representatives. (2017). *Joint Declaration for an ambitious EU industrial strategy*. Retrieved from http://www.acea.be/uploads/news_documents/Joint_Declaration_on_EU_Industrial_Strategy_Final_version.pdf

Kokkinidis, G. (2015a). Post-capitalist imaginaries: The case of workers' collectives in Greece. *Journal of Management Inquiry*, *24*(4), 429–432.

Kokkindis, G. (2015b). Spaces of possibilities: Workers' selfmanagement in Greece. *Organization*, *22*(6), 847–871.

Mayo, E. (2018). *What is the future of Europe? A co-operative contribution*. Retrieved from https://edmayo.wordpress.com/2017/09/08/what-is-the-future-of-europe-a-co-operative-contribution/

Marx, K. (1965 [1887]). *Capital volume 1*. Moscow: Progress Publishers.

Marx, K. (1973 [1939]). *Grundrisse*. London: Penguin Classics.

Merkel, A. (2013). *Speech at the World Economic Forum Annual Meeting*, 24 January, Davos, Switzerland.

Oberndorfer, L. (2014). From new constitutionalism to authoritarian constitutionalism: New economic governance and the state of European democracy. In J. Jäger, & E. Springler (Eds.), *Asymmetric crisis in Europe and possible futures. Critical political economy and post-Keynesian perspectives* (pp. 186–207). New York: Routledge.

Petroulakis, F. (2017). Internal devaluation in currency unions: The role of trade costs and taxes. *European Central Bank Working Paper*, No 2049, 1–61.

Pochet, P. (2016). From social pacts to productivity boards. *Intereconomics*, *51*(6), 321–324.

Poulantzas, N. (1978). *State, power, socialism* (P. Camiller Trans.). London: New Left Books.

Rosa Luxemburg Stiftung (Ed.). (2017). *Progressive industrial policy in the EU? Outmanoeuvring neoliberalism*. Brussels: Rosa Luxemburg Stiftung Brussels Office.

Sandbeck, S., & Schneider, E. (2014). From the sovereign debt crisis to authoritarian statism: Contradictions of the European state project. *New Political Economy*, *19*(6), 847–871.

Sandbu, M. (2016). *Europe's orphan: The future of the Euro and the politics of debt*. Princeton: Princeton University Press.

Schout, C., & Schwieter, A. (2018). *National fiscal councils, the European fiscal board and national productivity boards: New EMU independent bodies without much prospect*. Retrieved from https://www.clingendael.org/pub/2018/clingendael-state-of-the-union-2018/5-new-emu-independent-bodies/

Stockhammer, E., & Onaran, O. (2012). Rethinking wage policy in the face of the Euro crisis: Implications of the wage-led demand regime. *International Review of Applied Economics*, *26*(2), 191–203.

Tansel, C. B. (2017). Authoritarian neoliberalism: Towards a new research agenda. In C. B. Tansel (Ed.), *States of discipline: Authoritarian neoliberalism and the contested reproduction of capitalist order* (pp. 1–28). London: Rowman & Littlefield International.

Tansel, B. (2018). Reproducing authoritarian neoliberalism in Turkey: Urban governance and state restructuring in the shadow of executive centralization. *Globalizations*. doi:10.1080/14747731.2018.1502494

Vogiatzoglou, M. (2015). Workers' transnational networks in times of austerity: Italy and Greece. *Transfer: European Review of Labour and Research*, *21*(2), 215–228.

Wigger, A. (2017). Understanding the competition-crisis nexus: Revisiting US capitalist crises. *Rethinking Marxism*, *29*(4), 556–573.

Wigger, A. (2018). From dissent to resistance: Locating patterns of horizontalist self-management crisis responses in Europe. *Comparative European Politics*, *16*(1), 32–49.

Wigger, A., & Buch-Hansen, H. (2014). Explaining (missing) regulatory paradigm shifts: EU competition regulation in times of economic crisis. *New Political Economy*, *19*(1), 113–137.

World Bank. (2018). *Gross fixed capital formation (% of GDP)*. Retrieved from https://data.worldbank.org/indicator/NE.GDI.FTOT.ZS

Index

Note: Page numbers in *italics* denote figures.

For Product Safety Concerns and Information please contact our EU representative GPSR@taylorandfrancis.com
Taylor & Francis Verlag GmbH, Kaufingerstraße 24, 80331 München, Germany

www.ingramcontent.com/pod-product-compliance
Lightning Source LLC
LaVergne TN
LVHW080656011026
849160LV00014B/1452